Girls, Feminism,
and Grassroots Literacies

Activism in the GirlZone

Mary P. Sheridan-Rabideau

State University of New York Press

Published by
State University of New York Press, Albany

© 2008 State University of New York

For information, contact State University of New York Press, Albany, NY
www.sunypress.edu

Production by Kelli W. LeRoux
Marketing by Michael Campochiaro

Library of Congress Cataloguing-in-Publication Data

Sheridan-Rabideau, Mary P.
   Girls, feminism, and grassroots literacies : activism in the GirlZone / Mary P.
Sheridan-Rabideau.
       p. cm. — (SUNY series in feminist criticism and theory)
   Includes bibliographical references and index.
   ISBN 978-0-7914-7297-2 (hardcover : alk. paper) — ISBN 978-0-7914-7298-9
(pbk. : alk. paper)   1. GirlZone (Organization).   2. Feminist theory—United States.
3. Women's rights—United States.   4. Teenage girls—United States.   5. Young
women—United States.   6. Feminism—United States.   7. Women in community
organization—United States.   I. Title.

HQ1246.S44   2008
305.235'201—dc22
                                                                          2007013155

10 9 8 7 6 5 4 3 2 1

To Aimee, and the entire GirlZone community

Contents

Illustrations

Figures

Tables

Acknowledgments

I would like to thank Aimee and GirlZone for allowing me to reproduce several GirlZone documents: the photo of the GrrrlFest Auto Mechanic workshop; the front page of the GirlZone *Girl Zine 1.2*; a GirlZone flyer; and the GrrrlFest 2002 logo. I would like to acknowledge that the Radio-Girls photo (February 11, 1999) was reproduced by *The News-Gazette* Incorporated. Permission does not imply endorsement by the newspaper.

On and off for six years I played, studied, and worked with the girls and women of GirlZone. I am grateful for their enthusiasm, dedication, and desire to make the world as they want it to be. I am especially thankful to Aimee, for giving of herself so completely to a cause she believes in, and for sharing her time and talents with me as I tried to do the same.

My work at GirlZone began during my graduate work at the Center for Writing Studies at University of Illinois at Urbana. What a gift the Center was. I owe a particular debt of gratitude to Gail Hawisrher who modeled how to be a mentor and to Paul Prior who asked the tough questions. Supportively prodding my evolving sense of how to make my way in the world of research, Paul was all I could ask for in a Dissertation Chair. Starting with a summer class and continuing for years, Gesa Kirsh guided me though the process of academic publishing. Outside of the classroom, Teresa Bertram helped me negotiate colicky children and smoking computers. My wonderful cohort from the Center has continued to shape my thinking and I'd like to express my gratitude to Karen Lunsford, Lee Nickoson-Massey, Liz Rohan, Beth Suter and most especially Caroline Cole, all of whom have been generous and honest readers.

Over pizza and pomegranates, my Rutgers University writing group helped me reimagine my project and pushed me to think in new ways. Thanks to Chris Chism, Ann Coiro, Stacy Klein, Daphne Lamothe, Sonali Perea, Shuang Shen, and Edlie Wong. In years of hallway and more extended conversations, Harriet Davidson and Jackie Miller provided support for my project as well. I would also like to thank my Composition colleagues: Ann Jurecic, Richard Miller, Kurt Spellmeyer. Finally, two members of the Highland Park posse, Kim Hammond and Kara Donaldson, offered not only their nurturing friendship but also their professional eyes. I will always be thankful for them.

What has grounded and guided me throughout all of my work has been my family. My parents, siblings, and in-laws have cheered for me, even when they didn't know what I was doing. My sincerest thanks go to Mark, Mary Pauline, Luke, and Aidan. With their peals of laughter, cries for comfort, and questions about what I was doing, they continually remind me that my work matters only to the degree that it impacts the world.

Part One

Setting the Scene

1

The Telling Case of GirlZone

I arrived early on the first morning of *GrrrlFest 2002: Throw like a girl*, the second annual weekend-long "celebration of girls and women" that offered over forty hands-on workshops and panel presentations on topics ranging from skateboarding and web design to "Claiming your Anger" and "Minding your Mind over your Manners." As I meandered throughout the central Illinois Independent Media Center (IMC), the Fest's home site this year, I looked at the artwork and texts that transformed the IMC into GrrrlFest headquarters. In addition to GrrrlFest schedules and flyers were tracts urging the closure of the School of the Americas, pre-addressed postcards encouraging the local university to add contraception coverage to graduate student insurance policies, and, of course, the Powerpuff Girls-informed GrrrlFest logo. What most caught my eye were the easel boards in each of the three adjacent rooms. On these boards, GrrrlFest participants could respond to prompts such as: "Design your own 'Women's' sign for a bathroom"; "What did a teacher do?"; or, my favorite, "What do you say when someone says you throw like a girl?" All weekend, girls and women would gather around these easels. Some GrrrlFest participants wrote witty "comebacks" and funny anecdotes. Others discussed how misogyny and homophobia make the phrase "you throw like a girl," a taunt, an accepted "fact" that circulates in girls' everyday lives. On page after easel board page, girls and women poured out their thoughts, which then became stapled to the walls. Participants consistently checked for new entries, often dragging a friend or two along to see the newest "must read" response. Literally surrounding GrrrlFest participants, these responses made visible how texts mediate large-scale sociocultural forces that both reflect and construct who girls and women are on the one hand, and local ways girls and women redirect these forces on the other hand.

Exposing and redirecting damaging societal messages was a goal of GrrrlFest and its sponsoring organization, GirlZone. From 1997–2003, GirlZone and GirlZone-sponsored programs (such as GrrrlFest) offered over one thousand girls and women over four hundred hands-on workshops in activities they seldom had the opportunity or encouragement to explore elsewhere. Participants discussed the activity of hands-on work-shops (e.g., skateboarding, creative writing), yet crucial to GirlZone's success were talk and texts that mediated the social relations that shaped these workshops. *Girls, Feminism, and Grassrootss Literacies: Activism in the GirlZone* investigates these complex and, at times, contradictory social relations. In particular, this book examines how girls and women at one grassroots feminist organization used texts both to construct meaning and to construct themselves as meaningful in their everyday lives.

Throughout this research, I examine literate activities as a way to understand how people engage with the world, an approach that is beneficial for both literacy scholars and for those we study. For literacy scholars, *Girls, Feminism, and Grassroots Literacies* offers a model for studying literacy practices in out-of-school settings. My model provides a thick description of the broad cultural-historical contexts shaping how texts function and of the very local practices in and through which girls' identities and positions are being contested and reworked, especially through the literate worlds linked to this grassroots feminist organization. Through this model, I take up an engaged, praxis-oriented stance in order to better understand the complex phenomena at this site, and to work through the site to realize feminist goals of cultural and political change.

Understanding literacy as one way to make sense of and inform both local practices and cultural-historic contexts shaping these practices can also help those we study. For example, this understanding can help contemporary grassroots feminist activists develop tactics—from reworking girl culture to facilitating local activism—that foster social change on a local level. Consequently, *Girls, Feminism, and Grassroots Literacies* provides a case study for feminists, grassroots activists, and cultural critics considering how girls and girl culture have become cultural flash points, reflecting both societal and particularly feminist anxieties about and hopes for the future.

In the rest of this chapter, I contextualize these literacy and feminist projects before ending with descriptions of how the following chapters take them up.

LITERACY IN COMMUNITY SETTINGS

In her chair's address to the Conference on College Composition and Communication, Chair Anne Ruggles Gere issued a call to supplement composition studies' attention to the literate activities in the classroom with attention to literate activities outside the classroom. This call was part of Gere's argument that the field itself needs to be located in *and beyond* the classroom:

> Instead of a historiography based exclusively on textbooks used in schools and colleges, on the careers and works of prominent teachers

and scholars, on the curricular decisions made by universities and on texts produced by students, we can consider the various sites in which the extracurriculum has been enacted, the local circumstances that supported its developments, the material artifacts employed by its practitioners, and the cultural work it accomplished.[1]

In recent years, writing studies scholars have heeded Gere's call, addressing questions beyond the classroom in order to understand how people use literacy in their everyday lives. As we turn our attention to new research sites, this expansive understanding of everyday literacy transforms writing studies researchers from being composition teachers in the university to writing experts in the public realm.[2]

This shift indexes a definition of literacy, what I am calling "literate activities," that diminishes individual, decontextualized skills and foregrounds literacy as a social activity embedded in situated, cultural-historical contexts. This shift emerges, in part, from literacy research informed by anthropological/ethnographic traditions that focus on the diverse and interrelated activities surrounding the ways people use textual practices in particular settings.[3] Although theorists use different terms,[4] I use "literate activities" instead of "writing" or "literacy" to emphasize literacy's complexity. Sociohistoric theorist Paul A. Prior gets at this complexity when he describes the thinness of the term "writing":

> Usual representations of writing collapse time, isolate persons, and filter activity (e.g., "I wrote the paper over the weekend"). Actually, writing happens in moments that are richly equipped with tools (material and semiotic) and populated with others (past, present, and future). When seen as situated activity, writing does not stand alone as the discrete act of a writer, but emerges as a confluence of many streams of activity: reading, talking, observing, acting, making, thinking, and feeling as well as transcribing words on paper. . . . "Writing" is too partial, too contextually thin, a unit of analysis.[5]

Like Prior, I find traditional representations of writing—and literacy more generally—too limiting, as if literacy is primarily a mental activity bound in a moment's time and place. When writing, reading, and designing documents, participants draw on imagined and real people as well as what Prior calls "material" and "semiotic tools" that span time and space. The ongoing, interactive, and situated associations of "literate activities" better calls attention to both the spatially and temporally striated nature of literacy as well as the constellation of people, practices, and institutions that inform how people work with (and are worked by) texts.

When investigating how people engage in everyday literate activities beyond the classroom, scholars have primarily examined the workplace and the home. Scholars have paid far less attention to situated studies of community organizations—sites where, from the ground up, people imagine what they want and what structures they need to achieve their desire.

This lack of attention to community organizations is surprising. As David Barton and Mary Hamilton note, there are hundreds of these organizations throughout towns and cities everywhere and we know very little about how the literate activities at these self-chosen, everyday sites function.[6]

At community organizations, participants take part in a wide range of literate activities as they design, read, and distribute mission statements, logos, e-mails, and flyers. The literate activities of value to the grassroots GirlZone community itself were the activities I privileged. This focus meant that I examined not only the ways people engaged with texts, but also how they engaged with visual and aural documents, documents particularly pervasive in youth culture. While I accept the traditional definition of literacy that prizes close analyses of print-based texts, contemporary documents such as the websites, newspapers, and even school textbooks use multiple modes (e.g., text, icon) to convey their messages. Each mode carries a significant part of what communication theorist Gunther Kress calls a message's "functional load."[7] To be literate in the twenty-first century, therefore, means being able to understand and design multimodal documents.

This expanded view of literacy is rooted both in traditional literacy scholarship and in contemporary technological possibilities. As Gere has argued, for years women's groups have used literacy to shape pressing social questions, such as those surrounding immigration, suffrage, working conditions, race, and so forth.[8] GirlZone illustrates that, today, groups of women still use literate activities to address pressing social questions, especially to intervene in a sexualized and commodified girl culture. Nonetheless, understandings of literacy have changed. Technological advancements alter the production and distribution of texts as well as the multiple modes included in these texts. Similarly, globalized business practices and mass-marketing have ratcheted up the importance and altered the means of sharing information. Literacy scholars need to attend to these changes that include and exceed print-based documents.

In addition to expanding the traditional definition of literacy, I call for new methods to analyze literacy. Since literacy is inherently situated, analyses should attend to local practices and to broader socioeconomic dynamics that both make texts meaningful and authorize particular individuals to be creators of texts. This expansion means that analyses of literacy should investigate the issues surrounding participants' practices (e.g., tensions surrounding contemporary girl culture or feminist girl-centered organizations) and the issues surrounding literacy itself (e.g., a challenge to libratory literacy myths).

As participants imagine, develop, and sustain a grassroots project, these literate activities expose participants' struggles to balance their representations with their lived realities. These struggles raise important questions: what identities are textually foregrounded and how are these enacted; how do people negotiate the competing representations of in-your-face manifestos and institutionally conservative grant proposals to shape an organization's future, rewrite its past, and mediate its present; how do these representations and actions balance the demands and possibilities of institution building and of hands-on activism? *Girls, Feminism, and Grassroots Literacies* addresses these questions by examining the ways that one group of community girls and women used (and were used by), redesigned (and were redesigned by), and ignored (and were ignored by) "official literacies"[9] that shape this community organization.

As noted above, through this analysis, I complicate the enduring myth that literacy is liberating. This myth is supported by the disproportionate amount of literacy research that focuses on schools. As the sites of literacy research broaden and writing studies scholars explore the actual and not mythologized ways people use literacy, we see that literacy is far more complex than what many institutionally invested conclusions of school-based research may imply.

This research into literacy's complexity underscores how literacy does not necessarily work in ways writers anticipate. For example, GirlZone organizers wrote grant proposals to garner institutional resources. Although these literate activities successfully obtained funds, they also constrained organizers' ability to forward an innovative agenda for grassroots feminist activism by occasionally limiting what activities GirlZone would offer, an unintended consequence to be sure. This example also illustrates how the literate activities surrounding important institutional texts could powerfully draw participants and an institution into social relations that participants were unaware of.

Institutionally important texts reflect and construct what feminist sociologist Dorothy E. Smith calls "documentary realities."[10] People take up the expected ways of knowing and acting that these documentary realities construct. Examining these texts can reveal the social organization of knowledge and the social relations organizing power. Since we live in an increasingly knowledge-based and textually mediated world, it is critical to examine these textual realities in order to understand how these seemingly invisible constructions act upon us. For girls, women, and others who have generally been excluded from power and institutional knowledge-making, it is especially important to understand the ways that people take up these documentary realities in their everyday lives.

At GirlZone, the effects of documentary realities were evident, if not always recognized. There were the institutionally conservative grant proposals that linked GirlZone to national funding organizations, organizations that seldom had girls' organizations on their priority lists. There were also in-your-face manifestos and zines that linked GirlZone to radical feminist ways of producing knowledge and distributing information. GirlZone participants needed to negotiate their understandings of themselves and of their social relations within these contexts where divergent documentary realities at times overlapped and at times collided. Embedded in and shaped by a variety of institutional forces not readily apparent, GirlZone participants' literate activities index a complex cycle of textual production and reproduction that attracted and discouraged participants, business support, and funding opportunities in often unacknowledged ways. This book explores the dynamic struggle between the participants' desires to shape these realities and literacy's enabling and constraining impact on how people do so.

GIRLS AND GIRL CULTURE

Girls, Feminism, and Grassroots Literacies locates its examination into how people use literate activities in a decidedly feminist space. At Girl-Zone as at other feminist grassroots organizations during the 1990s, participants struggled to make sense of how girls and girl culture were influencing the feminist movement and the United States culture more broadly. Theorizing this sense making, both at and beyond GirlZone, is a second project of this book.

Although society now values girls' and women reading and writing, consumer culture and the mass-media send mixed messages and offer difficult rhetorical (textual, visual) conundrums for girls and women to negotiate. These difficulties can be seen in the multiple representations of girls that became highly visible since the 1990s. In national best sellers, on the cover of *The New York Times Book Review*, in Hollywood and independent movies, and on television programs as diverse as *Oprah*, *Law and Order*, and *The News Hour with Jim Lehrer*,[11] the quaint but powerfully residual sugar and spice representation of young girls was shattered by a spate of "mean girl" books and documentaries. In addition to girls' meanness, a second prevalent representation of girls centered on their increasing sexualization. From tabloids to mainstream news, pictures of the highly made-up six-year-old beauty queen JonBenet Ramsey perhaps unwittingly broadcast this sexualization of younger and younger girls. These "prost-i-tots" profoundly troubled traditional notions of who girls are and what they want. Why, for example, do eight-year-olds want thongs, preteens set up casual sex dates, and teens desire breast implants as the up-and-coming high school graduation gift? Although high profile media examples are easy to point to—the infamous Madonna and Britney Spears kiss at the 2003 MTV awards; the exposure of Janet Jackson's nipple as the most talked about moment of Superbowl XXXVIII and the most watched TiVo moment to date—these media eruptions are not the culprit. Rather, they reflect the changing options repeatedly offered to girls. Although these options were most visible in the media and consumer culture, their causes were far more diverse.

Part of this diversity is evident in the expanding age range of those self-identifying as girls. Not only were female youth from toddlers to preadolescents considered girls, but also droves of teens and twenty-something women took up this and related monikers, such as "girlie" "gURL," or "grrrl."[12] Ironically, this first generation of young women who grew up benefiting from second-wave feminist victories embraced a label that just a generation ago women rejected as an offensive attempt to infantilize them. Contrary to this assessment, twenty-somethings in the 1990s celebrated their "girl power." This girl power was made popular in the mid-1990s when marketers pumped out girl power T-shirts, body sprays, and parenting guides, yet girl power had emerged earlier out of both grassroots feminist activism, popular press, and academic books. In this latter context, researchers claimed that girls' power diminished when girls move into womanhood.[13] A new generation of "girls" wanted to reclaim that power and extend it to females beyond preadolescence.

The seeming desire to extend youth captured national and indeed international attention. Demographers, sociologists, psychologists and others are studying these 18–25-year-old "twixters"—women and men who are betwixt and between, unwilling and/or unable to leave youth and become adults. Some depict twixters as slackers. Because they lack financial and moral resources to make it on their own, this demographic rejects the trend of going to school, getting a job, and settling down with children. Others represented twixters as having the likely response to the changing socioeconomic times. Many have staggering college debt; face skyrocketing housing costs; and find fewer options for stable, well-paying jobs. Worldwide, this generation is living at home longer, getting married when they are older, and having children later in life. They will live longer and therefore will have to work longer than previous generations, so why rush?[14] As girls and women face new challenges, claim new identities, and seek new ways of being in the world, the emergence of these so-called twixters and the self-chosen "girl" moniker raises questions about how girls and young women understand and redesign the choices available to them.

These questions resonate far beyond girls and young women. Indeed, throughout the 1990s girls and young women functioned as cultural flash points that exposed society's schizophrenic anxieties and hopes within the global economy. On the one hand, marketers, the media, and doctors, especially in the early 1990s, represented girls in crises, taking up dangerous coping behaviors such as anorexia, cutting, and depression to escape from schools' "hostile hallways" and a "girl poisoning culture."[15] In these representations, girls appear vulnerable, innocent, and agent-less in the face of vitriolic and misogynistic messages washing over them. As stand-ins for other innocents, girls are left to negotiate an increasingly dangerous and unstable world in which social institutions withdraw their safety net and social problems become privatized. On the other hand, popular representations of girl power in the mid-1990s, such as the Spice Girls, depict girls as expressing their agency through consumerism. In these representations, girls gain access to power through their bodies and their credit cards. Represented as enterprising and entitled, young women project the wishful belief that in the marketplace everyone has equal opportunities for buying power.[16] Despite their divergences, these representations highlight how agency is framed within individualistic, often consumption-based models.

These competing constructions of girls and girl culture function not only as a tableau for societal anxieties and hopes, but also for enabling and constraining a new feminist generation. Contrary to the overrepresented generational tensions that have obscured racial, class, and other fissures about what it means to be a girl, a woman, and a feminist today, second-wave feminists have cleared a space for valuing and understanding women and girls. Since at least the 1970s, feminists have pointed out how scholars of youth culture marginalized, misrepresented, and profoundly misunderstood girls and girl culture.[17] Benefiting from this work, girls and young women are demanding to be seen and heard on their own terms. Instead of innocents needing to be saved, consumers duped by capitalism, or feminists-in-training, girls and young women argue that they are *present* agents who actively rework capitalistic and feminist frameworks that seek to configure options for girls and young women today. The ways that feminists of many generations and cohorts negotiate the representations and realities of girl culture will shape and already are shaping the current and future agendas of today's feminist movements.

An examination of literate activities provides one way to intervene in these important negotiations. As noted earlier, literate activities mediate the macro-level forces evident in "documentary realities" (e.g., the ways texts create—and not merely reflect—how people understand themselves and their relations to others) and the micro-level ways girls and women take up, modify, and/or reject these so-called realities. To understand this work requires extended, situated study of how people use (and are used by others') texts in their everyday environment and how large-scale forces enable and limit this work. *Girls, Feminism, and Grassroots Literacies* offers both a method for such a study and a range of applications for how this study can inform real-world matters, like developing organizations or intervening in girl culture.

The situatedness of this research means that there can never be a "typical case" able to stand in for all cases of literacy research or of grassroots feminist organizing. Instead, these situated and extended studies highlight the unexpected contradictions of everyday life and the unexamined assumptions of many typical cases. The potential of what Dorothy Sheridan, Brian V. Street, and David Bloome call "telling cases" is that they exceed what generalized theories might expect of them and work against the flattening theoretical appraisals that offer predicable answers.[18] Yet over time, even telling cases can become typical ones. For example, without using the telling-typical distinction, scholars in recent years have contended that Shirley Brice Heath's highly influential *Ways with Words*—an ethnographic account about the literate activities in several Appalachian communities—has shifted from a telling case to a typical one. At this point, Health's insights into the need to study literacy out-side of middle-class classroom settings have become commonplace.[19] Consequently, we need new telling cases that disrupt this typical flatten-ing, that lead to new theories, new ways of thinking about research, and new strategies to address real-world problems.

In *Girls, Feminism, and Grassroots Literacies*, my analysis of how GirlZone participants used literate activities functions as a telling case that addresses questions about literacy, girl culture, and the future of grassroots organizations/community activism far beyond this local site. My attention to girls' literate activities in community settings extends beyond the few previous studies that have focused primarily on girls in relation to the classroom.[20] This research complements research on women's literate ac-tivities outside the classroom, from writing clubs and public declarations to family parlors and commonplace books.[21] It also redresses the privileg-ing of boys in much research on the study of youth's extracurricular liter-ate activities.[22] This extended, situated study of how girls and women are shaped by the documents they read and produce both complements and complicates the cultural studies-informed work that has been so influential in girls' studies.[23] Moreover, my multiyear, ethnographically informed data collection and close textual analysis works against the trend in popular press books that address the perils of female culture that rely heavily on anecdotal evidence.[24] Through detailed analysis, *Girls, Feminism, and Grassroots Literacies* illustrates the mutual construction of a voluntary or-ganization like GirlZone and of the projected/enacted identities of a Girl-Zone girl.[25] In addition to investigating underresearched topics, *Girls, Feminism, and Grassroots Literacies* models an often voiced but seldom practiced goal of mediating macro and micro levels of analysis[26] by com-bining a cultural studies approach that examines large-scale political un-derstandings of praxis with cultural-historical approaches that examine the complexities of local praxis. This combination complicates and enriches generalized assessments of typical cases.

CHAPTER DESCRIPTIONS

Girls, Feminism, and Grassroots Literacies has two main sections. The first three chapters make up part one "Setting the Scene." Together these introduce the specifics of GirlZone and the broader feminist, activist frames necessary to understand the rise and fall of this grassroots organi-zation. The last four chapters and the coda make up part two, "Literacy in Action: Complicating Feminist Designs." These chapters investigate the complexities of the trends detailed in the first section by analyzing the messiness of how GirlZone participants used literate activities to pursue their goals.

In chapter two, "Building a Youthquake," I locate the place and the players of GirlZone within the disparate and largely uncoordinated activist movements during the 1990s. These movements laid the groundwork for what would become a "youthquake," an eruption of youth-based activism at the turn of the century that captured national and international attention. Responding in part to how multinational corporations construct and sell girlhood, third-wave feminists and others in this youthquake return to the local, including grassroots organizations, as a continuing and key site in which to educate future activists and to effect enduring social change.

In chapter three, "Representations of Girl Culture, Realities of Feminist Activism," I examine how the multiple and conflicting representations of girl culture informed a spate of girl-centered feminist activism at the turn of the twenty-first century. This largely third-wave project of alternately celebrating girlhood and lamenting its destruction was facilitated by the second-wave project of clearing a space for girls to be considered worthy of attention in their own right and not merely as ornaments needing protection from or in preparation for men. GirlZone emerged as part of this project.

In chapter four, "Founding Documents, Founding Feminisms," I examine how second-wave feminist resources both enable and constrain emerging third-wave activist projects. In GirlZone documents and in subsequent textual and material constructions of GirlZone based on these documents, participants negotiated internal feminist divisions as well as an external climate generally hostile to feminism itself. Despite these successes, the limitations of these negotiations were exposed in organizers' thwarted responses to one girl's unexpected suggestion that GirlZone put on a fashion show. This suggestion highlighted generational inflections of ongoing feminist debates as well as the significant fissures among Girl-Zone participants about who defines girl-centered feminist activism, an important issue as a new generation of feminist cohorts reshapes the practices of grassroots feminist activism.

In chapter five, "Circulations of a Feminist Pedagogy," I explore what an effective feminist pedagogy for 6–12-year-old girls might look like. I examine this question through a situated analysis of RadioGirl, a five-year biweekly radio program sponsored by GirlZone and a local radio station. Noting how RadioGirl was best attended when facilitators embedded their feminism within activities that built girls' skills in areas girls cared about, I argue against a pervasive pedagogy in many contemporary girls' programs that focuses on changing girls' awareness and affect. Instead, I argue for a pedagogy that encourages girls to be competent social actors, whether or not they take up the feminist label.

In chapter six, "Redesigning Girls' Image Stores," I argue that despite their ambivalence about engaging a consumer culture that elides an activist girl power into capitalistic messages selling nail polish and facial scrub, feminists need to develop strategies that resituate what Anne Haas Dyson calls youth culture's commercialized "image stores"[27] within feminist frames. This chapter examines the complications of such a project. Focusing on activities surrounding the logo for the annual GrrrlFests, this chapter studies how GirlZone organizers' redesigned consumer culture imagery and how GrrrlFest participants made sense of these remediations.

In chapter seven, "The Economics of Activism," I analyze the literate activities surrounding GirlZone's first and last grant proposal in order to investigate how socioeconomic forces make literate activities meaningful. GirlZone's first grant proposal exposed the ways in which remote funding organizations proleptically shaped this grassroots organization in far greater ways than organizers initially understood. Conversely, GirlZone's last proposal points to the inefficacy of literate activities in a funding climate where only 6 percent of "special population" foundation monies go to girls' organizations.[28] Taken together, these documents teach literacy scholars and feminists to acknowledge the uneven and often limited power literacy has in overcoming material shortfalls that chronically affect girls and women's organizations.

In the coda, "Success and Sustainability," I question how we should assess GirlZone. Should our judgment of GirlZone's success be based on the organization's sustainability? Or, should it be in terms of how people integrated the lessons of GirlZone within themselves or the communities they built? The effects of the latter assessment may require a long time to become visible and are sure to merge with other influences, making causal chains difficult to construct. And, if the effects of GirlZone are difficult to trace, the grounds of its success or failure may be even more difficult to determine. Consequently, this coda suspends a definition of success as permanence and investigates what GirlZone's closing can teach us about contemporary feminist and literacy practices.

2

Building a Youthquake

[What made me want to be an activist and a feminist] is a lot of emotion and just kind of looking around and seeing my little cousins, seeing my little sisters. You know, I've studied power structures for a long time, and you can't study power structures without looking at people who are outside the dominant power structure. And it causes me a lot of sadness. And sometimes since GirlZone started, it's made me, it's overcome some of that sadness. But sometimes it even makes me sadder that I'm giving, we're giving girls the ability to feel powerful but that the structure of patriarchy still exists to keep them down, you know to stunt their potential. But it's personal exploration and exposure to issues and studying culture. I can't imagine anything better to do with my time.

—Aimee, GirlZone co-founder, 1998

In describing what motivates her to be a feminist activist, Aimee weaves the local conditions of her life with larger cultural-historical forces that shape her life. Although she seems overwhelmed at times by the difficulty of changing oppressive structures, Aimee claims in her last sentence that she can find nothing more important than to challenge these structures in her own way, in her own time. This stance indicates how Aimee is like so many others who, without fully knowing it, were part of a surge in youth activism in the 1990s. Reinvigorating and reshaping local, global, and "glocal" causes, this activism emerged in large part from disparate grassroots attempts to reinvigorate historically Left causes, such as protesting war (this time the 1991 invasion of Iraq), or advocating for workers rights (this time in NAFTA's global context).

These less than efficacious political movements of the early 1990s proved to be training grounds and coalition builders that led to an explosion of activism at the turn of the century: the antiglobalization protests against the WTO and the World Bank; the demonstrations and sit-ins on college campuses that protested school paraphernalia made by sweat shops or child labor and agitated for a living wage for all school employees; the peace marches opposing the second U.S.-Iraq war; the online activism of Indymedia.org and MoveOn.org. Adrienne Maree Brown and William

Upski Wimsatt describe this forceful wave of activity that had been building for years yet that had gone largely unnoticed until it erupted as a "youthquake": "For the first time in a generation, there is an undeniable critical mass of young people who are aware of ourselves as part of a growing national—and international—movement."[1] This visibility was largely absent in the mid-1990s—when GirlZone emerged—but by the end of the 1990s, marketers and the media as well as businesses and political analysts were attending to the power and potential of this youthquake.

Knowing more about diverse local activist organizations would help explain how these disparate groups and actions gave rise to the youthquake Brown and Wimsatt describe. Unfortunately, there are few enduring representations of the largely uncoordinated groundswell that enabled later high profile activist eruptions; grassroots organizations are typically so focused on survival they seldom have time to record their processes. As the histories of these fleeting grassroots organizations disappear and those of more centralized, national organizations with institutionalized resources are overly represented, we lose a sense of how these movements were lived.[2]

Girls, Feminism, and Grassroots Literacies counters a repeat of this misrepresentative history in its attention to one grassroots activist organization that participated in this national youthquake. In particular, GirlZone provides a way to examine questions relevant to a feminist part of this youthquake: What made a group of feminist activists at this time and place start GirlZone? What made over one thousand participants, largely youth, attend any number of the hundreds of workshops? What were the local and national conditions that made a girl-centered organization thrive, and then disappear? To investigate these questions that situate GirlZone within the national contexts that are too often cordoned off in analyses of local organizations, this chapter provides an overview of both GirlZone's history, place, and players and the activist contexts shaping this grassroots feminist experiment. This overview understands GirlZone as one of many organizations that came to shape the future instantiations of grassroots feminist activism within the turn of the century youthquake. Focusing on a telling case, this analysis exposes both the promise of the youthquake's celebratory power-to-the-people goals and the less acknowledged difficulties of launching and sustaining these goals.

A BRIEF HISTORY OF GIRLZONE

In the fall of 1996, two community women, Aimee and Gina,[3] called together a group of twelve local activists in order to brainstorm ways to redress the sexism that girls and women in Champaign-Urbana, Illinois felt in the mid-1990s. Initially, these women thought they would form a collective to counter what Aimee called the "cultural hegemony that works against women, that works against females in our society."[4] As they talked, these women recounted how the limitations they felt started years earlier when, as girls, they faced intense pressures to conform to restrictive societal stereotypes. Without enough financial resources and cultural awareness to challenge socializing spaces, such as schools, that often exacerbated the deleterious effects of these cultural stereotypes,[5] these girls grew into women who felt undermined by previous hegemonic forces. Based on these conversations, the group decided to create a grassroots community organization to work with girls and young women; they would focus on adults later. Setting out with far more enthusiasm for than experience in running a grassroots organization, Aimee and Gina founded GirlZone with the rest of the women acting as a loose support structure.

After a few sparsely attended workshops in 1997, word of GirlZone spread. The local media publicized GirlZone and its mission—"a community grassroots program which engages girls and young women in weekly workshops which allow them to explore and celebrate their abilities and skills."[6] Resonating with school counselors, parents, business leaders, and girls themselves, the GirlZone mission interrogated both the popularized girl crises of the early 1990s and the girl power craze of the late 1990s.[7] Within months GirlZone was running weekly workshops twelve out of thirteen weeks on topics ranging from weight lifting to rock music, from improv to tai chi. This labor intensive project led to early challenges. For example, despite the fact that Aimee and Gina had been involved in a variety of activist, academic, and community groups, and despite the fact that they had found a not-for-profit sponsor with a free meeting space, Aimee and Gina would soon discover they were unprepared for the logistics of running an organization.

Early and persistent structural problems quickly became evident. First was the difficulty of making lasting institutional collaborations. Successful in short-term ventures, such as providing a RadioGirl workshop that allowed Girl Scouts the possibility to earn a badge, GirlZone had problems making these partnerships last. For example, after several cancellations, GirlZone organizers finally met with the coordinators of the local Girls and Boys Club to plan projects beneficial to both organizations: GirlZone could redress Girls and Boys Club's insufficient programming targeted specifically to girls; the Girls and Boys Club could provide GirlZone an institutional sponsoring with the African-American community, a community where GirlZone had consistent difficulty making inroads. Despite plans for one African-American woman affiliated with the Girls and Boys Club to serve on the GirlZone Steering Committee and for several GirlZone workshops to take place in the Girls and Boys Club building, neither came to pass; both organizations were spread too thin to devote the resources needed to make a new venture take off. Typical of grassroots realities, this experience illustrated how the energy and enthusiasm associated with a surge in grassroots activism is difficult to organize let alone sustain without funding to underwrite staff for outreach or volunteer coordination.

Lack of such funding emerged as GirlZone's main problem. Following the Do-It-Yourself approach of third-wave and other youth movements, GirlZone's $0–8 sliding fee was designed to cover the workshops' costs and to be accessible to all girls. In practice, however, the workshops lost money; volunteers either were too busy running workshops to collect the money or feared embarrassing a girl or parent who could not pay. In the end, Aimee and Gina paid GirlZone's institutional costs out of their own pockets.

To respond to the obvious problems in this system, Aimee applied for grants, receiving a $10,000 grant from the Chicago-based Girl's Best Friend Foundation to pay for programmatic costs. In addition, GirlZone moved to the University YMCA, which provided free copying—a key expense for GirlZone. These were important financial accomplishments, but organizers realized they most needed funding for staff positions; Girl-Zone's structural needs were proving greater than drop-in volunteers could accommodate and more overwhelming than the two founding organizers could manage on their own.

Similar to the life cycle of many grassroots organizations, GirlZone reached a critical juncture. After eighteen months of intensive creative activity, Aimee and Gina redirected their focus toward sustainability. Yet, the process of developing institutional structures squelched many volunteers' enthusiasm; volunteers signed up to change girls' lives or at least run workshops for and with the girls, not to lick envelopes or edit a database. When GirlZone organizers began privileging organizational needs they truncated what Aimee called the "organic nature of GirlZone development" and "left everyone frustrated." Sadly typical of many grassroots organizations, GirlZone's third year would either revitalize GirlZone, or show that the necessary interest and/or structures were not there.

The strain of this year took its toll on Gina and Aimee's collaboration. In the summer of 1999, with much to do, haphazard communication, and general weariness, Aimee and Gina had an acrimonious split. Tellingly, this split exposed what sociologist Verta Taylor believes is the underexamined role emotions play in social movement theory and in particular in feminist organizations that often openly acknowledge how emotions shape social movements.[8] At GirlZone, Aimee and Gina's falling out highlighted how central personal relationships are to grassroots activism—especially in the relatively small activist networks in nonurban settings such as Champaign-Urbana.

After the difficult rift, Aimee remained as the sole organizer of Girl-Zone and Gina returned to her art and to pursue her MA, hoping to recapture plans that she had put on hold while she devoted so much time to GirlZone. By the following summer of 2000, Aimee burned out, felt unappreciated, and took a job at the Girl's Best Friend Foundation in Chicago. This foundation allowed Aimee to pursue her commitment to problems faced by youth and girls in particular. She was paid for her work, had the structures that large organizations can provide, and could be nurtured by experienced mentors who shared similar activist causes. Even so, Aimee quickly realized she made a mistake. While appreciating the organizational structures that the foundation offered, she felt divorced from hands-on feminist activism. She returned to Champaign-Urbana, redoubling her efforts to make GirlZone viable. Overwhelmed with managing the daily operations of a grassroots organization, holding a job, and pursuing interests outside of GirlZone, Aimee offered fewer workshops (2 instead of 4 per month), sought interns from the University, and aggressively wrote for grant monies. In addition, Aimee began to view GirlZone as a clearinghouse that sponsored feminist activism for girls and women throughout Champaign-Urbana a shift most visibly manifested in the GirlZone-sponsored annual GrrrlFest—a weekend of hands-on workshops, discussions, and musical showcases celebrating girls and women.

Despite GirlZone's internal turbulence, the community publicly validated this organization: in the alternative paper's "Best of . . ." edition, GirlZone was voted the best nonprofit organization and won the best workshop award as well; the city of Champaign decreed April 22, 2000 "GirlZone Day" in recognition of GirlZone's accomplishments and importance to the city; GirlZone was featured in large media outlets such as *The Chicago Tribune* and National Public Radio. Beyond these public displays of support and interest, however, funding continued to be problematic. The community was more likely to offer space, volunteers, and materials than critical monetary support. Without funding for staff positions, GirlZone could not organize consistent forums for drop-in volunteers and girls, prompting Aimee to actively seek foundation monies once again. Unfortunately for GirlZone, foundations only offer about 6 percent of their "special populations" grants to girls' organizations and increasingly even these limited funds were directed to large urban areas.[9] In addition, these agencies often provided seed money, not support staff lines.

One organization in Champaign-Urbana did fund staff positions, and Aimee actively pursued these monies throughout 2002. Although crushed when she learned that this foundation had rejected the GirlZone application, Aimee was outraged when she heard through informal channels that GirlZone did not get the grant because of the funders' perceptions of Aimee herself. During the site visit, Aimee had carefully downplayed any "angry feminist" associations, feeling these might hurt her chances with the conservative funding agency. She was unaware and unprepared that it would be the funders' misperception that Aimee "smoked dope" that made her and therefore GirlZone less viable. As disturbed as Aimee was by this misperception, she was even more floored that funding decisions were made on such insubstantial grounds.

This foundation's response proved the death knell for GirlZone. Aimee concluded that GirlZone was no longer institutionally feasible. Saying she did not want to be part of a system that oppressed women and girls—a system that claimed the labor of meeting girls' and women's needs was valuable and should be continued, but was not worth funding—Aimee publicly announced that GirlZone would close at the end of GrrrlFest 2003.

Aimee idealistically hoped that GirlZone's ending would be a catalyst for increased action. No longer would the community be able to deny the needs and interests of girls; GirlZone had clearly proven that. As Aimee described in an email,

> i see our end, and the kick in the pants it might provide to those who have been wanting to get involved, or wanting to see change in certain areas, (as well as the mentoring-based awareness that it will bring through our informal exchanges and "lessons learned" sessions during grrrlfest on what worked, what didn't work, as well as major local obstacles to watch out for in creating and forging new girl-centric visions and action—and the physical evacuating of the all-too-assumed "this orgs got girls covered" seat in our community) at this point of time where GirlZone is so well knows [sic] and so well-respected, to be one of our strongest bids so far at success.[10]

GirlZone's greatest success, Aimee believed, would be to make girls able to explore their interests in a range of activities, at skating parks and basketball courts as well as physics classrooms and after school programs. To meet these needs, the community could no longer rely on volunteers, and especially not on the one volunteer who had given untold hours and personal funding for over seven years. Aimee would actively help others meet girls' needs, but the forum would no longer be GirlZone.

In this decidedly controversial act, Aimee chose to close GirlZone as opposed to pass the GirlZone torch to others. The crisis of GirlZone's closing had finally motivated people to step forward seeking to take up part of the workload, but Aimee found this act too late. As is always the case in organizational decisions, personal and institutional factors came into play. Aimee had started GirlZone in a particular moment in a particular place, and she wondered if that moment had passed. If she could not make GirlZone sustainable after seven years of on-the-ground training in grant writing, institutional organizing, and networking with media and local business owners; if she could not make it viable after years of largely working part-time jobs to support this passion and without competing obligations of a long-term partner or children, then Aimee felt it was time for GirlZone to close. Not all agreed with this decision. In the planning for GrrrlFest 2003, there were overt and covert confrontations between Aimee and some of the women who wanted to keep GirlZone running but, on September 14, at the completion of GrrrlFest 2003, Girl-Zone officially shut its doors.

GirlZone's closing raises questions about the possibilities and limitations of community activism at the turn of the twenty-first century. These lessons partially reflect the passion yet inexperience of GirlZone participants. GirlZone organizers had clearly tapped into a compelling problem, were able to motivate over one thousand participants, garner local and national press, and endure for seven years. But GirlZone organizers needed more training in a variety of areas, from educational outreach to grant writ-

Table 2.1
Timeline of Key GirlZone Events

Season	GirlZone Activity
Fall 1996	Community women discuss the lack of representation of women and their feelings of continued discrimination against women. Aimee and Gina decide to found GirlZone.
Spring 1997	GirlZone offers its first workshops.
Fall 1997	Aimee writes the first grant to Girls' Best Friend Foundation. GirlZone sponsors a RadioGirl workshop that eventually (1998) turns into a five-year biweekly radio program by and for girls.
Winter 1997–1998	I start researching at GirlZone.
Summer 1999	Gina leaves GirlZone and Aimee becomes the sole organizer.
Fall 1999	The original RadioGirl facilitator, Ayleen, moves to Portland, and Heidi begins coordinating RadioGirl.
Summer 2000	Aimee takes a position with the Girls' Best Friend Foundation in Chicago, returning after a few months with a revised vision for GirlZone.
	I move from Champaign-Urbana, participating in GirlZone remotely and in person at major events and summer workshops.
Spring 2001	GirlZone sponsors the first annual GrrrlFest: Throw like a girl!
Winter 2002–2003	Aimee learns of the United Way's rejection of GirlZone's grant application.
Fall 2003	GirlZone ends after the third annual GrrrlFest.

ing to business management. In this way, GirlZone reflects what academic and activist Eric Schragge sees as the professionalization of the community sector. This professionalization takes the power away from the local community and places it with experts who speak for the local community.[11] Like others who participated in the emerging youthquake during the 1990s, GirlZone organizers experienced how this shift poses significant dilemmas that might motivate and plague passionate community members seeking to make social change on a local level. At minimum, the telling details of the lived realities of GirlZone—from the difficulty gaining access to external resources to the charged emotional and personal internal relationships—

complicate typical celebratory "people power" stories that undergird the youthquake. These complications can inform the strategies of contemporary grassroots activists seeking to enact these inspiring narratives.

Fig. 2.1. GrrrlFest Auto Mechanic Workshop. *Note:* Permission courtesy of Aimee, co-founder of GirlZone.

Fig. 2.2. Off-air RadioGirl Workshop. *Note:* Reprinted from *The News-Gazette* (February 11, 1999) B—8. Photograph by Melissa Merdi.

GIRLZONE GirlZine   Special Web Edition
Winter 2000–2001   Volume 1, Number 2

active girls rock

The GirlZone GirlZine is a biannual publication that highlights the current events and thoughts of GirlZone along with the creative talents of local girls. This web version was edited down for the GirlZone Art Show on April 20, 2001. Contact GirlZone on the web at www.prairienet.org/girlzone, by e-mail at   @prairinet.org or call the GirlZone Hotline at 637-GIRL (637)-4475).

Fig. 2.3. Front Page of GirlZone *Girl Zine 1.2. Note:* Permission granted by Aimee, co-founder of GirlZone.

THE PLACE: ACTIVISM IN THE CORN FIELDS

Part of the "glocal" 1990s activist surge, GirlZone is nestled simultaneously in local efforts to build a community and in national and at times global trends that shaped concurrent activist eruptions.

Within the predominantly corn (and soy) fields of central Illinois sit the "twin city" towns of Champaign-Urbana. Since GirlZone began,

Champaign-Urbana has seen rapid development, with large houses on golf courses as well as Sam's Clubs and Target stores replacing tracts of farmland. Even with this development, both Champaign and Urbana have the occasional cobblestoned streets and a diminishing number of corn plots, used for farming and as a reminder that the state's flagship university, located in Champaign-Urbana, is a land grant institution in an agriculturally based region. This Big Ten university is the largest regional employer, with research hospitals and software companies as well as a Solo Cup plant and a Kraft factory offering a mix of white- and blue-collar work. Like many university towns, Champaign-Urbana has an activist and feminist presence more common to urban areas, like "upstate" Chicago. Frequently the only "downstate" areas to vote Democratic in national elections,[12] Champaign and Urbana are surrounded by more rural, economically depressed, and politically conservative towns.

Champaign and Urbana may look similar to a visitor, but there are important distinctions to those who live there. Champaign is larger in size, more densely populated, houses a greater percentage of the student population, and includes a notably poor section made up disproportionately by racial minorities. Champaign has two downtown areas. The city's downtown has a main strip surrounded by apartments and houses. The campus downtown has primarily student apartments and many bars that support the vibrant music scene affiliated with student bands and the university's strong jazz history. In a continual state of renewal, both downtowns benefit economically from the growing industry and new homes, as evident in new upscale restaurants, quirky coffee shops, and trendy secondhand clothing stores.

Champaign-dwelling college students dub Urbana the home of "arts and nuts," but those living in Urbana think of it more as an indie rock incubator. Urbana has a quiet downtown where one can buy "earthy" Birkenstock shoes, and stop for coffee and a poetry reading in a former movie theatre that had closed down. Less densely populated than Champaign, Urbana has predominantly single family homes and smaller apartment buildings that house many of the faculty, graduate students, and international students. Urbana's "faculty ghetto" is within easy walking distance to the university and its homes have overflowing, some might say unkempt, gardens. The seasonal farmers' market, held weekly in the parking lot of the frequently on the verge of collapse mall, brings in local produce and Amish goods.

Within the activist pockets of Champaign-Urbana, GirlZone had three "home" sites, each less than a mile apart from the others. The first two sites were on a tree-lined, well-trafficked part of the main campus where Champaign and Urbana abut. In its first space, GirlZone started as a sponsored organization of a community service organization called the Disciples Foundation. After a few months and a bitter controversy surrounding who would receive administrative costs in grant funding, Girl-

Zone changed its sponsoring institution and moved to a University YMCA where it spent most of its life. Echoing the large brick Georgian buildings across the street on the University's "quad," the YMCA offered office space for student-led initiatives, provided currents events programs, and sponsored initiatives on environmental and sustainable development as well as dialogues on diverse religious and ethical perspectives.[13] For GirlZone, the YMCA provided a level of support and stability as well as contact with more institutionally established activists and funders than it would have had if it were on its own. When GirlZone's founder Aimee graduated and thus no longer qualified as a current University member, the YMCA wanted GirlZone to pay rent or vacate their space. Surprised at the suddenness of what felt like an eviction, Aimee moved GirlZone's home base to its third site: the local Independent Media Center (IMC). Like the other sites, the IMC was on the free bus route. In a small storefront in downtown Urbana and adjacent to a big, paved parking lot that proved an excellent site for weekend workshops on skateboarding and car mechanics, the IMC was a warm, if a bit run-down site that overflowed with activists' tracts tacked to the walls and stuffed in nooks and crannies of this oddly shaped three-room space. GirlZone remained at the IMC for its duration, yet the IMC itself was closed down twice by the local government for contested code violations, a move seen by many in the activist community and beyond as an attempt to silence the IMC's critiques of the local government.

GirlZone's physical space in each of its three sites was generic and ephemeral, yet these were activist spaces where community members met to forward their agendas and learn about other causes. In none of these spaces did GirlZone have a room of its own. GirlZone had to make do with a mailbox, occasionally a desk and access to a copier. Nevertheless, these institutions provided GirlZone with two critical resources: a not-for-profit tax identification number (needed when applying for grants) and reserved access to public space that GirlZone organizers adapted to fit their needs—setting up chairs and tables for writing workshops or bringing in amps, drums, and guitars for music workshops. Even though GirlZone's home spaces varied in size and feelings of permanence, each space consistently exposed GirlZone participants to the thriving activist scene in Champaign-Urbana and physically and textually placed Girl-Zone participants within it.

In addition to these homesites, GirlZone often held workshops throughout the community in places appropriate to the workshop: a dojo for martial arts workshops, the community college planetarium for astrology workshops, and local restaurants for cooking workshops. Despite the appeal of physically enmeshing GirlZone throughout the Champaign-Urbana community, organizers increasingly held workshops in their homesite to lower the incidence of poor attendance and frustrated participants who could not find that day's events.

Outside of the workshops, GirlZone facilitators (including myself) held meetings throughout Champaign-Urbana to maintain community connections and, more commonly, to accommodate participants' competing demands, such as meeting at my house so that my children could nap. Even so, GirlZone organizers had a few typical haunts. These reflected GirlZone's explicit support of local and generally female-run organizations, notably the only female-owned coffee shop where many GirlZone workshop facilitators worked. These local organizations also assisted Girl-Zone, as when this same coffee shop hosted GirlZone film fests and prominently displayed flyers about GirlZone related activities. For Girl-Zone organizers, creating GirlZone meant building relationships with feminists, activists, and townspeople throughout Champaign-Urbana, in part by endorsing their causes and patronizing their shops.

Tightly nestled within its local community, GirlZone was also located in broader U.S. contexts, responsive to national activist trends. In retrospect, it is clear how these national trends would coalesce to form future youth and feminist activism. At the front end of these trends, however, things felt ad hoc and activists drew their lessons from diverse resources. For example, GirlZone organizers frequently referred to California's Proposition 187 (passed on November 8, 1994), which denied public social services, publicly funded health care, and public education to illegal immigrants in California. GirlZone participants opposed Proposition 187, but were most concerned about the disconnect between the discourses and the voting record of what GirlZone organizers considered the activist hotbed of Berkeley. In Berkeley, as throughout the state, those who supported Proposition 187 were often portrayed as racist, making it difficult for people to voice concerns without being demonized as bigots. This polarization, GirlZone organizers felt, fostered a mismatch between the public discourses opposing Proposition 187 and the voting results supporting this Proposition.[14] This mismatch exposed potential difficulties of transforming an idealistic, empowering philosophy into a lived reality. What GirlZone organizers took away from these events was the need to have spaces to hash out the complex issues involved in activism. Community members must have neutral spaces and multiple opportunities to engage each other even if, perhaps especially if, they disagree.

Since activism at GirlZone generally meant feminist activism, organizers wanted GirlZone to be a place where people did not take up predetermined "feminist" positions, whatever these might be. In sync with, yet initially unaware of, a new generation of feminist writers who felt that second-wave feminisms were essential but insufficient,[15] GirlZone organizers began the bumpy process of building a community that would question what "feminist" activism is, who gets to define it, and how to validate differences while staying unified enough to forward their agendas. To avoid the fate of Proposition 187, GirlZone organizers offered community-wide workshops, panels, and training sessions as well as GirlZone facilitator discussion nights and girl-centered and girl-run GirlZone panels. These were not always successful, and sometimes led to hurt feelings, such as when organizers doing the ongoing grunt work resented those who repeated the platitudes of activist discourses that did not reflect the lived reality of how issues played in specific settings. Like other grassroots organizations during the 1990s, though perhaps unlike romanticized assessments of the youthquake, GirlZone simultaneously struggled with internal differences and forged a (feminist) community that investigated what national activist eruptions could teach participants in their local context.

THE PLAYERS: PRIMARY GIRLZONE PARTICIPANTS

GirlZone was an organization deeply anchored in and defined by the lives of its participants who, at the time, would not have imagined they were part of a national youthquake; rather, participants thought of themselves as building a local community. In that community, there are four groups of participants critical to understanding GirlZone and this analysis of its literate activities: the two founding organizers, Aimee and Gina;[16] the facilitators who either ran the workshops or worked behind-the-scenes; the girls who attended the weekly workshops; and me, who acted both as a facilitator and researcher. With varying degrees of awareness of local and national trends, these participants worked together to create an activist community that, they hoped, might change at least the local culture of Champaign-Urbana.

The Founding Organizers: Building on Past Eruptions

Gina: Reverberations that Shape the Youthquake

When GirlZone began, Gina was in her thirties. A tall Caucasian woman, she worked odd jobs, such as cleaning houses, to support her work as an artist. Gina seemed most comfortable in small group interactions where she shared her art, her activist passions, and her encouragement in ways that girls clearly appreciated. As with other local leaders who informed the turn-of-the-century youthquake, Gina drew on lessons from previous activist eruptions, most notably second-wave feminisms, to shape the changes she hoped to foster.

Although Gina clearly valued the activism present in this university town, she had a fraught relationship with academics and even academic feminists who, Gina felt, talked more about feminism than did feminist work. For Gina, feminist work is shaped by acting on the insights of personal experiences. This is a lesson she took away from her feminist "click" moment, which occurred while reading *The Feminine Mystique* in high school.

> *The Feminine Mystique* by Betty Friedan. That's like an oldie, moldy book but that was a big book for me when I was younger. I felt like I was reading about myself and my family and this feeling of when I looked at

most of the women that I knew in suburban Cleveland, I didn't want to be like them. So it, reading this book sort of gave answers of why and what was going on. And it was just, I think it was big, probably the beginning of my identification as a feminist by reading that book. So it was just a big book. It was stuff that I knew intuitively like when I didn't want to take typing cause I would be destined to be a secretary, just to be sucked into the secretary karma. "No, I don't want to do that." So it's like stuff I knew intuitively and you read the book and you go, "OK."[17]

No longer feeling alone in being conflicted about her positioning or in desiring greater options, Gina felt that *The Feminine Mystique* provided both a language to understand her discontent and an imagined community in which she could participate.[18] Gina wanted this imagined community to become real for others. Her desire to foster such a community for women and especially for girls profoundly motivated Gina to start GirlZone.

In this GirlZone community, Gina wanted to expose and help make sense of the continuing problems girls and women face today. For example, thirty years after *The Feminine Mystique* was published, Gina was frustrated at what she considered the false offers of possibility that obscure how women and girls are still being excluded and discriminated against:

People don't want to just see guys in a band and they don't want to just see guys skateboarding and they don't want to, I mean, as an adult, seeing a competent woman passed over at the office for a man. You know, I worked in the printing trades and I was using equipment to do film output. I was the second woman to do it and one guy said, "they put you in that department to see you fail." I mean it's like incredible, like personal things that we are all coming up against that just, it's just a very real issue.[19]

Despite expanded opportunities, Gina recognized that women continue to face overt as well as covert discriminations whether on the music stage, at the skate park, or in the workplace. Gina believes girls today face similarly limited options in schools, "where the gender stereotyping tends to be reinforced," and boys "are doing the science experiments; they are playing basketball when girls are sitting back."[20] Second-wave feminist goals, such as eliminating discrimination against girls in the classroom and women at work, clearly inform how Gina understood her activist commitment to develop a community that examines and opposes these limiting personal experiences.

In shaping a local instantiation of the contemporary youthquake, Gina hoped that GirlZone participants could learn from earlier disruptions, even if the origins of these disruptions were not fully visible to younger activists. Until her dramatic departure from GirlZone, Gina shared this project with GirlZone's other founding organizer, Aimee.

Aimee: A Product and Harbinger of Feminist Activism

Around the same age as many of the activists writing in Adrienne Mareé Brown and Wilham Upski Wimsatt's collection described in the opening of this chapter, Aimee was in her early twenties, athletic, and continually trying new things when she co-founded GirlZone. Personable and quick to smile, with usually blond hair—sometimes in cornrows, sometimes in a kerchief, pigtails, or just down—Aimee was charismatic and motivating, able to encourage others also to try new things. When GirlZone first started, Aimee was pursuing her MA in the Quantitative and Evaluative Methodologies Division of Educational Psychology at the state university. During her tenure as co-founder of GirlZone, Aimee took some time to be a researcher for the Girl's Best Friend Foundation and eventually became the Program Coordinator for the Women in Engineering Program at the university. Although Aimee worked within feminist philanthropic and academic institutions, she preferred the immediate responsiveness of grassroots activism to directly address the questions and needs Aimee saw around her.

Unlike Gina's "click" moment, Aimee was like others in her third-wave cohort, growing up with feminist accomplishments paradoxically infused and lacking throughout her childhood. On the one hand, Aimee remembers a Chicagoland home where the work was evenly distributed and both her mother and father actively encouraged each of their four middle-class Caucasian daughters to believe they could do whatever they set their minds to do. This support continued as Aimee's sisters and mother participated in key GirlZone events. For example, Aimee's older sister led a workshop on songwriting, bringing information about her activist efforts to close the U.S. Army School of the Americas; ARTCAR!, a program that encourages women to participate in music; and, the New York City-based Hen Foundation, which she co-coordinated as a site to support grassroots activist artists. The activist, feminist, and educational networks that Aimee's family brought to GirlZone workshops highlighted both how feminist activism can be part of participants' everyday and how even local activists are situated within and need to build communities across a range of global and local causes.

On the other hand, the initial feminist accomplishments Aimee benefited from exposed the need for continued feminist activism. For example, Aimee preferred playing tennis with her male friends when growing up, because boys played competitively without fearing they would be called mean or would hurt their opponent's feelings. She attributed her reluctance to associate more with strong women to a culture that limited available roles for women and made women jealous of other strong women.[21] Already benefiting from Title IX's support of girls and women's athletics and long before the girl culture buzz phrase "relational anger" became commonplace, Aimee struggled to think beyond legislative equality toward the multiple internal and external structures that keep women from supporting other women. Although Aimee did not articulate this meta-awareness, her activism was both enabled by recent feminist work and called for future feminist work. For Aimee, this future work drew on national trends but was enacted locally. This was the case in founding GirlZone.

Despite the many steps that made GirlZone seem long in coming, Aimee claims she wanted to start GirlZone when, in the summer of 1996, she realized she no longer wanted to be President of the United States because she no longer thought that a woman could.[22] In an almost clichéd moment, Aimee railed against this limitation. Beyond writing checks or letters to members of Congress, and beyond supporting The White House Project, which seeks to change the cultural climate so it becomes common for women to be in positions of power such as the President,[23] Aimee wondered what she could do. She concluded that acting locally seemed her best option.

This impetus for local action typifies much Do-It-Yourself (DIY) feminist activism central to the 1990s youthquake. High schooler Erica Gilbert-Levin captures the feelings behind this activism when she describes her decision to start a feminist group in her high school:

> Of course, compared to issues like global poverty, ever-increasing violence against women and a lamentable dearth of affordable heath- and child-care in the United States, these issues [gender oppression in high school] seem small. But while feminists fight to end sexist oppression around the world, I felt that the best thing I could do—as a seventeen-year-old with a year and a half of high school left to go—was to start a feminist club and raise awareness about both the sexist conditions around the world and the subtle forms of everyday sexism within our own small community.[24]

As Erica Gilbert-Levin points out, despite the necessary feminist work on national and international levels, feminisms are still lived in the everyday.

To put this in less personal terms, as Nancy H. Naples does, local activism provides an important entry point where people build communities, name problems, and work toward solutions in order to shape community engagement with the state, with corporations, with discriminatory and limiting forces of everyday life.[25] For these reasons, even in a time of globalization, attention to local grassroots activism is still important. Unbeknownst to Aimee and Gina, their decision to act locally—to found GirlZone—mirrored the youthquake and, more specifically, the third-wave, girl-centered activism that emerged during the late 1990s (see chapters 3 and 4).

Their decision also enacted contemporary theories of learning. In disciplines as diverse as cognitive psychology, anthropology, science studies, and education, scholars developed learning principles not as abstract shifts of an individual mind but as social practices within a specific community. Aimee and Gina asked the same question as many educators: what types of social interactions would offer effective contexts for learning to take place? Like scholars Jean Lave and Etienne Wenger,[26] Aimee and Gina felt one answer was to help participants become viable social actors able to create a community, what some call a "community of practice" or a "community of learners," which in GirlZone's case could create resources that help girls and women to explore options that seemed foreclosed to them.

Throughout GirlZone's institutional life, groups of women and girls helped Aimee and Gina think through this project.

The Facilitators: Forging Community Across Generations and Allegiances

Of the many who supported Aimee and Gina's work, "facilitators" are those who helped form GirlZone and who later ran workshops. Among the facilitators, there are at least three groups of women of varying ages and allegiances to GirlZone's feminist agendas. Like participants in other activist movements, these facilitators negotiated their differences in order to sustain the GirlZone community (see chapter 3).

The first group of women is largely comprised of feminists who had been active in Champaign-Urbana for years, such as the director of the community college's Women's Studies office, an editor of the local newspaper, and local business owners. Through the causes they shared, these women had known each other informally perhaps for decades. Seeing GirlZone as a resource their community needed, this group of facilitators was instrumental in creating GirlZone and in running early workshops that tapped their positions in the community, such as a state representative facilitating a political writing workshop. Although these women were stretched thin—spearheading various activist efforts, maintaining full time jobs, and juggling packed personal lives—these facilitators were role models and mentors; they provided an activist community that younger facilitators would draw upon and eventually shape. Gina and particularly Aimee became part of this core group of women that community members would seek out when looking for allies in local feminist or activist projects.

The second group of activist facilitators was generally younger and more transient. They were also committed activists, yet these women were living in Champaign-Urbana while thinking about what to do next: the RadioGirl facilitator Ayleen left Champaign-Urbana to travel to Africa for a month with a friend in the Peace Corps before moving to Portland; Andi, a longtime workshop leader, assembled a portfolio and moved to New York in hopes of going to art school. Many in this second group would self-define as third-wave, perhaps even alternative, and frequently performed their alteriority through body piercing, unusually colored hair, thickly soled shoes, and generally hipper styles of dress—a look that appealed to girls attending GirlZone.[27] This second group of facilitators organized and ran many of the workshops the girls suggested and became the main group of facilitators as GirlZone institutionally aged. GirlZone provided this group a community where they could interact with other young feminist activists as they struggled to understand themselves within and against the existing and emerging feminist activist frameworks.

The third group of facilitators was undergraduate university women who volunteered at GirlZone to meet the community service requirements in their Women's Studies, Psychology/Family Development, Education, and other course work. Dipping into Champaign-Urbana's activist, feminist community, perhaps for the first time, these facilitators chose to meet their academic requirement at GirlZone because of their interest in GirlZone's mission. They might support existing workshops or run a workshop in an area of expertise, whether dance, creative writing, or football. This category also includes a rotating group of university interns at GirlZone from 2000–2003, who were learning about the nitty-gritty work of developing institutional structures, writing grants or solicitation letters to the community, creating databases, or interacting with volunteers and volunteer training. Although often energized by their activist experiences, facilitators in this group seldom continued after the semester. In general, those women were either just beginning to openly call themselves feminists or took a stance best described as "I'm not a feminist, but . . . [I believe in feminist ideals]." GirlZone provided a way for them to envision themselves as feminist activists, if even for a short time. The women in this group were the most transient in GirlZone, yet they linked GirlZone to communities beyond girls and their parents and beyond communities of self-identified feminists/activists. This link has been crucial yet difficult to sustain in many contemporary feminist projects.

These three groups of facilitators offer a window into how GirlZone provided a space for a community of women, of various generations and degrees of feminist identification, to learn from and with each another. Facilitators found the idea of GirlZone compelling, but beyond a group of facilitators from the second group, this community remained quite loose. Indeed, GirlZone facilitators were like those of many grassroots activist communities in the youthquake, with high casual participation but few people moving into leadership positions. These facilitators—stable but overtaxed older activists, committed but transient younger feminists, and interested but "feminist" leery younger women—left GirlZone organizers with the responsibility of nurturing this community as well as building and running GirlZone. This difficulty dramatically shaped how GirlZone developed as an institution, and played a central role in GirlZone's demise.[28] Despite this profound limitation, for years GirlZone allowed participants to imagine possibilities for feminist activism and to work to enact their visions on a local level.

The Girls: Building and Recognizing Youth's Agency

Central to the turn-of-the-century youthquake was building alliances across many groups. And, although GirlZone focused on girls, "girls" was anything but a monolithic term. In fact, GirlZone consciously struggled to serve and attract girls with diverse education, age, economic status, ethnicity, and interest. To do this, GirlZone organizers used flyers, conducted classroom presentations, made personal contacts, and publicized GirlZone in a variety of settings. These pitches combined with other factors—the activity, the groups of friends attending, a girl's ability to get to a workshop, and even the season[29]—to inform girls' participation.

For organizers, schooling was one of the most surprising aspects of diversity. Most girls attended the local public schools, yet the many home- or alternatively schooled girls highlighted the biases of the adult participants who had normed school socialization, such as ways of working in groups or listening to directions. Although GirlZone texts claimed GirlZone encouraged girls to think for themselves and not be afraid to speak out, workshop facilitators frequently discussed home-schooled Cyan because she continually "disrupted" workshops when she questioned facilitators' ideas and activities, thought of alternative ways to do things, or spoke out when she disagreed. Cyan complicated the libratory image that facilitators and organizers had made of a self-confident, nonconformist girl.[30] With fewer constraints than schools have, GirlZone organizers could address these disruptions by asking girls to shape the practices of this institution and determine acceptable ways GirlZone participants should act. Some of the eleven "GirlZone Participant Expectations" reinscribed school behavior (e.g., "6. Raise hands when talking in a group"), but many focused on reasons for actions (with an emphasis on respect) and fostered socialization atypical of school girls (e.g., "10. Voice their opinion if they disagree").[31] In developing their community norms, these GirlZone girls imagined what practices they needed in their extracurricular education in ways that echoed school, but with a slant. This slant recognized that girls could and should be seen as agents who have the power to shape community norms.

Other factors of diversity also proved important. One factor organizers correctly anticipated was that the divergence in girls' age would significantly inform their interests and concerns.[32] For example, in the cooking workshop, seven-year-old Samira challenged the workshop leader by asking, "If bread is a living organism, where does it go poop?" Far away from the ensuing pandemonium of first graders' talking about eating poop, fifteen-year-old Elizabeth challenged the creative writing and publishing workshop facilitators by talking about depression, friend and boyfriend trouble, and suicide. To address such different concerns, younger girls (6–12) met from 1:00–2:30 P.M. and older girls (13–16) met from 2:30–4:00 P.M., with many exceptions when all the girls worked together on larger projects or at outside facilities, such as meeting at the local newspaper to publish *The GirlZone Times*.

Another important factor in achieving diversity was reaching girls with varied access to feminist messages. Because organizers imagined that daughters of university faculty were more likely to have heard feminist messages and may therefore be more predisposed to an organization like GirlZone, organizers targeted girls they imagined were less likely to hear about GirlZone. To become known to these girls, organizers advertised in the local alternative and daily papers, put up flyers in the university and in less economically well-off areas of town, announced workshops on the Radio-Girls' biweekly radio program, and managed to be highlighted in other community venues, such as the community college's "Go Girl" Conference or GirlZone's own GrrrlFests. Ironically, organizers' commitment to girls other than faculty daughters (e.g., indirectly, often lower-class girls) may have undermined opportunities for GirlZone to gain greater access to faculty who could have influence and expertise with funding circles in Champaign-Urbana. Such access might have better enabled GirlZone to remain institutionally viable, and therefore reach a greater range of girls over a longer period of time.

Among the thousand-plus participants attending GirlZone and GirlZone-sponsored events, a core group of seven girls participated in most of GirlZone's early workshops regardless of the activity. Their diversity reflected the multiple enactments of a GirlZone girl. Four of the seven core girls were Caucasian (Sophia, Thai, Faelyn, Chloe); one, African-American and Caucasian (Samira); one, African-American, Caucasian, and Latina (Sage); one, Caucasian and Native American (Cyan).[33] None were daughters of faculty. All were aged 6–12. Two came from areas surrounding Champaign-Urbana, and four were alternatively schooled (two were home-schooled and two sisters attended an alternative school that seemed Montessori-based). In my first two years of data collection, I focused on these girls because their consistent attendance at GirlZone meant that they were the central girls influencing what it meant to be a GirlZone girl. Through our sustained contact, I earned their trust and the trust of their parents, helping me overcome potential research obstacles, especially when working with minors.[34]

Table 2.2
Core Girls, Estimated Age (1998), Schooling, Participation at GirlZone

Cyan (7)	Home-schooled; Consistent GirlZone participant and part-time RadioGirl participant
Sophia (10)	Home, alternative, and public schooled; Part-time GirlZone participant, active RadioGirl and 2003 GrrrlFest participant
Samira (7)	Public schooled; GirlZone participant and occasional RadioGirl participant; Cyan's friend
Sage (10)	Public schooled and later attended alternative high school; GirlZone participant and later part-time RadioGirl participant; Sophia's friend
Thai (8)	Alternative Montessiori-based schooled; GirlZone participant
Faelyn (5)	Alternative Montessiori-based schooled; GirlZone participant
Chloe (6)	Public schooled; GirlZone participant, and part-time RadioGirl participant; Sophia's sister

Of these seven, Cyan and Sophia are most represented in *Girls, Feminism, and Grassroots Literacies*. Both were extensively involved in GirlZone and RadioGirl, and Sophia in GrrrlFest. Through their involvement, Cyan and Sophia influenced GirlZone's multiple purposes, those stated by the organizers as well as those imagined by the girls.[35] Both girls were highly articulate, alternatively schooled, and middle to lower-middle class. And, as noted earlier, at the start of my research, both were in the 6–12-year-old age range, the same age as the majority of GirlZone girls.

Cyan began coming to GirlZone when she was only six. Extremely bright, she wrote poetry about her mother and her cats, spoke English, Spanish, and possibly other languages, and was home-schooled. One-sixteenth Native American, Cyan was involved in a range of Native American causes, such as opposing the state university's mascot as an unwelcome appropriation of Native American culture. She came from a more rural town outside Champaign-Urbana and, for at least part of her time at GirlZone, did not have a home phone. In addition to complementing her home-schooling and providing an opportunity to be in and build community with girls and women who may share her (activist) interests, GirlZone provided Cyan with weekly contact with girls her age, particularly another core girl Samira.

Sophia was a Caucasian girl, living in Champaign-Urbana with a range of schooling practices. Describing her public middle school experiences, Sophia could not hide her disdain for the truly "hostile hallways" documented in literature:[36] from boys snapping girls' bra straps and groping girls on buses to vapid social interactions with girls primarily seeking boys' attention. She changed to an alternative middle school, but also found this wanting. Finally, Sophia was home-schooled until she was old enough to attend the "ongoing experiment" that is The School For Designing Society.[37] Unlike Cyan, Sophia's home schooling often made it difficult for her to come to Saturday afternoon workshops; as part of her home-schooling, Sophia visited an elderly woman on Saturdays, often reading her mail or running errands during the time when GirlZone workshops were held. Although Sophia's attendance at GirlZone workshops became increasingly sporadic, she was a regular and, eventually, a leading member of the weekly Sunday morning RadioGirl workshops. She herself became interested in chronicling GirlZone and GrrrlFest history in her stint as a RadioGirl "airshifter" and an IMC correspondent. In addition to frequent contact at GirlZone and RadioGirl workshops, Sophia and I maintained limited contact via our interviews and her sending me some RadioGirl recordings after I moved out of state. Through Sophia, I kept loose tabs on other core girls, such as her younger sister Chloe and Sophia's friend Sage, both of whom initially attended public schools and offered different perspectives about girlhood, schooling, and GirlZone. More than any other GirlZone girl, Sophia's eventual participation in antiglobalization protests and her IMC reports on agribusiness and censored media located her squarely within the youthquake movements that would erupt just a few years after GirlZone began.

Despite their diversity, girls at GirlZone shared a struggle to be recognized as agents. Whether protesting racist mascots or caring for the elderly, these girls countered the limiting and inaccurate constructions of girls and of youth more generally.[38] As this chapter's epigraph makes clear, GirlZone organizers recognized and fostered girls' sense of agency. Indeed, acknowledging and representing youth as agents is an underlying project of much girl-centered activism, and of the *youth*quake more generally. Yet, as the epigraph also indicates, girls still feel stunted. To better understand what thwarts and enables girls' agency, the following chapters analyze the interactions between GirlZone participants, in part by providing depth often missing in typical accounts.

My Position as Researcher and Facilitator: Observing and Participating in Local Disruptions

At GirlZone, I held many roles beyond a researcher seeking to understand how literate activities help and hinder people as they pursue their grassroots feminist activism. The girls constructed me as a fun provider who brings in electric guitars and amplifiers; a participant who may or may not get a vote in determining workshop procedures; an adult who enforces rules such as respectfully listening to a workshop leader. With the facilitators and organizers, I participated in fairly prominent activities: helping with grant proposals, serving on the Steering Committee, and acting as Volunteer Coordinator and Curriculum Coordinator. In August 2000, after more than two-and-a-half years of weekly participation, I moved eight hundred miles away. Until GirlZone closed three years later, I continued to attend GirlZone special events and periodic summer workshops, to meet with Aimee and facilitators during the year, to be in personal contact with some core girls, to participate on the GirlZone listserv, to serve on the GrrrlFest Web Committee, to be a contact person for journalists writing articles on GirlZone and GirlZone-related events, and even to write letters of recommendation for facilitators and an organizer. Although no longer participating in the everyday life of the organization, I remained remotely but strongly connected with the people and institution of GirlZone. My continued participation at GirlZone both honored my debt to the organizers and girls of GirlZone and allowed me to support an organization I valued. In these roles, I was guided by calls for praxis-oriented research and for giving back to the people (and organizations) that support our academic labor.[39]

The complexities of my multiple positionings were perhaps most visible when, during my first two years at GirlZone, I gave birth to two children. No other participant was visibly pregnant at that time, let alone repeatedly so. After the girls and their parents (primarily mothers) saw me pregnant or with my children at GirlZone workshops, they often displayed increased interest in my project; similar to feminist ethnographer Lila Abu-Lughod's experiences,[40] my pregnancy and motherhood provided access to people and practices that I previously had not noticed missing. Girls offered advice about how to understand girlhood and suggestions about how to be a mom. Mothers felt that my having a daughter bonded us in the shared quest of finding healthy options for our daughters. As mothers variously discussed where to buy cute clothes, how to find a good midwife, and which alterative medical remedies to try, my pregnancies highlighted how assumptions about women as mothers and as feminist activists interanimated as well as bumped against each other. For example, I felt a certain irony in that mothers who brought daughters to an explicitly feminist site devoted to social change were more likely to approach me as a pregnant woman or as a new mother than to approach me as an activist. This blurring of social roles, as a Girl-Zone participant, an academic researcher, and a mother, exposed the situatedness and multiple social relationships that shaped both my research and myself as a researcher.

I was motivated to participate in and pursue research at GirlZone because its mission encourages young girls to see themselves as socially recognized do-ers, to explore activities to increase girls' personal sense of capability, to improve their self-esteem so they can decide for themselves whether to participate in such activities. Family and friends provided me many opportunities while growing up, but I was surrounded by explicit and implicit messages about the limits of girls' ability; little league was for boys only and my high school physics teacher told me to "ask a boy" when I had a problem. GirlZone offered a way to redress these messages.

In addition, GirlZone provided a way to publicly perform my feminism. Sensitive to the allegations of elitism made against academics, I was struggling to connect my academic feminist theory with an activist feminist agenda. How was feminist theorizing impacting public debate and political action? What would girls find compelling about feminism and about Girl-Zone? How could I perform my activism with family and career responsibilities? Questions such as these are not new and were certainly being asked by others in the youthquake,[41] yet I found them compelling. As a feminist living in the second- and third-wave tensions of the mid-1990s, I believed feminism was still relevant, but was unsure how to understand and represent this relevance.

While thinking through these questions, I particularly valued Girl-Zone's feminist community, loose as it was. Instead of the powerful but short-lived feminist events of my early twenties (e.g., Take Back the Night rallies), I wanted ongoing involvement with women and girls about pressing topics that were both serious and fun. GirlZone provided that in a way that felt both less emotionally draining and more sustaining and sustainable. This sense of community infused my weekly routine and encouraged me to join with others to explore contemporary feminist possibilities.

Those at GirlZone could not have known that this emphasis on community as something both needed and underdeveloped would become a national topic of discussion. For example, just a few years after GirlZone started offering workshops, Robert Putnam published the national best-selling book, *Bowling Alone: The Collapse and Revival of American Community*, in which he argued that community involvement was diminishing at an alarming rate. Specifically examining United States youth culture, Steven Mintz makes a similar observation, claiming that changing societal structures (e.g., an age-segregated and highly structured childhood) means a loss of freedom and a loss of chosen community for youth.[42] Years before popular press books brought this topic onto talk shows, reading groups, and news programs, grassroots organizations like GirlZone were countering this loss of community. Even with their own difficulties sustaining a GirlZone community, girls and women of many ages came together as a community, trying diverse activities and exploring what it meant to be a girl, a woman, and/or a feminist today. Through these activities, GirlZone participants were offered a feminist community and an activist education. Participants accepted and built upon this invitation in uneven ways.

Like the pending youthquake, GirlZone emerged in response to a range of local and national trends: the reestablishing of activist networks; the increasing visibility of generational differences within feminism; the changing understanding of childhood, children's agency, and youth culture; the loss of community and civic participation; and, of course, the continuing painful effects on girls and women of patriarchal practices. And, while sharing the energy and successes of much of the turn of the twenty-first century youthquake, the story of GirlZone also exposes just how hard it is to launch and sustain this energy and success. By examining how one group of grassroots feminists enacted their activism, *Girls, Feminism, and Grassroots Literacies* makes sense of GirlZone and through GirlZone provides a window onto understanding the struggles, failures, and successes of local organizations in what would come to shape these larger activist eruptions.

3

Representations of Girl Culture, Realities of Feminist Activism

[Starting GirlZone] was really an exciting time and what we, what we were thinking about is a lot of the material discussed in *Reviving Ophelia*. And then the statistics about girls valuing themselves for their appearance and finding their appearances to be the thing that they consider most important about themselves. And considering this [was] very upsetting. And knowing that girls face a lot of pressures. And then reading about how the age where girls tend to lose themselves is adolescence. So we [initially] decided to target girls between 7 and 12.

—Gina, GirlZone co-founder, 1998

From its founding GirlZone was informed by multiple, often contradictory, representations of contemporary girl culture. These representations ranged from an underground punk revolution to marketers courting girls' consumer dollars and from girls dying of anorexia to The Cartoon Network's Nick-at-Nite's playful programming. Out of this alternative, consumeristic, medicalized, and popular culture matrix, two broad categories emerged: girls in crisis and girl power.[1]

Various representations of these categories circulated at GirlZone, complicating how participants defined themselves and the activism this grassroots feminist organization hoped to foster. Initially, GirlZone organizers took up the girls in crisis representations that depicted girls as hamstrung by deficient cultural resources and adults as reviving these troubled and overwhelmed victims. As Gina's opening quote indicates, GirlZone organizers were strongly affected by these texts, particularly by Mary Pipher's *Reviving Ophelia: Saving the Selves of Adolescent Girls*.[2] As the institution of GirlZone aged, participants reworked the crisis-based frameworks by linking them to the proliferating girl power ones. Whereas the organizers tended to invoke the RiotGrrrl inspired representations of girl power that playfully and aggressively focused on grrrl solidarity and on changing harmful societal structures, the GirlZone girls tended to prefer commercialized representations of girl power that organizers found problematic if not antifeminist (e.g., Spice Girls). At GirlZone, girl power was a deeply contested idea.

Despite their many differences, depictions of girls in crisis and girls in power similarly confined girls to what Barrie Thorne describes as "the realm of conceptual privatization."[3] GirlZone was one of many girls' and other youthquake organizations that contested this confinement, in part by articulating more complex interpretations of girls' agency. Using GirlZone as a telling case, this chapter examines how activists worked with and against the chaotic representations and realities of girl culture that on a local level gave rise to GirlZone and on a broader level became a site to imagine new possibilities for feminist activism. After providing an overview of girl culture during the 1990s and of the academic, activist, and popular representations of this culture, this chapter argues that these representations profoundly influenced the ensuing girl-centered activism that sought to ratify girls' agency and to call girls into a greater range of active if not activist identities.

THE RISE OF GIRL CULTURE

Traditionally, girl culture has been denigrated,[4] viewed as "insipid and insignificant, unworthy of close attention."[5] During the 1990s, this assessment was changing. Part of this change reflected an increased societal attention to youth in general and youth violence in particular. The killing sprees of white males who opened fire at their schools seared the national imagination,[6] yet girls' physical violence also received national attention—early in the decade were reports of predominantly African-American girls and Latinas joining gangs and going to jail and, at the turn of the twenty-first century, were reports of generally middle- to upper-class white girls participating in hazing rituals such as "powder puff" football games turned violent.[7] Despite these often sensationalized reports that shocked middle-class sensibilities, much of the early 1990s attention to girls focused on violence from within. In particular, anorexia, bulimia, cutting, and other self-destructive behaviors received significant publicity, which not only described existing problems, but also facilitated doctors, psychiatrists, educators, and parents, as well as documentarians, best-selling authors, television producers, and magazine editors as they tried to make sense of and represent the dramatic increase in girls' injurious behaviors. As adults struggled to determine the cause of these crises, girls received much needed attention.

Girls also received attention from another group of adults: marketers. Aggressively courting these young consumers in hopes of capturing their brand preferences early, marketers represented girls as actors based on their consumption habits. Girls took up this agency, with teens and tweens[8] spending *billions* of dollars annually.[9] Tweens were a particularly attractive market because they had the financial resources to make large purchases without the responsibilities of older women.

Whereas girls received widespread attention from marketers, doctors, and activists, girls received uneven attention from academic feminists in the United States. Girls are generally absent from 1990s feminist collections that largely continued the trajectories set in the 1980s: theorizing ethical relations among differences, increasingly within transnational and global feminist frames.[10] While transnational feminisms used international United Nations human rights language,[11] such as discourses on "the girl child," this transnational shift left little room to talk about issues for girls in middle America. Those who did explore girls' issues tended to be institutionally dispersed in academic fields already studying girls and girl culture, such as education, psychology, or cultural studies.[12] Challenged by their home departments about whether girls and girl culture were viable sites of research, these scholars crossed disciplinary lines to find communities in which they could chart converging areas of critical inquiry.[13] Coalescing under the term "girl studies," academics attended to girls' often-troubled development, their engagement with multiple media, and their relationship with consumer culture.

GIRL IN CRISIS

Since the 1990s there have been two distinct but overlapping phases of the girl crisis: girls as victims and girls as aggressors. Like other feminist activism of the time, GirlZone emerged out of and sought to intervene into conversations central to both phases.

Girls as Victims

In the early to mid-1990s, representations of girl culture portray girls as victims. Within the primary socializing space of schools, hostile hallways make girls feel unsafe; classroom practices diminish girls' confidence; and disincentives discourage girls' participation in fields such as math, science, and technology. Girls receive less attention than boys; face biased curriculum and tests; and balance conflicting demands, such as be successful, yet act feminine and defer to men.[14] These schizophrenic messages put girls in no-win situations. Often focusing on the alarming rates of eating disorders, depression, and self-mutilation, research on girls out of school found girls struggling with similar schizophrenic messages. The message these studies share is that girls are victims of alienating relationships, indifferent institutions, and dangerous cultural representations that surround them. In this research, girls' withdrawal into isolating or dangerous coping behavior is explained as a fairly straightforward product of girls' responses to gender discrimination and harassment.

Representations of girls as victims of patriarchal structures set the terms and frameworks that would come to shape feminist activism surrounding the girl crisis. Carol Gilligan's work is considered foundational in this regard. Gilligan's early work exposes the biased structures that take males (largely white, monied males) to be the standard and mark females as deficient when they do not measure the same.[15] Mis-measures such as these, Gilligan argues, are more than simple tests; they are damaging cultural tools used to reinforce a belief that women are inferior. The consequences of these representations are significant since they shape how participants imagine themselves and what they can do. With the rise of girl culture, feminists returned to representations of girls as outlined by Gilligan, to lament and counter the culture forces that distort girls' strength (á la girl crises) and to revel in and bolster the existing power of girls (á la girl power).[16]

Academics and professionals drew on this research to write crossover academic-popular texts that reached large audiences with profound effects. As noted earlier, clinical psychologist Mary Pipher popularized and expanded many of these ideas in her highly influential, *Reviving Ophelia*. Loosely continuing Gilligan's assessment of biased accounts that do not serve girls well, Pipher documents the tremendous difficulties girls face as they navigate adolescence. According to Pipher, this navigation seems more angst ridden than that of girls just a generation ago:

> At first blush, it seems things should be better by now. After all, we have the women's movement. Hasn't that helped? The answer, as I think about it, is yes and no. Many of my friends, middle-aged and middle-classed women like myself, are entitled in ways few women have been since the beginning of time. Many of us are doing things our mothers never dreamed of doing.
>
> But girls today are much more oppressed. They are coming of age in a more dangerous, sexualized and media-saturated culture. They face incredible pressures to be beautiful and sophisticated, which in junior high means using chemicals and being sexual. As they navigate a more dangerous world, girls are less protected.
>
> As I looked at the culture that girls enter as they come of age, I was struck by what a girl-poisoning culture it was. The more I looked around, the more I listened to today's music, watched television and movies and looked at sexist advertising, the more convinced I became that we are on the wrong path with our daughters. America today limits girls' development, truncates their wholeness and leaves many of them traumatized.[17]

As Pipher points out, feminism has given privileged women even more privilege, yet all kinds of girls face an increasingly oppressive adolescence. Pipher wants feminists, psychologists, and people who care about girls more generally to "save girls' selves" in large part by helping girls understand themselves as active and valued in ways that girls do not normally see validated. Although feminisms would seem to provide this corrective, when Pipher points out that girls are doing poorly, she indirectly asks how feminists who have been active for decades can help girls become viable social actors able to withstand today's "junk culture."

One response is to publicize the girl crisis. Pipher engaged in this work, exposing the pervasiveness of girls' problems on the national stage. On the

New York Times best seller list for 154 weeks and number one for twenty-seven weeks,[18] *Reviving Ophelia* became a "must read" for people working with, raising, or studying girls. In fact, Pipher's representations became a gloss for the girl crises more generally. This gloss still resonates. Ten years after *Reviving Ophelia* was published, the critically acclaimed movie *Thirteen* both updates *Reviving Ophelia*'s description of girls in crisis and shows the continuing problems Pipher's work exposes. As this movie details, girls of a similar age to those Pipher studied seem to have agency through their autonomy and money. Yet that agency is largely channeled into the destructive options they see available: the pursuit of drugs, sex, and self-mutilation (i.e., cutting). Since *Reviving Ophelia*'s publication, Pipher's representations have profoundly influenced how activists recognized the girl crisis strand of girl culture and, consequently, how activists sought to create more beneficial identities and practices for girls and women.

Girls as Aggressors

If the 1990s representations of the girl crisis depicted girls as victims of "girl-poisoning culture," "hostile hallways," and "schools that short-changed them,"[19] the 2000s representations of the girl crisis positioned girls as victims *and aggressors*, locked in a debilitating oppressed/oppressor relationship within supposed friend circles. In this second phase of the girl crisis, academic research grounded largely in psychology and education focuses on girls' "relational aggression."[20] This research argues that dominant cultural scripts do not allow girls (predominantly monied white girls who are disproportionately documented in the research) to be aggressive and, therefore, do not teach girls how to handle aggression productively. To deal with this bind, girls create a culture of manipulation (power + passivity), using relational aggression to hurt others.

Naming this unacceptable behavior "relational anger," researchers exposed not only the complexities of girls' struggles to pursue sanctioned ways to express their agency but also the social strictures that led girls to perpetrate such abuse. As these researchers made clear, relational anger represents both maladaptive ways girls seek to resist the sanctioned roles of the sweet, ultimately powerless and victimized Ophelias, and girls' desire for a greater range of agency than sanctioned roles allot. The resulting studies captured national attention with numerous books about "mean girls" variously called Alpha Girls, R.M.G.'s (Really Mean Girls), and Queen Bees.[21] In addition to being cover stories on teen magazines as well as *The New York Times Magazine*,[22] the topic of relational anger was featured everywhere: newspapers across the nation, Oprah's talk show, self-dubbed "ripped from the headline" prime time television drama, and films.[23] Yet, while these representations of girls and young women as powerful in their meanness enabled girls to identify the relational anger they experienced, they prohibited girls' legitimate exercise of anger for fear of being labeled a R.M.G.

Even as the constructions and representations of these girl crises documented and explained the perils of girlhood, popular discourses often represented girls and women in an all-too-familiar binary: victim or aggressor. While many females would agree that primary cultural institutions and expectations often shortchanged them, they were less willing to embrace their role as victim. Where was their agency? Similarly, while feminists readily recognized that females are often placed in a double bind and forced to develop unhealthy coping skills, did they want to accept a "really mean girl" identity? These troubling representations mobilized grassroots feminists to understand and help girls understand girls' anger and agency.

Activists' Engagement with Representations of the Girl in Crisis

In designing GirlZone, organizers drew from representations of the girl crisis that chronicled how dominant cultural messages limit girls. GirlZone organizers and facilitators referenced this research both formally in Girl-Zone's grant proposals and informally in weekly workshops.[24] Not surprisingly, Mary Pipher's *Reviving Ophelia* was the most influential of these texts; it was the first book chosen for the GirlZone women's book club and, according to the girls, the book that teachers and counselors recommended at school. GirlZone participants echoed Pipher's questions (e.g., "how [can] we encourage our daughters to be independent and autonomous and still keep them safe?"[25]) and enacted some of Pipher's solutions (e.g., providing adolescent girls with protective spaces to try out roles other than that of sex objects; strengthening girls before they get to adolescence by having them become aware of, critique, and redesign cultural messages).[26]

After the "mean girl" representations thoroughly saturated girl culture, GirlZone organizers felt enabled and, in fact, obligated to interrogate the supposed prohibition of "good girls" showing aggression in order to help girls identify and handle relational aggression in themselves and others. For example, at GrrrlFest 2002—the year popular culture bombarded girls with representations of these mean girls—there were workshop sessions expressly devoted to this topic. For girls, there was a session entitled "Are Girls Mean: a conversation about Girl Aggression with XX," which gave participants the opportunity to address the complexity of this representation: How do girls handle it when they or others are mean? Do girls think they have other ways of expressing their feelings? For women, there was a session "ANGRY WOMEN: Challenging the stereotypes, claiming realties," which allowed discussants to address how representations of anger positioned women and feminists in difficult binds, and to explore strategies for owning and using their anger productively. Such workshops made explicit a question that

GirlZone organizers had tried to investigate for years: how do popular representations construct and/or obscure girls' and women's experiences? Providing girls and women with feminist forums to "claim their anger," GrrrlFest organizers hoped participants could interrogate these representations and the structures that make these representations seem so powerful, in part by using Fest activities to imagine themselves as more powerful than these popular representations.

GirlZone organizers were hardly alone in the way their activism was influenced by popular representations of girls in crisis. As journalist Margaret Talbot argues, "a small industry of interveners has grown up to meet the [widely depicted problem of girls' relational aggression]."[27] The Erie, PA-based Ophelia Project is the most explicit in its lineage, but this program is one of many activist responses that sought to redress the continuing destructive institutional and cultural forces to help girls today avoid the fate of Shakespeare's heartbroken and self-destructive Ophelia. This national non-profit credits Pipher's book as a catalyst for their work to publicize and deal with relational anger, initially with girls but over time with boys, parents, educators, and counselors across the country. Authors of popular "mean girl" texts similarly sparked girl-centered activism. Rosalind Wiseman, author of *Queen Bees And Wannabes: Helping Your Daughter Survive Cliques, Gossip, Boyfriends, And Other Realities Of Adolescence,* started the Washington DC-based Empowerment Program to help youth understand and stop violence in schools. Rachel Simmons, author of *Odd Girl Out: The Hidden Culture Of Aggression In Girls,* worked as a national trainer for The Ophelia Project and as director for The Girls' Leadership Institute at a private school in Washington, DC. These twenty-something activists and authors had their fingers on the pulse of a broad cultural trend, which urged adults to take girl culture seriously and to intervene in the destructive but culturally sanctioned patterns that debilitate girls.

Representations of girls in crisis and the activism these representations sparked were generally made by adults, yet girls themselves also initiated such projects.[28] For example, seventeen-year-old Sara Shandler edited *Ophelia Speaks: Adolescent Girls Write About Their Search for Self,* a nationally available collection by teen and tween girls that, according to Shandler, sought "to enable girls to tell their own stories and to hear the stories of other girls. I hoped to take the adult intermediary out from between us. I wanted us to see one another's intelligence and experience, pain and power directly, free from adult interpretation."[29] Depicting girls as actors within situations not of their choosing,[30] the textual representations in Shandler's collection construct an imagined community in which girls can blunt the injurious parts of girl culture for others like themselves.[31]

Such collections indicate that, while the desire for girls to define their own agenda may not be new, the degree to which girls could publish these representations and promote girl-focused activism certainly was. These previously rare forms of agency were facilitated by a variety of influences: the previous generation of feminists who named girls as agents in their own right and defined their pleasures and problems as worthy of study; the resurgence of the Do-It-Yourself ethic where girls were encouraged to control their own message and address their own needs; an explosion in the cottage industry of parenting guides that told this generation of parents how to raise their daughters with feminist victories as the backdrop; and, consumer culture's fostering of girls as agents.

Despite the forces that encouraged girls' agency, for most of the 1990s representations of the girl crises were written by adults. In many of these representations, adults were the privileged actors who helped girls navigate their crises, a depiction at odds with the current process where, as Henry A. Giroux argues, adults were shirking their responsibilities to youth (e.g., the government's evacuation of programs that support youth).[32] For girls' activists, these crisis representations called all adults to rethink, first, the ways girls come to understand girl culture and, second, the possibilities for cultivating girls' agency within and against these understandings.

GIRL POWER

During the same time period that the girl crises captured the popular imagination, so did the girl power movement. In practice, these representations intertwine, yet girl power more frequently represents girls as agents and more thoroughly infuses girls' perspectives. In addition, girl power is predicated on the idea that girls are not broken and don't need fixing. Such representations sparked their own activist responses, at Girl-Zone and beyond.

In the academy, the field of cultural studies is most involved with this project. For example, twenty years before GirlZone, Angela McRobbie and Jenny Garber helped bring attention to girl culture by roundly criticizing cultural studies for equating youth culture with boy or "lad culture."[33] In so doing, they cleared a space to focus on how girls are more than objects related to male youth culture. Later, in the 1980s, scholars examined how key sites of youth culture (e.g., magazines or music) constructed girls as *active* consumers who read and interpretered of cultural messages, creating their own pleasure and meaning from the intended messages.[34] During the 1990s, cultural studies research focused more extensively on girls' own production of girl culture,[35] from altering secondhand clothes to making pastiche zines. Linked to the increasingly popular phenomenon called girl power, this research further recognized girls as agents.

This academic work intermingled with and co-informed the work of explicitly activist feminists, specifically new cohorts who were charting their vision for feminisms (see chapter 4). These activists argued that, even if they didn't adopt the feminist label, girls and young women are agents in their world. By creating foundations, writing zines, and going on national music tours, they were advancing an image of girl power that aligned with and shaped feminist identities, often in relation to the forces of consumer culture.

In popular culture, girl power typically meant girl solidarity and the idea that girls can be powerful actors in their own worlds. Girl power championed the idea that girls were not merely sidekicks to boys or ornamentation until adulthood; rather, girlhood was a time to be celebrated and girls were agents in that celebration. For an extended age range of "girls" raised on 1980s anthems such as Cyndi Lauper's "Girls Just Want to Have Fun" and Madonna's "Material Girl," play and pleasure were a central part of this celebration, themes commonly linked to consumer culture. And yet, consumer culture's girl power exploited these themes to sell a product, essentially empting girl power of its focus on resistance and repackaging it as a commodity able to be bought in a wonder bra. These multiple and fundamentally contradictory representations of girl power aligned with and bumped up against each other, enabling and limiting feminist identities and activism throughout the 1990s, as exemplified by three of the most well-known representations of girl power of the decade: the RiotGrrrls,[36] the Spice Girls, and the Powerpuff Girls. Separately and collectively, these varied and, at times opposing, representations of girl power indicate the conflicted possibilities for understanding girls' agency and girl-focused activism, concepts evident at GirlZone.

RiotGrrrls

In the early 1990s, the RiotGrrrls embodied grrrl (girl with a growl) power. Perhaps best known as a group of mainly female bands that initially rallied under a "RiotGrrrl" banner to open the International Pop Underground convention in August 1991, the RiotGrrrls also include writers (often of zines such as *GirlGerms* and *RiotGrrrl*) and activists supporting progressive causes. Primarily located in the Pacific Northwest and later in Washington DC, the RiotGrrrls sparked and reflected a renewed sense of grassroots activism as youth developed an increasing political awareness, evident, for example, in their opposition to the first Gulf War.

The RiotGrrrls' activism included offering teach-ins before concerts, claiming space for women in mosh pits at punk concerts, and rethinking girlhood. For this last project, RiotGrrrl bands such as Bikini Kill, Calamity Jane, and Bratmobile exposed the tumult of girlhood by performing contradictory and highly sexualized, girlish identities. Their punk screams captured both the agony of being the object of sexual abuse and the ecstasy of flaunting their sexuality. Similarly, their album graphics offer nostalgic, iconic images of happy youth that contrast with their songs detailing the harsh limitations girls still face today. In order to create new ways to be powerful within the contradictory representations of a contested girl culture, the RiotGrrrls exposed personal and institutional forces that limit girls, grrrls, and women, but more forcefully advanced the idea that girls and women can be aggressive, active, and in control.

Key to RiotGrrrl was the Do-It-Yourself (DIY) mentality. DIY indicates a desire to take care of ones own needs without relying on corporate intermediaries. As the author of the grrrl zine *Bikini Kill #2* states, girls and young women "Must take over the means of production in order to create our own meanings."[37] Sharing punk's aversion to the commercialism of rock music, RiotGrrrl bands reacted to the increasing commercialization of alternative music within the DIY framework: most RiotGrrrl bands stuck with independent labels, used new modes of production such as zines for publicity, and encouraged alternative consumption of media messages. When the mainstream media decided these "angry women of rock " were the next big thing to follow on the heals of the Grunge scene's skyrocketing success, the RiotGrrrls imposed a media blackout, refusing to give interviews to protest what they felt to be a commodification of their ideas and the media's construction of a star system they opposed. Despite these measures, the media frenzy persisted, quickly overwhelming the fledgling RiotGrrrls who had difficulty handling their unexpected rise to fame. Within just a few years after their 1991 meteoric rise, hardly any of the original bands were still performing.

Although RiotGrrrls wrote and sang about race and class issues, RiotGrrrl USA remained largely white and middle class, unlike their counterpart RiotGrrrls UK, with whom they shared messages and methods. Whereas U.S. bands such as Bikini Kill or Bratmobile were formed primarily by middle-class women who met through college contacts, RiotGrrrl UK bands such as Huggy Bear were credited with breaking class barriers. Similarly, the overwhelmingly white RiotGrrrls USA reappropriated girlhood for feminist critique, fruitfully imagining alternative identity possibilities for women and girls yet problematically situating this critique within a nearly exclusive focus on gender; women without the assets of middle-class white privilege needed to negotiate this critique within class and race discourses as well.[38] Diminishing if not obscuring how girlhood must be reimagined within multiple identity frames, the important work of the RiotGrrrls was limited by the unmarked class and race privileges common in the girl power movement.

Even with these significant limitations, the initial wave of RiotGrrrl music inspired girls and women across the country to come together as grrrls who could participate in this largely male music world and control their own message. Popularizing the mantra "Revolution Girl-Style Now!," the RiotGrrrls ushered in a grrrl-centered decade and are credited with fostering a new generation of feminist activism.

Years after most RiotGrrrl bands ceased, their representations and representations of them became important resources for feminists to draw upon. For example, the RiotGrrrls' claiming of play and desire, of critique and designing something new resonated strongly at GirlZone. In fact, despite the dangers of linking to the RiotGrrrls' in-your-face messages, Aimee came to publicly align GirlZone with the RiotGrrrls, in part to counter the commercialization of girl power that became popular in the mid-1990s. Although GirlZone organizers could not overturn the consumeristic understandings of girl culture, Aimee's decision to connect GirlZone's texts and hands-on workshops to the RiotGrrrls at least exposed girls to a greater range of girl power history and girl-centered activism. Ironically, even as representations of RiotGrrrl grrrl power inspired activists such as those at GirlZone, these same representations came to benefit marketers in ways that activists would abhor.

Spice Girls

The mid-1990s saw a radically altered representation of girl power: the Spice Girls. Highly choreographed and commercialized, this all-women British band tapped a groundswell of interest in a tamed girl power. Singing catchy pop tunes addressing "a girl's world" and "a spice revolution," the Spice Girls sent the message that girl power and feminism were a necessary and fun part of everyday life. With explicit ignorance of feminist history and theory, the Spice Girls forwarded a pragmatic and practical version of feminism based on their own experiences: addressing interracial relationships and multiracial identities; valuing girl friends over, or in spite of, relationships with boys; and, encouraging girls to make their own fun with other girls without relying on men.[39]

Despite these grassroots feminist tenets, the Spice Girls seemed to be created in a marketing office, designed to fit a preexisting sales plan that equated girl power with consumerism. While calling the buying of goods "empowering" is not new, the degree to which this took off in the tween market is. As journalist Kerry Gold describes, "In 1998, the year the Spice Girls were at their peak, tweens spent $1.4 billion per year, according to a YTV Tween Report. In 2002, the figure had gone up to 1.7 billion per year, showing strong, if not a consistent market. The Spice Girls, it seemed, had taught little girls to shop." Although Gold gives the Spice Girls perhaps an unreasonable amount of power, she also reveals how marketing trends aimed at girls in general and how "products" like the Spice Girls ushered in an era of targeting tween girls.[40]

Not surprisingly, the Spice Girls' many critics questioned the depth of their feminist message, focusing on the production of the Spice Girls' message and their relationship with consumer culture. While singing about girl power, the Spice Girls modeled that girls do not make their own message; rather, they voice others' message of them, a representation of girl power that contrasts sharply with the RiotGrrrls. Not only did the Spice Girls *not* reject the consumeristic values generally pushed by the media, but they also courted the media and marketers, arguably for their own advantage. Through their music, image, and the media—the main resources available to them and accessible to their young fans—the Spice Girls forwarded their message and their commercial success. And indeed, the Spice Girls were phenomenally successful, selling out concerts around the world, putting out movies and videos, and marketing untold products primarily to tween girls. Girl power Spice Girl style—enabling a revolutionary feeling to be safe, perky, and for sale—was very powerful. For better and worse, the Spice Girls' vast exposure and appeal made representations of girl power common in both conversation and in image, adding girl power to the image store of mainstream youth culture.[41]

At GirlZone, as at many girl-centered spaces, the Spice Girls represented a commercialized girl power that many adults opposed. Girls, however, loved the Spice Girls. For example, although tween GirlZone participant Sage was extreme in her devotion to "Scary" and "Sporty" Spice, Sage was like many girls in that she managed to make the Spice Girls central to workshops as diverse as philosophy, zine writing, and football. Even as organizers shared girls' pleasurable and problematic relationship with consumer culture, and even as organizers recognized they could not merely dismiss nor denigrate consumeristic representations such as those surrounding the Spice Girls, organizers struggled to find ways to interact productively with these representations. At GirlZone, these struggles indexed concerns about how to forward feminist messages within a largely anti- and/or post-feminist consumer culture.

Powerpuff Girls

Toward the end of the 1990s, the Spice Girls' staying power waned and a crime fighting cartoon trio called the Powerpuff Girls was again reinflecting the concept of girl power.[42] Fueled by global media and an increasing interest in Japanimation, the Powerpuff Girls appealed to girls and boys, as well as tweens, teens, and twenty-somethings within the United States and abroad. *The Powerpuff Girls* was one of the highest rated shows on The Cartoon Network and this trio infused youth culture through their CD, *Game Boy* videogame, full-length movies, monthly comic books, and untold childhood items like school supplies, clothes, and bedding.

As the introduction to the cartoon makes clear, Bubbles, Blossom, and Buttercup were created to be typical girls, made of sugar and spice and everything nice, yet through the accidental addition of the mysterious Chemical X—what in an earlier version of the show was a can of Whoopass[43]—, these perfect little girls were also mutants with super powers. As mutants of an old-fashioned ideal, the Powerpuff Girls became the latest representation able to mix traditional constructions of girlhood with the explosive potential of girl power.

Unlike the perfection of previous superheroes, such as Wonder Woman during the supermom 1980s, the Powerpuff Girls are more complicated, playful, and flawed. Both good and bad in a single episode, the Powerpuff Girls work for justice, naughtily eat too much candy and play when they should be sleeping. During all episodes, adults such as the Mayor call upon these girls to save Townsville, USA. Despite inverting the typical roles of who has agency,[44] these superheroes are simultaneously contained by societal strictures; Bubbles, Blossom, and Buttercup powerfully save the world yet they do so before bedtime. Just as a new generation of feminists foregrounded their multiple and contradictory identities, the Powerpuff Girls do not try to resolve their seeming contradictions; rather they take them as a starting point. They will save the world their way. With humor, smarts, and girl power, the Powerpuff Girls became superheroes of a new sort.

GirlZone girls frequently talked about *The Powerpuff Girls* television show, movie, and merchandise, but this animated trio did not have the same hold on the girls as the Spice Girls had. For GirlZone organizers, however, the playful Powerpuff Girls gained icon status; facilitators even digitally modified these superheroes for the logo of the annual GrrrlFest, indicating that some activists no longer sought to opt-out of consumer culture (e.g., the RiotGrrrls), or primarily critique a commercialized girl power (e.g., the Spice Girls). Instead, feminist activists at GirlZone worked with the best representations of girl power they could find as they sought to provide an opening for feminist interventions into consumeristic notions of girl culture.

As these examples illustrate, during the 1990s, girl power became mainstream. In the early 1990s, representations of girl power depicted an activist feminist project first known to local punk musicians who were working to counter both the commercialization of and the gender discrimination in the music industry. In just a few years, representations of girl power were everywhere, becoming integrally linked with consumer culture; the images and phrase of "girl power" were imprinted on folders and pillowcases, T-shirts and advertising campaigns. The edge of the early message—where RiotGrrrls wrote SLUT across their belly, sang about child abuse, and campaigned against commodified images of girls—changed into perky songs played in shopping malls and into doe-eyed superheroes that girls and parents alike could embrace.

Mass-marketing had watered down the growing RiotGrrrl movement to a more palatable girl power. This mainstreaming may help girls become recognized as actors, yet as part of the neoliberal focus on individuals with equal opportunities, especially in the market place, the logic of consumer culture has no interest in redistributing social or economic resources that might facilitate the long-term changes that early girl advocates sought. Therefore, the pervasiveness of consumerism within United States culture presents feminist activists with a profound dilemma: how can activists reshape widespread representations of girls and girl power when they cannot out shout the media nor outspend the marketers? This question is less concerned with whether these changes in representations of girls are good or bad. Rather, it prompts additional questions that focus on what now can be done: why are various representations so popular? What are the implications for feminist identities and practices facilitated and hindered by these representations?

These questions expose the need for feminist activists to negotiate the ambiguous and contradictory identities of girl culture, the pleasure and exploitation of consumer culture, and the reworking of girls' agency. As a telling case, GirlZone highlights how such negotiations preoccupied a new feminist generation and informed their activism in the 1990s and beyond.

REPRESENTATIONS AND REALITIES
OF GIRLS' AGENCY

Although representations of both the girl crisis and of girl power vary significantly, they provide an opportunity to reexamine the realities of contemporary girlhood and womanhood. In particular, they expose the need for feminists to theorize girls' agency. This lack of agency can be seen in girls' absences as much as their presences. Where, for example, are the girls in 1990s feminist theorizations of labor markets, public policy, and activism? This absence may reflect that girls' agency has been imagined primarily in the private realm, making girls difficult to study. This absence also reflects that girls' agency has been defined in typically three adult-centric ways.[45] First, as in the girl crises, girls are innocent victims, stand-in for all females who are oppressed by patriarchal structures, such as androgynous standards and deficient, even dangerous cultural, economic, and institutional resources offered to females. Second, as with "mean girls," youth are dangerous agents adults need to control, yet, even here, girls' agency is limited to the "realm of privatization," expressed behind closed doors and within friendship circles. Third, the amalgam of girl power images construct girls as learners of a consumerized adult culture, as truly blank slates whose romanticized (and commodified) agency is able to be appropriated by adult girls/grrrls. These adult-centric representations are partially true, yet they obscure how youth, like adults, are both agentive and subordinated in complicated ways. This recognition pushes activists simultaneously to acknowledge girls as actors and to lobby for girls' interests, explaining and altering structures in order to redistribute material resources to better serve girls' needs.

To ratify girls as public actors beyond the realm of conceptual privatization, activists need also to heed girls' own representations which resonate beyond girl culture. For example, despite the many constructions that disproportionately focus on how consumer culture socializes girls into womanhood, the question of socialization remains open. In fact, girls seem ambivalent about being socialized into feminist, consumeristic, and other images of womanhood.[46] As chapter 1 describes, twenty- and thirty-year-old "twixter" women share this ambivalence.

Celebrating the power and the play of girl and grrrl cultures, these adult women are redefining girl culture and womanhood in today's changing socioeconomic conditions.

At GirlZone, an activist organization designed to offer girls useful identities and practices, twixter-aged women helped girls navigate the conflicting representations and realities of an increasingly dangerous, playful, sexualized, media-saturated, and consumer-driven girl culture. As the following chapters detail, the creation and continuation of GirlZone responded to these conflicting conditions, providing a telling example from which to understand the often hidden ways that girls and women work with and against representations of them in order to pursue their everyday, often activist, agendas.

Part Two

Literacy in Action:
Complicating Feminist Design

4

Founding Documents, Founding Feminisms

> We invented [GirlZone] from us seeing a need, like a need from what we experienced and knew what was happening now. But there wasn't, there were no models that I knew of. . . . I think these [girl centered organizations] are cropping up spontaneously because it's like, it's reflecting a shared experience. It sort of speaks of an environment that is ready for something to happen.
>
> —Gina, 1988

In an environment ready for something to happen, how does a feminist community organization write itself into existence? What sort of identities and practices should it foster? How do literate activities reflect and participate in its formation? Like others at girl-centered organizations that were, according to Gina, spontaneously cropping up in the mid-1990s, GirlZone organizers struggled to answer these questions, in part by articulating how their organization was a feminist project needed in a changing environment. At this moment in GirlZone's creation, organizers were most aware of the second-wave feminist resources they grew up with: the discourses taught in Women's Studies classes and those made familiar by feminists coming of political age in the 1970s when many at the initial GirlZone brainstorming meeting "discovered" feminism.[1] And yet, in this mid-1990s environment, new textual and feminist practices were becoming increasingly associated with an emerging generation of feminists that would come to call themselves the "third-wave." Working with the resources at hand and with the understanding that these resources may not be appropriate, organizers struggled to textually and materially construct a socially relevant organization. This chapter investigates these constructions by examining both how GirlZone participants defined their social competency within and against feminist frameworks and how literate activities played a role in this social action.

The first part of the chapter outlines the privileged projected identities and social practices—what sociolinguist James Paul Gee calls "social competency"[2]—of various feminisms operating at GirlZone. Informed by the convergence of multiple factors, social competencies guide how people define and address pressing issues. Given changing environments and social problems, feminists of different cohorts tend to privilege diverse social competencies. Negotiating which social competencies are most appropriate for specific contemporary concerns is an important if not fully articulated project for grassroots activists at the turn of the twenty-first century.

The second part of this chapter examines how GirlZone's foundational documents served as pivotal resources that momentarily stabilized these multiple feminisms in order to forward a coherent feminist agenda. One of GirlZone's foundational documents, a grant application to the Girl's Best Friend Foundation, described GirlZone's mission, organization, and practices as a necessary corrective to the societal limitations girls and women still face. A predominantly second-wave liberal feminist text, this grant proposal emphasizes how patriarchy limits girls' opportunities and hinders the discovery of true selves. The grant application's critique was quite successful externally, bringing in grant money and participants to what had recently been only an intriguing idea of local women. Internally, the grant proposal detailed GirlZone's first cohesive articulation of its practices and participants. However, new workshop facilitators and a changing relationship with second-wave goals meant that this early articulation soon began constricting how organizers saw themselves and the goals for their workshops. GirlZone's other foundational document, its logo, represents an alternate understanding of the social competencies GirlZone privileged. GirlZone's logo redesigned images from male-dominated skater magazines such as *Thrasher* to depict what would become classic third-wave imagery of a skater girl. Created in the mid-1990s when a spate of third-wave manifestos were written, this foundational document encapsulates a feeling about girls, feminisms, and the possibilities for new social competencies needed at the end of the twentieth century.

The third part of the chapter analyzes the lived realities of running this grassroots organization, realities that were far messier than the imagined futures outlined in GirlZone's foundational documents. In particular, this section examines the organizers' responses to a girl's unlikely proposition that GirlZone put on a fashion show. This telling case exposes the bind organizers faced when layered personal relationships and competing institutional demands challenged the feminist identities and practices GirlZone privileged, as laid out in GirlZone's founding documents.

Taken together, these sections detail the possibilities and difficulties of fostering feminist social competencies at moments of profound transition when typical responses no longer address contemporary needs.

COMPETING AND COMPLEMENTARY COHORTS

The waves metaphor has historically been a privileged trope describing the most visible phases of U.S. feminist activism: first-wave (1848–1920); second-wave (1960s–1980s); third-wave (1990s–present). While meant to honor the women's movements' various struggles for social justice, "waves" is contested because it obscures the important and continuing work that extends beyond typical participants and time-frames. Sociologist Nancy Whittier provides an alternative metaphor that seeks to capture the variations within and continuities across this movement's troughs and peaks.[3] According to Whittier, movements are made up of political "generations" containing multiple "cohorts." These constantly forming cohorts construct collective identities that differ from each other but can converge to become a political generation with a shared sense of "the way things are" that is perceptively different from a previous generational assessment. Because these emerging cohorts push established movements to address developing concerns, new cohorts are both disruptive to and needed for the survival of any movement.

Taken too strictly, Whittier's metaphors are also problematic. As Rebecca Munford notes, defining differences in a movement as a generational disagreement implies a typical family rebellion, which diminishes their political import. In the trope of mother-daughter conflict, generational differences are seen as a psychologized drama.[4] While psychological factors form part of the larger sociohistoric context, the struggles over what it means to be competent in the changing conditions that feminists face today are far more complex than a stereotypical mother-daughter conflict. What is at stake in these generational negotiations is the vibrancy of feminism needed to address continuing social injustice. What are the privileged feminist identities and practices that will serve feminists well at this moment? How can feminists foster these for themselves and for others? Limiting answers to these questions within terms of generational conflict obscures participants' focus on addressing the material context that makes feminisms so important.

Although overstating generational commonalities can misrepresent generations as coherent, rather than as comprised of multiple cohorts, Whittier's metaphors illuminate what Raymond Williams describes as the emergent and residual influences among the various groups and the mix of movements.[5] This nuance is particularly useful in the conflicted moment of the mid-1990s when significant changes coincided with the emergence of a new generation of feminists and their third-wave organizations.

At GirlZone, participants operated out of what they considered second- and third-wave feminisms that at times coincided and at times conflicted. The ways prevalent feminisms played out at GirlZone can be seen in the literate activities surrounding GirlZone's foundational documents.

Participants created and drew on these textual and visual documents to help them negotiate feminists' shared mission to redress social injustice. And yet, the differences within these documents index generational tension about what social competencies should be privileged and how social competencies are best represented. An analysis of the literate activites surrounding these documents can expose how local activists worked with and against the emergent and established resources available to them in this time of generational transition.

Second-Wave Feminisms

In the United States, the feminist generation generally referred to as second-wave attempted to redress the oppression that women felt due to patriarchy. This generation saw evidence of male privilege continually built into the structures of society from the stultifying limitations placed on women post-World War II to the thwarted participation of women in civil rights and antiwar activism of the 1960s and 1970s. Although diverse feminist cohorts (e.g., liberal, radical, Marxist, eco-Socialist, French, womanist, etc.) contested each other's foundational terms—liberal feminism wanted equal access to existing structures, while radical feminism wanted to dismantle these structures; separatists wanted to create utopic, all-women spaces while womanists pointed out women's racism and elitism—these early second-wave cohorts functioned as a political generation because they shared the idea that patriarchy oppresses women as a group; despite their differences, women, need to unite to redress it. For more than a decade, this central tenet enabled a range of cohorts to function as a loosely united women's movement that pursued actions generally recognized as feminist. These actions changed cultural attitudes as well as led to legislation for equal opportunities and rights, and these successes radically altered the social and political landscape for men and women in the United States.

For many, the Equal Rights Amendment (ERA) represented the promise and unraveling of this generation's attempt to codify their social activism.[6] With the words, "Equality of rights under the law shall not be denied or abridged by the United States or by any State on account of sex," the Equal Rights Amendment attempted to write gender equality into the constitution. The spectacular failure to pass ERA cast a long shadow, and during the 1980s United States' feminists pondered what had gone wrong and what to do next. The generational movement often identified with the concerns of white middle-class women[7] fractured, making some cohorts feel that feminism had failed while others felt that feminism was finally expanding to more fully value and include diverse perspectives of women from many locations and of many colors, classes, and sexualities. These internal shifts were paired with the externally difficult "defensive consolidation" of the 1980s when feminist organizations representing varied cohorts needed strategic cooperation to survive the hostile economic and political climate.[8] Feminisms internal splintering and external pressures radically altered feminist practices to such a degree that, as Misha Kavka argues, feminist activism during the 1990s seemed almost unrecognizable, almost invisible.[9] Looking toward the turn of the twenty-first century, feminists were left wondering, What is the current and future state of the feminist movement? Who gets to represent the agendas? What are the consequences of these representatations?

A New Political Generation

Coinciding with feminists' struggles to articulate a new understanding and public representation of themselves, the early 1990s was punctuated by numerous sensational stories of women, sexuality, and feminism. Susan Faludi detailed how powerful antifeminist forces distort feminism and misinform the public in her 1991 national best seller, *Backlash: The Undeclared War Against American Women*.[10] This text proved a harbinger of a series of events that highlighted fraught gender and racial power relations: the Anita Hill-Clarence Thomas hearings (1991) publicized how those who allege sexual harassment in the workplace may be treated; the 1992 Naval sexual abuse scandal at Tailhook exposed the continued harassment women face; the 1992 court decision surrounding the videotaped police beatings of Rodney King raised questions surrounding racial justice; the 1992 Supreme Court case *Planned Parenthood versus Casey* continued the recent erosions of women's rights to abortion.

Other high profile events offered hope and despair about whether earlier feminist victories were bearing fruit. In United States politics, 1992 was dubbed The Year of the Woman: a record number of women won local and national public office; feminist-friendly Bill Clinton was elected president; and, Hillary Rodham Clinton, Janet Reno, Madeline Albright, and other women attained prominent roles in national and foreign policy.[11] Just two years later, however, the possibilities of these feminist political openings were brought to a swift and forceful foreclosure when Hillary Rodham Clinton was sidelined and her national health care initiatives were in shambles. More dramatically, the election of the Republican 104th National Congress in 1994 exemplified a conservative, antifeminist swing in national sentiment. This sentiment was challenged, however briefly, by the widely publicized images of Mia Hamm and the U.S. women's soccer team. Confirming that legal victories such as Title IX were having an impact even in the traditionally male bastion of American sports, the 1996 images of these athletes successfully competing on an international stage showed what girls and women with funding and support could achieve, a message GirlZone organizers heeded as they first met that very same year.

At this conflicted moment, when the need for feminist activism was clear and when the seeds of previous activism were alternatively coming to fruition and being stamped out, the question of how to foster effective feminist social action seemed pressing. Out of such events emerged a confluence of cohorts that would self-define as a new political generation within the feminist movement. Under the umbrella term third-wave, this new political generation shared a focus on hybridity and on the multidimensionality of identity that simultaneously addressed race, class, gender, sexuality, religion and a host of other identity markers.[12]

Despite this generation's focus on multiplicity, the media generally portrayed relatively homogenized images of feminists who combined success, good looks, and previously male roles. These representations have many labels such as postfeminists, girlie feminists, Do-Me feminists, "I'm not a feminist but . . . [I believe in feminist tenets]," to name but a few.[13] Less frequently, the media portrayed those in the third-wave who challenged clear identity categories (including "feminist") and aligned with a range of causes, from protesting national and international policies, such as those associated with the World Bank, the International Monetary Fund, or the School of the Americas, to challenging the indirect and often overlooked cultural consequences of these policies, such as misogyny in hip-hop and mainstream media's exclusion of dissenting voices.[14]

As varied as these representations are, girls and women in this political generation have at least two things in common. First, they come to feminism with past feminist achievements as a given. As described in Jennifer Baumgardner and Amy Richards' *Manifesta: Young Women, Feminism, and the Future*, "For our generation, feminism is like fluoride. We scarcely notice that we have it—it's simply in the water."[15] This generation grew up with explicitly feminist ideas, organizations, and role models evident in their everyday. Paradoxically, a second thing defining this generation is that it came of age when the feminist movement was generally portrayed as dead. In "The Semiotics of Premature Burial: Feminism in a Postfeminist Age," Mary Hawkesworth notes "between 1989 and 2001, for example, during a period in which the number of feminist organizations grew exponentially, a Lexis-Nexis search of English-language newspapers turned up eighty-six English language newspapers referring to the death of feminism and an additional seventy-six articles referring to a postfeminist era."[16] Faced with these contradictory pressures—on the one hand, benefiting from second-wave victories and believing in the feminist agenda of working for social justice with particular attention to gender and, on the other hand, being bombarded with messages that either denied the present existence of feminist movements or that vilified feminists as angry, bitter, and anti-male—many in this political generation focused more on living their feminism than on calling themselves feminists.[17]

This generation's struggle with adopting the feminist label came not only from hostile responses to feminism in the general public, but also from wanting to push feminist movements in new directions. This goal, especially evident in the mid-1990s when GirlZone was just forming, is articulated by a highly influential third-wave text, Rebecca Walker's *To Be Real: Telling the Truth and Changing the Face of Feminism*. Walker writes:

> [I]t has become clear to me that young women are struggling with the feminist label not only, as some prominent Second Wavers have asserted,

because we lack a knowledge of women's history and have been alienated by the media's generally horrific characterization of feminists, and not only because it is tedious to always criticize world politics, popular culture, and the nuances of social interactions. Young women coming of age today wrestle with the term because we have a very different vantage point on the world than that of our foremothers. We shy from or modify the label in an attempt to begin to articulate our differences while simultaneously avoiding meaningful confrontation. For many of us it seems that to be a feminist in the way that we have seen or understood feminism is to conform to an identity and way of living that doesn't allow for individuality, instantaneously pitting us against someone, forcing us to choose inflexible and unchanging sides, female against male, black against white, oppressed against oppressor, good against bad. . . . we find ourselves seeking to create identities that accommodate ambiguity and our multiple positionalities: including more than excluding, exploring more than defining, searching more than arriving.[18]

As typical of other third-wave feminists, Walker describes how this generation wants new practices, not only the heavy critique associated with earlier generations. Similarly, third-wavers want to expand traditional identity categories, a desire highlighting that although feminists have for years actively worked to redesign rigid, binary identity categories, that is not how many younger feminists experienced this movement.

Feminists of this generation responded to the dilemma of self-defining in a variety of ways. Some avoided the quagmire of naming by doing feminist work without using the feminist label. As Jennifer Baumgarden and Amy Richards write: "It's a sign of the times that feminists today are more likely to be individuals quietly (or not so quietly) living self-determined lives than radicals on the ramparts. They are experts in their fields—media, politics, advertising, business—rather than expert feminists (though they are often that, too)."[19] This choice to live yet not talk feminism avoided draining energy away from accomplishing feminist work, but it also obscured the importance of feminist frameworks that enabled and made sense of this work.

Both validating and altering the focus of feminist movements has been an ongoing project for third-wave feminists. Writing almost a decade after her earlier call to understand what a new generation of feminists wants their agenda to be, Rebecca Walker retrospectively assesses third-wave struggles:

I am not alone in my assessment that capital *F* Feminism needs an overhaul. By 1992 Feminism has been roundly critiqued by the majority of the world's women, including but not limited to indigenous women, Third World women, American women of color, and working-class women. Even among the privileged and/or converted, there is a resistance to identifying with its rebel yell. Sure, there are those "I am not a feminist but . . ." girls who don't have a clue, but then there are the rest of us, who are feminists but not Feminists. We came to our radical consciousness in the heady postmodern matrix of womanist texts, queer culture, postcolonial discourse, Buddhism, direct action, sex positivity, and so much more. We are intimate with racist feminists, sexist post-colonialists, and theorists who are so far removed from the street they can't organize their own wallets, let alone a rally. We find that the nexuses of power and identity are constantly shifting, and so are we. We find that labels which seek to categorize and define are historical constructs often used as tools of oppression. We find that many of our potential allies in resistance movements do feminism but do not, intuitively, embrace Feminism.

In the context of all this, to call oneself a Feminist without a major disclaimer seems not only reductive but counterproductive. While this complexity makes for meetings full of fervor and supreme sensitivity to differences of all kinds, it also leaves many of us at the forefront of a movement with no name.[20]

The non-"clueless" third-wave feminists, according to Walker, built on the work of earlier generations and embraced the complexity of contemporary life. Although this embrace has problematically hindered their ability to propel a coherent movement forward, it also spotlights how a new generation of feminists privileges different identifies and practices than the ones they perceive as representative of mainstream Feminism.

Baumgarden and Richards as well as Walker—three oft-cited third-wave feminists—detail different ways and reasons why the feminist label may be overtly omitted, even as the work of feminism goes on. As an emerging feminist organization led primarily by feminists in this generational cohort, GirlZone struggled with similar issues. And, as should be expected, the tensions surrounding a new generation's feminist identifications were apparent in the ways that GirlZone's participants created and used their foundational documents.

THE TEXTUAL CREATION
OF AN EMERGING ORGANIZATION

According to Stephen Doheny-Farina, foundational documents invoke a desired future as already established in the present. Because these documents seek to guide an organization to an imagined future, they both enable and constrain the subsequent practices and identities of the documents' authors and the institutions they found.[21] Written by different authors, targeting different audiences, and using different modes (text and image), GirlZone's initial grant proposal to the Girl's Best Friend Foundation and GirlZone's logo fit this description. This grant application is formed in a loose collaboration with Girl's Best Friend; their potential funding called GirlZone to articulate its goals in ways that engaged the foundation's ideas about girls and patriarchy, and Girl-Zone willingly took up many of this foundation's second-wave liberal feminist frameworks that focused on critique. When creating the logo, organizers were less constrained, and this image privileged third-wave practices of redesign. Despite their differences, both pivotal documents proleptically project GirlZone as an organization that can help girls become socially competent. Participants continued to refer to these documents when seeking funding and members, illustrating that the constructions laid out in these founding representations shaped GirlZone's future iterations.

The Girl's Best Friend Grant Proposal: Social Competency as Critique

Early in GirlZone's history, Aimee and Gina openly called GirlZone a "feminist organization" when talking to workshop facilitators and other volunteers. What "feminist" meant in a context ready for something to happen was a project GirlZone organizers wanted to explore. GirlZone participants frequently pursued that exploration through a range of second-wave discourses. For example, at an organizational meeting with core facilitators, Aimee used radical feminist discourses to whip up enthusiasm by saying, only partially tongue-in-cheek, that GirlZone would continue, "until the patriarchy had fallen!"[22] This call for radically restructuring the systemic injustices of a patriarchal society was energizing and familiar to those in the room, yet it was less well received by the general public. Consequently, when talking to girls, their parents, and the Champaign-Urbana community, organizers privileged liberal feminist discourses, which criticize how patriarchy limits girls' opportunities by diminishing their ability to discover and celebrate a Romantic sense of self. In liberal feminist discourses, feminists appropriate the liberal discourses so central to American culture by, for example, making the "all" in "equality and justice for all" actually include women.[23] In addition to believing in liberal feminist goals, GirlZone organizers believed that exposing 6–12-year-old girls to more accepted liberal frameworks through fun Saturday afternoon workshops would diminish the backlash that might come if they used the more controversial radical frameworks. As arguably the most visible and enduring feminist discourse of this generation, liberal feminist discourses provided GirlZone organizers with acceptable ways to imagine and describe their project.

These ready-to-hand discourses were apparent in the most important internal document in GirlZone's early history: their grant proposal to the Girl's Best Friend Foundation. Begun in 1994, this foundation supported girls-only programming that also impacted local communities. Although Girl's Best Friend shifted its focus to Chicago-based organizations in 2002, from 1994–2002 it funded diverse programs throughout Illinois, including theatre and multimedia projects, work with trade organizations, and girls and women leadership courses. In each case, Girl's Best Friend supported community organizations that helped girls create their own messages and alter existing social structures.

GirlZone's practices aligned with this foundation's mission, which was to "support those who challenge the status quo by offering alternatives to the societal messages girls receive."[24] GirlZone organizers' judiciously highlighted their obvious overlap with this mission. For example, in the grant proposal, Aimee stated that GirlZone provided girls with opportunities to challenge what girls felt they could do:

> By stressing girls' innate sense of power and personal strength, GirlZone challenges popular images of females as primarily submissive, polite, passive figures whose duty lies in supporting, rather than doing. One GirlZone participant who built a web page, played the drums and learned self-defense techniques with GirlZone succinctly paraphrased our program's mission by stating: 'I did things in GirlZone that "I thought I couldn't do."
>
> GirlZone works to transform society by encouraging females to claim and express their full potential. By offering experiences in which girls learn to actualize their power of self-determination and choice, GirlZone works to undermine the cultural hegemony which is the root of pervasive societal violence toward women. What girls experience at GirlZone contrasts with restrictive stereotypes that girls might encounter in real life. The program creates an environment in which girls are able to test and develop faith in their own resources through the participation in a positive, affirming experience which calls to question gender stereotyping and societal norms.[25]

This passage constructs GirlZone workshops as places that expand the limiting options the status quo offers girls, a construction that astutely echoes what the Girl's Best Friend Foundation funds.[26]

GirlZone's grant proposal privileges liberal feminist discourses that articulate two intertwined foci. First, the grant emphasizes "choice." Typically the idea of choice is associated with liberal feminism's "pro-choice" stance on abortion rights, but Aimee emphasizes a more general sense of choice. Throughout the grant, Aimee writes that girls: "make reflective choices"; lay "claim to their own power of choice"; "choose from the full range of occupations, activities and expression"; and, "actualize their power of self-determination and choice."[27] GirlZone's grant proposal argues that girls should have the choice to become powerful and self-confident, interested in social issues and intent on dismantling patriarchal limitations.

Second, the grant emphasizes that individual girls should become self-actualized by discovering their talents and desires and by celebrating their true potential. For example:

> GirlZone strives to support girls' personal development and self-expression by encouraging girls to look beyond the culturally constructed boundaries of femaleness, and into their own individual realm of possibilities when grappling with their concept of self. In these skill-building workshops, girls learn to question the validity of gender-role activities while at the same time laying claim to their power of choice. Gender roles

demystified, girls understand that there are no activities that a girl can not do, and that the choice to be involved in any activity lies with them.[28]

Aimee portrays GirlZone as helping girls discover and trust their Romantic sense of self, largely by helping girls see that they have the power of choice over their lives. The grant makes these arguments by invoking easily recognizable second-wave slogans: "GirlZone forwards the notion that the personal is political. Through exercising their inherent rights to strength and choice, GirlZone participants act upon their potential while becoming irrefutable challenges to the validity of institutional sexism and patriarchy."[29] These calls for individual rights to choice, self-determination, and "discovery and celebration of true potential" are paired with critiques of patriarchy.[30] Thus, this grant proposal takes up the Girl Best Friend's mandate to challenge the status quo through a typical liberal critique of patriarchal "truisms."[31]

These textual representations initially tailored to match a funder's mission began to profoundly shape how GirlZone developed, a goal of Girl's Best Friend and something GirlZone organizers came to appreciate. For years, the articulations of GirlZone's mission and goals made in this grant proposal established GirlZone's priorities and eased everyday activities: descriptions from the grant proposal became blurb material for flyers, fodder for solicitation letters, and a touchstone for workshop possibilities; Aimee repeatedly referred volunteers to this grant proposal for descriptors and background information; and, facilitators lifted complete sections from the grant proposal to justify GirlZone to the community and to publicize its programming. This complex interaction between the textual representations of GirlZone still as a largely imagined organization and the actual practices that constructed how GirlZone came into being exposes the proleptic power that founding documents, and in this case remote funding sources, have on emerging organizations.

GirlZone's overlap with Girl's Best Friend frameworks was not always productive. Misalignments exposed past contradictions and buds of future, divergent trajectories.[32] As evident later in the chapter, the problematic implications of such misalignments revealed that while the grant proposal (and implicitly the organizers' values) initially located multiple feminist understandings of GirlZone largely within second-wave liberal frameworks, as time wore on, these representations less accurately captured the everyday social competencies that GirlZone participants sought to foster. These social competencies were better represented in GirlZone's other foundation document, the GirlZone logo. A sketch of desired reality, GirlZone's logo illustrates the third-wave feminisms present from GirlZone's beginning but unrecognized as organizers continued to reproduce liberal feminist discourses in new GirlZone documents. Despite the fact that participants did not initially identify as third-wave, the associated social competencies became increasingly important as GirlZone institutionally aged.

The Logo: Designing a GirlZone Girl

Center left in the frame, the GirlZone girl is caught in mid-motion, perfectly poised on her skateboard with her pigtails flying and her arms skillfully maintaining balance. She moves of and by her own power without protective gear as shafts of light emanate from her. She is the center of energy and is about to skate past us. Flying through the air above the reader, the Girl-Zone girl is not looked down upon by anyone. Instead, her eyes focus downward on us, making clear that she does not define herself as the object of others' gaze, at least not a gaze that defines girls as lacking choice and self-determination. The "Girl Power is Invincible" patch on the bottom of her skateboard is for us to read; her body language makes clear she is girl power embodied. The GirlZone wording floats below her, almost buoying her, and uses a comic-like font that invokes associations with superheroes. This GirlZone girl gives the impression that she is her own superhero.

With this image, Gina wanted to invoke

> a feeling of power and freedom and grace, and then I came up with that [logo] because I was looking through things like *Thrasher* [a skateboard magazine] and stuff and I was just thinking very beautiful. It's a really beautiful sport. And it's also a sport that is generally a guy thing, so I thought it would be really nice to see an image of a girl doing that.[33]

While the grant proposal requires textual references to actual girls or published research, the logo constructs its argument by tapping, even producing, others' desire to see girls embody power, freedom, and grace through remade exclusionary visual images. In magazines, seasonal competitions, and on the streets of Champaign-Urbana, skateboarding is a sport dominated by males. Positing a new representation of what skateboarders should look like, this logo highlights both the material exclusion of girls and women in skating competitions and the representational exclusion of girls from skating magazines. Without making its feminism explicit, the logo signals this feminist critique by redesigning available though traditionally male images in order to better suit GirlZone's agenda.

The image of this skateboarding girl captures this sentiment. Describing her approach to designing the logo, Gina makes this clear when she notes the image of the skateboarder

> was me thinking of a symbol and what would speak to girls now and also sort of an intuitive way of summing up what the program is. It's sort of a little bit of a rebellious take too. . . . [It's] the idea that you can be what you want and it doesn't have to be supported by the mainstream and I think that's what we are sort of after too with GirlZone.[34]

In designing the logo, Gina wants girls to know they don't need to follow mainstream conventions; they can be rebellious and reconfigure representational systems of meaning making as well as material practices. Through the logo, Gina argued that GirlZone could help girls pursue this possibility.

GirlZone is a community non-profit organization which encourages girls to
explore and celebrate their individual abilities and competencies.
GirlZone is proud to be co-sponsored by Parkland College's Department of
Women's Studies and the University YMCA.
For more information, call   e-mail   .

Fig. 4.1. GrrrlZone Logo on a Promotional Flyer. *Note:* Reproduced by
permission of Aimee, co-founder of GirlZone.

Girls took up this idea, citing the logo as what influenced them to participate at GirlZone. In fact, for many the logo seemed a material artifact
of feminist possibility, a scarce resource girls needed to grab in general,
and perhaps more so in 1996–97 in central Illinois where such images and
the implicit third-wave feminist messages were still uncommon. As Aimee
noted, when GirlZone first started advertising, "We were losing all our
flyers because kids were taking them home and putting them on their re-
frigerators and on their bedroom doors . . . and it was less for the information of it than the fact that it was really cool looking."[35] Some GirlZone
participants specifically mentioned this cool looking image as what first attracted them to GirlZone: after a school counselor displayed the GirlZone
flyer, "the image of the skateboarder just was so attractive to the girls . . .
[that] a group of about four older girls started to come [to GirlZone] and
now [after the GirlZone rock music unit] they have their own band
[Feaze]."[36] These girls in Feaze were initially attracted by GirlZone's image
of a girl mastering a traditionally male practice, a desire of feminists
in many generations. Feaze embodied particularly third-wave projected
identities and social practices, however, when they attended both GirlZone

rock and skateboarding workshops, prefiguring the coming merger of skater girl imagery and girl rock seen a few years later in the hit videos of Pink and Avril Lavigne.

Created years before this imagery became mainstream, the GirlZone logo made visible what would become a widely sought after construction of girls' agency. This construction became more prevalent as third-wave feminisms (and the activism of the coinciding youthquake) came into wider circulation. For example, almost six years later Shuana Pomerantz, a Canadian columnist who probably never knew of GirlZone, wrote about girl skateboarders in ways that echo and expand on Gina's earlier comments:

> Why are there so few girl skaters out there? Isn't this the era of girls who rule, rock, and kick ass? Aren't grown women embracing a girly ethos because of how exhilarating girlhood is these days? Aren't we all wearing powerpuff T-shirts just to grab us a taste of youth culture. And then it occurred to me that you just don't hear much about this kind of girl culture—the everyday kind, where girls are living an embodied and implicit kind of feminism. . . . Girls on skateboards are knowingly and deliberately engaging in a sport that has been dominated by men and boys since its conception in the 1960s Californian surf culture. . . . Girl skateboarders are the perfect example of an implicit feminist politics that may slip under third-wave's radar . . . [In this third-wave feminism] girls can begin to think about themselves as powerful, political, and part of the process of change. Why should all the youthful feminist glory be reserved for girls who play in a band? Plus, girls on skateboards are so darn cool. It's just an incontrovertible fact.[37]

Distinguishing skater girls from the explicitly feminist and better known third-wave rockers (e.g., RiotGrrrl), Pomerantz argues that a skater girl exemplifies one third-wave cohort's practice of enacting feminism without explicitly calling oneself a feminist. Her mere presence is an everyday challenge to male culture. By participating in a supposedly male sport, a skater girl symbolizes the social change made possible by second-wave feminism, such as Title IX. Even so, her confident and playful embodiment of youth culture makes the skater girl's performance of feminist politics distinctly third-wave. The organizers of GirlZone sought to help women and girls participate in this kind of playful, embodied, and entitled feminist politics.[38] The logo captured this project.

Examining the ways GirlZone organizers used literate activities to figure out what type of grassroots feminist organization GirlZone could and should become links GirlZone's local texts to the broader shifts that communication theorist Gunther Kress associates with the globalization. According to Kress, rapidly changing social, economic, communicative, and technological environments require people to move beyond critique of existing structures to redesign given materials that meet contemporary demands. This shift from critique to design is hardly a direct line. Rather, emerging and residual components overlap and diverge, at times conflicting and at times cooperating.[39] Nonetheless, a shift is clearly underway.

GirlZone's foundational documents make both the textual and feminist shifts clear in their attempt to locate GirlZone within various feminist frameworks. The text of the grant proposal to the Girl's Best Friend emphasizes critique. It envisages an organization that meets the needs of individual girls whose collective gender roles have been demystified by challenging patriarchy. It imagines girls freed to be themselves by no longer being denied the full compass of cultural potentials. The logo takes on a similar project, but the social competencies center not on critique but rather on designing something new. With the third-wave "Girl Power is Invincible" motto, the comic font, and the powerful but pigtailed girl image, the logo remakes cultural imagery to provide a snapshot of reconfigured possibilities, graphically depicting girls designing acceptable social practices for themselves. The logo is less about demystifying gender roles than it is about blasting through or over gender barriers. For example, even though the logo responds to limiting constructions of girls based on their bodies—what the grant proposal calls the "mirror effect"—the logo does not show an anorexic girl or a girl in a beauty pageant. Similarly, even though the logo implicitly critiques institutional sexism, it does not depict the "hostile hallways" of middle schools.[40] Instead, the logo redesigns sexist imagery and practices, using third-wave feminist frameworks to create newly recognized identities and practices for girls.

As organizers used foundational documents to mediate the projected identities and social practices GirlZone hoped to foster, these documents reflected and participated in the not-always-smooth redefinition of these social competencies within GirlZone's own feminist activism, as the next section details.

THE CONFLICTED AFTERLIFE
OF FOUNDATIONAL DOCUMENTS

The initial production of GirlZone's foundational documents reflected the haphazard construction of GirlZone based on the resources at hand. And, although GirlZone's grant proposal and logo sought to temporarily situate GirlZone within feminist frameworks, the practices and identities posited in these documents were redeployed in new texts and activities. In these everyday contexts, Aimee and Gina tacitly recognized that explicit feminist references could be as dangerous to feminists as they were to patriarchy.[41] Consequently, when engaging the public and the girls, GirlZone organizers obscured their feminisms by privileging liberal discourses about choice and self-development or by foregrounding third-wave imagery and practices without overtly discussing feminisms at all.

Organizers hoped that at GirlZone feminism would be apparent, so they decided to focus on what Gina describes as the "work" of feminism (e.g., hands-on "fun with physics" or "rock music" workshops) and not the "theory" of feminism, what for Gina seems to be explicit discussions of systematic obstacles females face (e.g., entering and remaining in the sciences or in punk bands).[42]

This omission of explicit feminist references was motivated by various reasons. Those at GirlZone who privileged second-wave frameworks coded feminist references in order to model feminist social competencies within a social environment often hostile to overt feminism. For those at GirlZone who privileged third-wave frameworks, this absence of overt references reflected participants' ambivalence about the Feminist label and anticipated third-wave writing that encourages people to be experts in their fields rather than expert feminists. Despite divergent rationales, feminists of various generations and cohorts shared this tactic in the hopes of providing girls with implicit feminist frameworks and feminists with a way to straddle generational and cohort differences.

Even though this coding is an understandable response to the constraints feminists faced in the mid-1990s—that the past paradigms evident in the grant proposal felt dated in the emerging environment; that feminists of a new generation were conflicted about the feminist label and searched for new ways to express feminist-informed social competencies, as the logo implies; that many generations of feminists wanted to avoid the knee-jerk antifeminist sentiment—it bred fraught dilemmas. For example, by leaving feminist analyses implicit, Aimee and Gina risked that the girls would not make the connections that could help them challenge sexist societal stereotypes in a more systematic manner; without explicit feminist frameworks, girls are not provided with the tools to redesign given resources to create new social identities. In addition, although coding explicit feminist frameworks can build consensus, it can also allow participants *not* to address key differences about feminists' desired goals, such as desired practices and identities that comprise what it means to be socially competent in this community. This avoidance can lead to unanticipated consequences, as happened in 1998 when a preteen GirlZone girl offered the unlikely suggestion that GirlZone put on a fashion show.

"Let's Do a Make-Over"

At least once a semester, organizers and the Advisory Board (essentially any girl attending GirlZone) met to suggest what activities GirlZone should offer the following semester. According to GirlZone's 1999 grant proposal to the Girl's Best Friend Foundation,

> The Girls' Advisory Board is responsible for creating workshop topics, as well as providing input to program development. Advisory Board

members have collectively selected the workshop units for both the Fall 1998 and Spring 1998 schedules. They will continue doing so in the future . . . GirlZone's Girls' Advisory Board encourages self determination, while fostering creativity and political skills, and allows girls to align the program with their needs and wants.[43]

In practice, organizers attempted to enact what was initially an imagined structure. Sitting on metal folding chairs or even on the snack-ladened tables in the comfortable but quasi-institutional space of the YMCA's common room, the Advisory Board playfully brainstormed about dream—even implausible—activities (e.g., horseback riding through the streets of Champaign-Urbana) as well as realistic but challenging activities that girls may have been scared to try before (e.g., snowboarding, pool playing, starting their own businesses). Girls offered far more suggestions than could be fulfilled, leaving organizers to decide not only what was possible, but what was desirable. At this stage, organizers tried to find both a space and a facilitator to lead as many of the girls' suggestions as they could.

At one of these meetings, nine-year-old Ann Marie suggested that GirlZone put on a fashion show. Like many girls attending GirlZone at that time, Ann Marie simultaneously giggled and shared secrets like a young girl and seemed interested in exploring puberty's immanent changes like a tween wanting to be a teen. Ann Marie was squarely within GirlZone's target audience, and her suggestion of exploring new looks enacted much of what organizers hoped GirlZone could be— a place where participants would investigate a range of possibilities for how to be and act in the world. Even so, organizers feared that Ann Marie's fashion show suggestion imagined a pervasive, superficial, appearance-oriented project that would, in a few years, be visible in an explosion of television shows that sought to "make over" people (e.g., *The Swan*; *Extreme Makeover*), cars (e.g., *Pimp My Ride*) and homes (e.g., *TLC Trading Places*).

Despite these concerns, the diverse facilitator responses exposed cohort and generational fissures of a feminist movement in significant transition. To some organizers, putting on a fashion show would contradict GirlZone's mission. To others, the fashion show suggestion indexed questions about the level of agency to grant girls. To still others this suggestion raised a concern about whether Girl's Best Friend, a foundation that helped girls challenge the status quo, would also sponsor GirlZone if it put on a fashion show. The representations laid out in the grant proposal made at least some of those who wanted to pursue this suggestion feel ensnared. The organizers' mixed reactions to Ann Marie's suggestion illustrates GirlZone participants' changing understanding of how a social organization with an activist and educational mission should deal with the knotty problems girls see as integral in determining who they are and what feminism is today. Moreover, these responses highlight how deeply

divided GirlZone organizers were about GirlZone's desired social practices and projected identities and how best to communicate these.

Fashionable Critique: Take 1

Ann Marie's suggestion came about one year into offering workshops and
provided facilitators a concrete example through which to discuss how
GirlZone should meet the needs of contemporary girls. Debates about the
fashion show were particularly lively within the weeks after Ann Marie offered this suggestion, but facilitators and organizers returned to it on and
off for months. As noted earlier, some facilitators argued against the fashion show suggestion, citing GirlZone's mission to critique stereotypical experiences that value girls for their appearances. Gina similarly argued that
fashion is an oppressive force on U.S. women, yet her strong personal con-
nection to Ann Marie made her seek a way to recast Ann Marie's suggestion as something possible. Her solution was a critique of fashion:

> I am totally wrestling with [the fashion show suggestion] because it's
> like, is it possible to have feminist values in that venue? And we sort of
> came out with a compromise that we could do something with a fiber
> student at the U of I. But Ann Marie wanted to do like makeovers. . . .
> I was thinking that maybe we could do like a deconstruction of fashion,
> show different fashions through history and different cultures. . . . If you
> look at the 20's it was the thin flapper and before it had been the buxom
> butt bustle and then even further back the women who were heftier
> were considered wealthier and that was beauty and how standards of
> beauty are continually changing. Also, you could show like facial and
> body modifications, like the Thai women with all the rings, the long
> neck, and just show how incredibly relative it is. That may be a way to
> approach it.
>
> I'm probably the most for [doing the fashion show] because I have a
> connection with Ann Marie and I would like to see her thing be done in
> some way that would be constructive. But doing it is gonna be kind of
> tricky. So I have to watch, you know, am I letting my attachment to a
> particular person sort of make me do something that I would probably
> never, ever, ever, ever, ever do under another situation (laughing). So that
> is kind of where I'm at on it, trying to figure out a way to, and also, it is
> sort of a reality that girls are dealing with ideas of beauty and attrac-
> tiveness and how do you wind your way through all of that material.[44]

Like many at GirlZone, Gina wondered if there could be a feminist engagement with the fashion industry. While Gina wanted to see the suggestion of a girl she felt close to undertaken in a constructive way, doing
so would go against her feminist beliefs, something she "would probably
never, ever, ever, ever, ever do under another situation." Within Gina's
second-wave feminism, it was *not* fine to do makeovers, and thereby implicitly value girls for their appearance—even if you were emotionally
close to the person who suggested it.

As a person who claimed she found feminism in the 1960s–70s, who avoided make-up, dresses, and heels, Gina in many ways embodies a stereotypical second-wave feminist position described by feminist activist Wilma Mankiller. In discussing the differences between feminist generations in the conclusion of a third-wave activist collection, Mankiller notes: "Nowhere is the line between second and third wave feminists clearer than in the editors' desire to make feminism 'hot, sexy, and newly revolutionary.' While those of us in the second-wave like to believe we were once hot, sexy, and newly revolutionary, that has never been a widely held perception of feminism."[45] Although stereotypes are never universally accurate and many have changed or became more nuanced over thirty years, early negative images of feminism remain vibrant even today, as Mankiller points out. Fashion is one site where stereotypical and actual feminist differences roil about.

Compelled to come up with an alternative in part because of her attachment to Ann Marie, Gina suggested what could be read as a stereotypical second-wave compromise: help GirlZone participants consider fashion via the cultural construction of gender. Through this activity, Gina hoped girls could become critics of fashion, able to deconstruct both the practices and the projected identities the fashion industry inspires.

Gina's attempt to reframe Ann Marie's suggestion into a critique of fashion ran into problems. The primary problem with this proposed solution was that girls weren't interested. Representing the fashion show as an opportunity to deconstruct conventions was *not* what Ann Marie had in mind. As Gina noted, Ann Marie rejected the deconstruction-of-fashion suggestion and asserted her makeover suggestion instead. A second problem alluded to earlier centered on acknowledging girls' agency. Organizers claimed the Advisory Board would determine workshop topics, and generally they did. Now that the Advisory Board picked something that the organizers would not have chosen, organizers had to decide whether they would still validate this choice. Ignoring girls' right to choose their own activities seemed an example of the discredited second-wave "false consciousness" arguments: if the girls knew what the organizers did, girls would not have chosen fashion-as-makeover. In this line of thinking, instead of supporting girls' desire for and inquiry into fashion, organizers should lift the girls' blinders. While hardly prevalent, this false consciousness sentiment was apparent at some early organizational meetings that addressed the fashion show suggestion.

Gina's more complicated argument, however, recognizes girls' interest in "beauty" and "attractiveness." Feeling committed yet conflicted about how to help girls wind their way through these laden issues, Gina's deconstruction-of-fashion suggestion led to a final problem: girls' inability to assume the projected identity of a critic. Because organizers elected to code their feminisms rather than state them outright in the weekly banter surrounding the workshops, girls heard about their power of choice but not about the social structures that shaped girls' choices. Without feminist analyses that made sense of the feminist social competencies GirlZone forwarded, girls did not link their projected identities to the complicated social forces shaping these feelings, which, in turn, meant that girls were unable to play the role of an informed feminist critic.[46] Thus, the fashion show suggestion raises a fundamental question about what it means to be a socially competent feminist organization: For feminists privileging social competency based on critique, what should they do when girls are unwilling and/or unable to take-up the projected identities and social practices of girls-as-critics?

Whereas Gina saw the fashion show as a workshop to radically reframe or avoid, Aimee, who also wrestled with Ann Marie's suggestion, saw it as a charged opportunity that required significant time for reflection on how to make fashion better suit girls' desires:

> [We] had a lot of people who said that we should not do fashion. You know, "fashion is an industry that creates anorexic girls, that creates models of beauty that other people feel like they have to adhere to in order to be satisfactory, that creates this weird dynamic of 'mirror effect.'" And I guess what my personal stance on it is that [the] fashion industry in itself isn't evil. What the fashion industry has become is evil. To give the girls a chance to explore it might be helpful but the amount of time that we give to each workshop makes it difficult. If we do an hour and a half, if we do two hours just trying to create fashion, that won't allow that much reflection, so if we do something like this volatile subject, then I would like to see it in kind of an expanded form where people talk about different images and media. . . . But heck, we do skateboarding, we do cooking. This is something girls should explore. And if we shut it off as an option, they are going to explore it on their own. You might as well explore it with people around that they could ask questions to.[47]

For Aimee, the fashion show suggestion provided an opportunity for girls to imagine what social competences they want to pursue within the multiple definitions circulating at GirlZone. In one scenario, the fashion show critiqued an evil industry that values girls for their bodies. This emphasis on critique and in particular on critiquing the projected identity of girls-as-body is made explicit in the grant proposal. In that text, Aimee describes the "mirror effect" where "girls internalize the beliefs that their self worth comes from their attractiveness—a superficial and fleeting trait at best."[48] But as Aimee describes in the quote above, this focus on critique did not represent the possibilities fashion presented. Aimee, like Gina, recognized girls' struggles to understand their relationship to beauty, and Aimee wanted GirlZone to provide girls with a forum that afforded them "time for reflection" in order to tackle loaded questions about body and self worth. Implicitly and perhaps indirectly, Aimee wanted to provide girls with the space and feminist frameworks to gain critical sensibilities. Without structured time for reflection, however,

Aimee wondered how to validate this suggestion so that girls explore fashion in ways they might not think of on their own. How could GirlZone bring to light the overdetermined popular constructions of makeovers to advance feminist ideas about social competency?

Without an answer to this question, Aimee investigated another way girls could productively understand the multifaceted fashion industry: have girls build stages, design runway lighting, work with fabrics, and understand women's bodies as art.[49] Aimee hoped that by allowing girls to explore the many facets that go into a fashion show, girls could see themselves as designers and not objects of fashion within GirlZone's feminist frameworks. For Ann Marie, such an identity could combine her interests in fashion and inline skating, an unusual activity for a preteen girl, but an activity with a following after local speed skater Bonnie Blair won her 1988, 1992, and 1994 Olympic medals.

Despite its potential, Aimee's plan also had problems. First were logistics. There was no place to house a runway-in-progress for a semester, organizers did not know a lighting designer, and, when working with electricity, questions about safety and insurance seemed at best unresolved. Ultimately, however, the problems with this suggestion rested on the structure of GirlZone itself. GirlZone's weekly drop-in format lacked the "expanded form" to examine a "volatile subject" like fashion; in other words, GirlZone's institutional configuration didn't allow for sustained participation in social practices such as designing a fashion show that might allow girls to posit new projected identities.

On and off for eighteen months, the fashion show suggestion complicated organizers' understanding of how GirlZone, as an activist and educational community institution, could forward relevant feminist social practices and projected identities. In 1998, when Ann Marie first proposed the fashion show, Aimee and Gina did not have resources and models about how to productively redesign (instead of critique) fashion, especially within GirlZone's projected institutional identity as outlined in the grant proposal. Consequently, when this fashion show suggestion asked organizers to negotiate the many, and at times contradictory, social competencies the organizers and girls sought to pursue, Aimee and Gina were at a loss for how to proceed.

This significant dilemma indexed profound uncertainty about what practices and identities GirlZone would privilege, but on an immediate level participants were busy with more pressing issues: Aimee and Gina put on dozens and dozens of workshops that were perhaps less controversial and were certainly easier to staff and obtain local materials; Gina left GirlZone; Aimee took a temporary leave to work at the Girl's Best Friend Foundation in Chicago; and, Ann Marie stopped coming, ironically largely because of her participation in sports. Nonetheless, the fact that GirlZone facilitators returned to this suggestion highlighted how the fashion show suggestion continued to be a Rorschach test that reflected participants' choices about what social competencies GirlZone should foster.

Future Designs: Take 2

In the fall of 1999—a year and a half after the initial suggestion, as Girl's Best Friend funding was winding down, and after third-wave feminist activism and theories of design became increasingly foregrounded at GirlZone[50]—GirlZone put on a series of three "fashion workshops." The first workshop focused on making costumes. Held the week before Halloween, this workshop encouraged girls to imagine what they wanted to be, not what marketers offered them. The second workshop focused on fashion design. Facilitators explained texture, materials, and sewing techniques. Pushing the girls to design their own fashion "line," in part by modifying already existing fashion, such as putting patches on pants and purses, the workshop facilitators encouraged girls not to disparage fashion, but rather to remake something given into their own design.

The last workshop was Fashion Marketing. While neither the makeover Ann Marie wanted nor the semester-long series of workshops Aimee hoped for, this Fashion Marketing workshop represented a two-hour engagement with competing constructions of fashion and beauty. The workshop started with the facilitator inviting girls to define fashion by looking through magazines devoted to girls their age. The regulars, like Cyan and Sage, as well as the many sporadic attendees loved sharing their reading preferences and practices, discussing how they and their friends took-up the styles, attitudes, and identities outlined in these magazines. Like the "social queens" and "tough cookies" in Margaret Finders's study of middle-school girls,[51] the girls at GirlZone used teen magazines to mediate their social relationships with their friends and with their imagined futures not only at this workshop but also, it seemed, throughout these girls' lives.[52] This workshop facilitator wanted both to validate girls' pleasure in reading these magazines and to help girls analyze, critique, and redesign what she felt were their unhealthy messages. Consequently, she acknowledged how fun reading these magazines with friends can be, yet also asked the girls what they thought about the fact that the models were overwhelmingly skinny and tall, and had clear skin, perfect teeth, and blond hair—a description that did not fit anyone in the room. Why, she asked, might these representations occur, who fostered them, and what impact did these have on girls their age. Soon the girls themselves discussed not only the "coolness" of the ads, but also how the magazines constructed unrealistic and unhealthy standards of beauty that made girls feel inadequate.

This jumbling of pleasure and critique in the first part of the workshop provided a launching pad for the rest of the session when girls designed their own ads. Sprawled on the floor, alone or with a friend, girls created ads for watches that told the future and magic perfumes that responded to each person differently. When girls portrayed models, they looked more like those in the GirlZone workshop and less like the girls in the magazines. Based on participants' reactions, this workshop was a success. Girls had fun on a Saturday afternoon and through talk, text, and play, the facilitator constructed a learning environment where girls could explicitly question and remake fashion and advertising possibilities. At GirlZone, this messy social engagement with difficult topics allowed girls to redesign girls' relationships with fashion, at least for the moment. As girls determined what it meant to be socially competent within these relationships, they found accessible ways into what organizers considered this "volatile subject."

LESSONS FROM FASHION'S DO'S AND DON'TS

Throughout GirlZone's history, participants struggled to determine what a feminist organization might mean in a context ready for something to happen. In this struggle, GirlZone's foundational documents functioned as a case study of how literate activities shape and are shaped by on-the-ground responses to rapidly changing social conditions at the turn of the twenty-first century. With few third-wave models of how to articulate feminisms' responsiveness to contemporary conditions, these documents and the way GirlZone participants used them illustrate a conflicted moment when second- and third-wave feminist frameworks forwarded diverse social competencies able to meet the challenges of the changing social trends that organizers knew to be occurring.

The dynamics of emerging and residual notions of social competency are evident within both a social movement like feminism and the social practices surrounding literacy. Similar to fluctuating, alternating currents, these dynamics coexisted from GirlZone's foundational documents to the last of GirlZone's fashion workshops. The change in emphasis, indicating shifting conceptions of social competency, can be seen in GirlZone's textual construction (via the production and consumption of its founding documents), and in GirlZone's feminist activism (via the workshops Girl-Zone offered). As the textual and material practices at GirlZone indicate, negotiating these shifts in representational and social practices can be bumpy. GirlZone participants responded with debate and reflection, and the co-founders worked seriously at the edges of this tension, trying, for example, to find ways to repurpose the social competencies laid out in suggestions such as Ann Marie's. In the end, a series of workshops on fashion offered a hybrid blend of critique and design. In these workshops, design does not so much supplant critique as encompass it.

GirlZone's practices coincided with ongoing changes within feminist movements and representational systems; new social competencies in textual practices and feminist activism are emerging and these changes are important for feminists, activists, and educators seeking to prepare youth for fuller participation in the changing world. While representational theories of use and design do not neatly map onto second- and third-wave feminisms, their shifts form patterns that call for literacy scholars and feminist activists to rethink the privileged practices of education and activism today. To make sense of these patterns requires attention to the multiple factors that affect how people take-up textual representations. These factors expose complications that all too often get flattened out in narratives about learning, whether in school or in grassroots feminist organizations. Without attention to these complications (e.g., cohort divisions, material limitations), the hopeful possibilities laid out in GirlZone's foundational documents cannot possibly guide the messy realities that make up contemporary feminist activism.

In the next chapter, we'll see how the girls and organizers engaged these messy realities in their public performances at RadioGirl.

5

Circulations of a Feminist Pedagogy

The RadioGirls grace the airwaves with force every other Sunday from 10–11 A.M. Topics covered have included: the controversy of the crayola color Indian red; the movement to eliminate the Chief as a symbol of the U of I; celebrating Black History Month: African American musicians and the saga of Dr. Martin Luther King, Jr.; celebrating women of various backgrounds for Women's History Month, including mothers and local women; poetry they [RadioGirls] have written, short stories, and much more. Interviews with: the founders of GirlZone, Gina and Aimee; women involved with a local resource book for women geared at incoming freshmen students of the U of I; a teacher from the Howard school who is from England; a woman U of I hockey player who is anti-chief; Susie Hofer, a local jazz vocalist; a woman from A Woman's Place who organized weekend workshops on rape awareness around Take Back the Night. And if you are a regular listener of the show, you know many other topics as well. Their interests are diverse and they want to be active.

—Ayleen, RadioGirl founder, 1999

Ayleen's representation of RadioGirls as diverse reflects her desire to expand the social identities currently available to girls in the twenty-first century. In the above description, Ayleen highlights how the biweekly radio program RadioGirl (RG)[1] provides a space for girls to be writers and reporters, researching sports, history, and music as well as investigating community resources and local engagements with national trends, generally with specific attention to race and gender. In this space, RG organizers shared GirlZone's pedagogies, such as using hands-on workshops as opportunities to help girls recognize and represent themselves as social actors capable of pursuing projects they care about.[2] Over time, however, RG organizers' pedagogies ran into problems. First, although both of RG's two facilitators identified themselves and their work with RG as feminist, the RadioGirls themselves were mixed about this label, a response that is hardly surprising in a time when feminist identities are maligned.[3] Second, RG's pedagogies worked against what Henry A. Giroux might call a "public pedagogy," or highly visible representations—in this case of girls in the media—that teach the public how to understand and interact with those represented.[4] Whereas most public pedagogies sought to pathologize youth and disparage girls in particular as self-centered, consumer–driven, capatilistic, or apolitical,[5] RG sought to ratify girls as citizens engaged in social activism. In light of these two problems, the dilemma RG facilitators needed to consider was how to foster feminist-informed pedagogies when girls were conflicted about feminisms and awash in negative public pedagogies.

As GirlZone's longest running single activity, RG provides an example of the profound predicaments facing many feminists pedagogies both in and beyond the classroom learning environment. This telling case encourages us to rethink learning, shifting from primarily individualistic, mental constructions to largely social ones. A socially-informed pedagogy acknowledges that the practices and identities surrounding learning are not cordoned off to discrete times and places but rather they inform how participants learn as they align with some people and ideas and oppose others. This shift in emphasis, I propose, does not aim to create or reinforce dualistic goals, but rather seeks to integrate the place of the social in ways that traditional learning environments do not accommodate.

For feminists, this shift in privileging calls for pedagogies that help girls design identities they desire (a primarily social project) even as teachers expose the facts that make feminisms so necessary (a primarily mental project). To experiment with and redesign the social identies that prevalent public pedagogies make abundantly available, girls need safe spaces that allow them distance from the expectations public pedagogies present. And yet, girls cannot stay in these spaces, even if they wanted to; rather, girls and representations of them travel in the world, and girls need to understand these representations in both supportive and objectifying contexts.

To investigate pedagogies that can address these needs, this chapter first evaluates feminist responses to public pedagogies about girls in general. The chapter then examines the socio-cultural trends and local idiosyncracies affecting RG by analyzing the pedagogies of RG's two facilitators, the RadioGirls' responses to these pedagogies in their biweekly radio productions, and how/if the local newspapers depicted the identities these pedagogies and productions sought to foster. This analysis highlights the complex work required to foster girls' identities as public actors and the ways that imagined identities become remediated and reimagined as they travel. In the end, this chapter calls for a pedagogy that interanimates popular representation of girls. Since words shift meaning given their context not only in a sentence, but also in the world, interanimation works to alter the meanings of words, ideas, and social competencies by eliding them into new contexts. This strategy seeks less to overpower the pervasive but limiting public pedagogies about girls than to infuse feminist understanding into them. For feminists, these pedagogies model ways girls can reinflect what it means to be a girl.

FEMINIST ENGAGEMENTS WITH
PUBLIC PEDAGOGIES ABOUT GIRLS

The project of constructing girls' social identities is part of what sociolinguist James Paul Gee considers the construction of "cultural models," the "images, storylines, principles, or metaphors that capture what a particular group finds 'normal' or 'typical' in regard to a given phenomenon."[6] These generally tacit understandings of "the way things are" are reflected in and created by material representations, such as magazines and newspapers, the words and actions of others, and public policy and legal codes. When cultural models are manifested in widely available representations that reach large numbers of people, they function as public pedagogies. Without overt instruction, these pedagogies teach audiences how to make sense of who and what is depicted.

Although there are always multiple public pedagogies interanimating each other, current public pedagogies tend to discourage girls from actively participating in the social and political realm, particularly when such participation appears to have activist leanings. Instead, popular public pedagogies encourage girls to adopt social identities in the private realm.[7] These largely individualized and depoliticized identities are most apparent in the consumer-based identities of the late 1990s girl power discourses (see next chapter). Besides these consumed-with-consumerism public pedagogies, girls' studies scholar Jessica K. Taft[8] argues for critical attention to three other interrelated public pedagogies that draw upon "girl power" in problematic ways. "Antifeminist" representations, according to Taft, define girl power by denigrating this movement, as when the Spice Girls claimed they wanted to update feminism in the form of kicking it in the "arse."[9] In addition to its violence toward feminists, this public pedagogy focuses on cultural aspects at the expense of political ones. In a second "postfeminist" pedagogy, girls no longer need feminism since gender equity supposedly already exists. This problematic assertion, Taft contends, both hides the continuing gender oppression and hinders girls from developing tools for structural analyses of oppression that could help them understand and work toward social change. A third public pedagogy pushes individual power. Focusing on personal responsibility and meritocracy, Taft explains that this cultural model evokes American rugged individualism and obscures cultural factors and likely alliances that could help challenge the status quo. United through an exclusion of girls' political selves and the creation of barriers to girls' social and political engagement,[10] these pedagogies may not be taken up as they are given, but Taft's central point is important: the prominent girl power public pedagogies reaching vast audiences of girls in the late 1990s depoliticized girl power; they focused on self-esteem and individual consumption at the expense of social analysis and political participation.

Aiming to expand social identities so that girls see themselves as competent social actors who are able to take part in social, political, and other issues, feminist pedagogies develop spaces where girls can reflect upon and challenge the teachings of prevalent public pedagogies. Extracurricular organizations often provide these spaces.[11]

In recent years there has been much research on feminist pedagogies of the extracurriculum, particularly in such fields as science, technology, engineering, and mathematics. As individual scholars and feminist associations investigate the myriad factors that have led to significant gender imbalances in these fields, their research reveals that extracurricular activities (e.g., meeting professionals in desired fields, taking field trips) have much to offer in the way of redressing these imbalances.[12] Even with the limitations of many extracurricular programs—for example, their ad hoc nature, their lack of institutional resources, and the tenuous status of organizational survival—extracurricular sites provide the kinds of structures that can foster effective pedagogies for advancing active if not activist social identities for girls and young women.

In extracurricular and school settings, feminist pedagogies, like other pedagogies, have often been based on the assumption that learning is primarily a mental activity. This assumption manifests itself in feminist pedagogies that teach the facts about the interlocking systems that thwart girls and women's political, economic, and social power to motivate people toward feminist activism. And yet, the number of girls shying away from the feminist label exposes the fallacy of this pedagogical approach. The central problem is not the feminist logic that something is wrong and those interested in social justice should want to change it. Rather, the problem is privileging a cognitive construction of learning (i.e., learning facts about a problem) at the expense of a social construction of learning, which encourages people to be competent social actors within the groups of their choice. For pedagogies of all kinds, attending to the social motivations for learning illustrates that the development of social identities beneficial for and desirable to students is at least as important as the information being taught.

Since many girls and young women who might share feminist beliefs do not desire what they imagine to be feminist identities, one response is to embed feminist frameworks within activities that foster identities girls desire. Many contemporary activist organizations, which may not be overtly feminist but which share the feminist goal of encouraging girls to be socially active, already do this.[13] For example, while the long-standing organization Bikes not Bombs supports and cultivates peace as well as environmentalism on a local level, it also explicitly addressed gender issues in its 1998 pilot program Girls Action Initiative, a program designed to help girls participate more fully within Bikes not Bombs, as well as within the local environmental, community, and peace initiatives this organization facilities.[14] Similarly, the Freechild Project, started in 2000, connects young people with a range of local and national initiatives that help them become social actors, whether redressing racism, homeless youth, or illegal labor practices. Like so many youth-focused organizations, the Freechild Project also has a special section devoted to girls' activism that addresses issues that are not gender-specific such as reducing substance abuse and increasing school achievement, and that allows participants spaces to explore how gender expectations inform these activist projects.[15] Perhaps this embedding of gender issues within activist organizations reflects that a focus on gender is too fraught at a time when girls are both struggling with gender norms and wanting to fit in. Or, perhaps it reflects that gender is an important but not primary way girls self-define. Either way, at the turn of the twenty-first century, activist organizations often provided girls with the resources to try out a range of social identities focused on being public actors.

Although such opportunities can help in general, feminist organizations fear the difficult choice of obscuring or foregrounding feminist identities when encouraging girls to be social actors. RG exposes the dilemmas one extracurricular organization faced when pursuing such a project.

ORGANIZERS' PEDAGOGIES AT RADIOGIRL

In September 1997, GirlZone and the community radio station WEFT sponsored an "airshifter" workshop that sparked the girls' interest. Almost a year after this workshop, a rotating group of approximately ten 6 to 15-year-old girls and young women met with a facilitator most Sunday mornings from 10:00–11:00 A.M. in the well-worn WEFT common room. Each radio program represented the work from one week's off-air brainstorming meeting and the next week's live, on-air broadcast. In theory, RG was a place where girls could learn about airshifting/radio production and radio journalism; over the two week cycle, girls picked music, read background material, wrote their own segments, edited others' writing, and, to varying degrees, worked the controls. In practice, however, RG was many things to the participants: a place to try "cool" activities with friends; an opportunity to learn a skill that would set them apart, and perhaps provide an edge in college admissions; a chance to produce and be heard on the radio; and, indirectly, a space where they would be exposed to feminist identities and activities. Among these many motivations and with a facilitator's guidance, girls hosted a radio program and developed identities of themselves as RadioGirls, active producers of their own cultural representations.[16]

Like GirlZone participants, RadioGirls varied significantly over time and within workshops. Initially and sporadically, RadioGirls were GirlZone regulars (e.g., Cyan, Sage, Samira, Chloe, and most especially Sophia), but for extended stretches RadioGirls formed a distinct group that generally had a greater age range than did most GirlZone workshops and included more ethnically and religiously diverse girls, perhaps because RG's Sunday 10:00 A.M. time slot conflicted with many Christian services. RG also asked for more commitment that GirlZone did. Girls often researched in pairs or planned segments weeks in advance and each workshop linked one week of preparation to the following week's show; to skip a session could mean letting down other RadioGirls. Finally, RG attracted girls interested in learning about radio journalism, a topic of particular interest to girls such as Miriam, or girls interested in researching, writing about, and publicizing topics of their choosing without having to learn the technicalities of radio production.

In its over five-year run, RG had two phases based on its two facilitators, Ayleen and Heidi. Both facilitators fostered girls' sense of competency and self-determination, asking RadioGirls to define the meaning of their radio program as one by and for girls in central Illinois. Ayleen and Heidi differed, however, in the privileged social identities and practices (social competencies) they thought RG should foster. The differences and similarities of their pedagogies and girls' responses to these pedagogies expose tactics of and challenges to recent feminist pedagogies.

Ayleen: Privileging Social Competency

RG's founder and first facilitator was Ayleen, a calm, quiet, quick-to-smile twenty-something who stayed in Champaign-Urbana after graduating from the state university. When she was young, Ayleen had to overcome the teasing of her siblings, her own insecurities, and what she describes as her "squeaky" voice when she pursued her interest in radio. Her perseverance paid off and she gradually surprised herself with the range of her curiosity and the development of her ideas, even when participating in what she considered traditionally adult forums such as radio station staff meetings. At the time she founded RG, Ayleen was a WEFT "airshifter" who deejayed her own weekly program, "Jivin' with Java." A few months after she and a friend led one of GirlZone's early workshops that taught girls how to build their own CD racks, Ayleen decided she wanted to provide additional opportunities for girls. Based on her past experiences and present resources, she started RG.

In this first phase, Ayleen embedded her feminism in the weekly talk and activities. Instead of "pushing her own agenda,"[17] Ayleen provided girls with structured opportunities to compose their own meaning, participate in public forums, and build a community in which they could pursue their own interests. Too many organizations, Ayleen argued, were focused not on girls' programming, but rather an adult programming voiced by girls: "It's generally thought that it's a fun program for kids if a bunch of adults sit around and script it out for them and have them read it and trying to cater to the kids. But the only way to know what girls want to hear about is to actually let them come on the air and plan it themselves."[18] In the hopes of countering the common trend in which girls simply ventriloquize ideas thought up by adults, Ayleen did the bulk of the preparation and sound engineering, which freed girls to learn to be journalists and radio airshifters.

To help girls understand themselves as social agents during the closed, off-air, biweekly meetings and then again more publicly in the alternating on-air, biweekly broadcasts, Ayleen validated girls' interests that prevalent cultural models had demeaned. Ayleen explained:

> They've got these ideas that other kids their age aren't necessarily talking about, like science and what's going on in Kosovo, and they are finding that nobody around them really wants to hear about it so they can't get in discussions at school cause people would be like, "Oh, why are you talking about that," "Who wants to hear about that?" But yet, when it's presented as part of the radio show, it's like an important piece, because they are pieces for the show. And all of a sudden it becomes more. It kind of gives them a space to talk about ideas that they don't necessarily have [a place] to talk about somewhere else.[19]

With encouragement, girls wrote strikingly complex and insightful pieces that Ayleen found atypical of girls this age. By understanding girls as public "voices" in "an ongoing girl-centric dialogue with the community,"[20] Ayleen created a space where girls could explore public identities largely unavailable elsewhere.

Whether or not they could fully articulate Ayleen's pedagogy, the Radio-Girls seemed to appreciate it. A bit older than many RadioGirls and notably more interested in radio journalism as a career, Miriam captures a common sentiment:

> The nice thing about RadioGirl is that the girls who are participating in it are not told what to do or what they have to do. They are free to talk about or read things that interest them or that they think will interest other girls. I think RadioGirl represents a good program that is not very common unfortunately because there is not a lot of initiative or interest that people have to get it started. I think it's a good chance for girls not only to get a chance to voice their own opinions, but also to learn about broadcasting and journalism and the radio in general.[21]

Girls appreciated an environment that fostered their ability to decide what to do and they liked learning the skills that could help them become competent public actors, in part by adopting an implicitly feminist stance of taking other girls' interests seriously.

As broadcasters and journalists, RadioGirls constructed their social identity as actively addressing a range of social and political issues. For example, RadioGirls with Islamic backgrounds, such as Miriam, Mudita, and Nghana, challenged the media privileging of Christian holidays by researching and writing a special report on the Islamic holy days of Ramadan, Ede, and the Night of Power.[22] Similarly, a RG interviewee challenged heteronormativity by highlighting the irony of being told that she "could be President of the United States but [she] couldn't go to prom without a [male] date."[23] Moreover, in this supportive environment, Radio-Girls felt able to question their own and others' activist commitments, as when RadioGirl Sarah lamented that although RadioGirls researched and reported on African-American women in Black History Month, these same girls diminished African-American's contributions to Champaign-Urbana during Women's Awareness Month, a problem Sarah wanted to correct.[24] These RG segments broadcast a public pedagogy that encouraged RadioGirls to be public actors who oppose discrimination in their everyday. RadioGirls themselves took-up what were in practice activist social identities, without publicly acknowledging the fact they were doing so.

Although these issues could clearly be framed as feminist, Ayleen seldom used that word in her interactions with the girls. Like many of the 1990s third-wave, Ayleen chose to enact her beliefs rather than discuss them. Even without a "feminist" label, girls read Ayleen and, in some ways, RG itself through this lens. The girls, therefore, had to negotiate Ayleen's pedagogy with their own perceptions of feminisms—perceptions engendered by public pedagogies that tended to depict feminists as anti-religious, generally white, and holding both irrational and negative attitudes toward men. Ayleen described how she helped the girls discard one of these stereotypes:

> In the beginning they felt they had to, they would say, "do I need to find a woman musician?" And I would say over and over again, "No. We decided that we are not going to focus in that way. It's going to be music in general." But the one time they did [focus on music all by women], the issue came up about boys somehow and it was that we don't need them. We can do things on our own. . . . They didn't take the typical just putting down the other sex aspect of it. And they really, they found a really nice way to go about it. It's just like they are trying to empower other women and they are not trying to knock boys out of the picture, they are just empowering each other.[25]

Through Ayleen's guidance, RadioGirls learned not to take-up "typical," or more likely stereotypical, stances. Girls followed Ayleen's lead and focused less on an imagined feminism that tried to "knock boys out of the picture" and more on a lived feminism that encouraged girls and women to be social actors.

To develop these feminisms, Ayleen provided repeated opportunities and a supportive environment for RadioGirls to become socially competent, whether they perceived this competency as feminist or not. Girls responded positively to this pedagogy and, as they learned new skills in radio production, they also began to imagine themselves as journalists, airshifters, and producers. Becoming a RadioGirl was an identity the girls wanted, and Ayleen capitalized on this desire by obliquely teaching the girls about versions of feminism other than those foisted upon them through negative public pedagogies.

Heidi: Privileging Feminist Identities

Before moving to Portland in the fall of 1999, Ayleen actively sought her replacement. Among those Ayleen solicited was another WEFT airshifter, Heidi, who was also involved in a range of local activist organizations, from the Independent Media Center (IMC) to the School for Designing Society. After it became apparent that if she did not accept this weekly commitment no one else would, Heidi became RG's second facilitator, adopting a pedagogy that encouraged different social identities and practices than those Ayleen's encouraged.

Whereas Ayleen provided the structural support and continuity for RG's drop-in format, Heidi wanted girls to assume greater responsibility and control for what RG would become. In fact, when Heidi presented RG to the WEFT Programming Committee at RG's annual review in 2000, the first full year Heidi ran RG, Heidi described RG as a "collective" (instead of a workshop).[26] This shift to a collective had a decidedly DIY feminist, activist tone, and she wanted the "you" in the Do It Yourself to mean the girls.

The fact that Heidi was more overt about her activism and feminism with the girls than Ayleen had been was a second shift. For Heidi, self-sufficiency in technical, often male-dominated, forums was a feminist issue. Heidi wanted girls to learn radio technology and, in practice, to become active social agents who design and produce their own meaning. This required girls to reject traditional social identities that, in the mid-1990s, associated at least computer technology with a-social males.[27] The pervasiveness of these associations reflects and perpetuates stereotypes that girls are unable to compete successfully in such areas as technology, math, and science, reinforcing stereotypes evident in the much publicized "math is hard" Barbie and the "shrinking pipeline" of women in science, technology, engineering, and mathematics. For Heidi, girls' interactions with emerging technologies created new sites to address long-standing issues, such as the trend where girls use given technologies but less frequently understand and design them.[28] To counter this trend, Heidi wanted to give girls entrée to a public, technology-mediated world in order to break the limitations of debilitating everyday stereotypes. As Heidi describes on-air,

> with things like computers or technical equipment in general I've found the boys tend to take over the boards and push all the knobs and buttons and things like that. And women have generally been involved as voices and front performers and things like that. So, one of the reasons I'm interested in RadioGirl is because I want to introduce girls to this world of composition, composing their own shows, of working the boards and of putting together a radio show, which involves quite a bit.[29]

The RadioGirls either followed Heidi's lead into more independent and overtly feminist frameworks, or they left. One girl who particularly valued Heidi's pedagogy was Sophia. A member of what she considered the radical schooling movement, Sophia appreciated RG's current "project based" orientation where participants made things happen. Although this required a high commitment of participants, it also allowed them a high degree of control. For Sophia, this contrasted with the "classroomish" pedagogy of RG's first phase. Since Ayleen ensured things kept moving regardless of others' participation, Sophia felt this RG first phase encouraged participants to think "of RG as an institution, like, if I leave it's not going to fall apart."[30] For Sophia, this assessment required low investment and provided RadioGirls with little control.

Perhaps Sophia preferred Heidi's approach because Sophia, like Heidi, was at the end of RadioGirls' feminist-activist spectrum. Sophia went to an alternative school called the School for Designing Society;[31] wrote feature pieces for the local IMC, such as the one opposing Monsanto's genetic modification practices; and attended national feminist and activist conferences when middle and high school aged. Few other RadioGirls shared this background, especially in RG's first phase, and few other RadioGirls had the skills and interest in pursuing a deep knowledge of radio production. With Heidi's encouragement, Sophia reported on her own participation in protests against the IMF or against the U.S. invasion of Iraq. Sophia felt strongly about these topics and wanted to use RG as a vehicle to let girls know that they too could join in such activism. Indirectly, Sophia forwarded a public pedagogy that encouraged girls to do so.

Although Sophia strongly endorsed Heidi's pedagogy, few other Radio-Girls did. In time, friends of Sophia came to RG, including former GirlZone participant Sage after she and Sophia re-connected at the School for Designing Society. In the short term, however, most girls commented that they did not want to do such activist shows, and they soon stopped coming to RG altogether. Sophia acknowledged that this activist push may have "scared the other girls away," and their departure presented a paradox for Sophia: "It's kind of weird, because on the one hand we must be hanging on the edge because we only have two people [participating in RG]. And on the other hand, our shows are going better than before."[32] For Sophia, this "better" reflects how RG's second phase encouraged and supported participants to become invested in an overtly activist, feminist technology training ground, a rare resource Sophia in particular valued. At that moment, Sophia found the benefits of this resource outweighed the cost to RG in fewer participants. This cost, however, soon proved too high. Gradually, RG's few but loyal participants recognized that their radio show no longer represented a range of girls' voices; participation dwindled from about ten regular RG participants toward the end of RG's first phase (March 1999) to two, what Sophia called the "Sophia and Heidi show,"[33] almost a year into RG's second phase (July 2000). RG aired its last program just months after GirlZone closed.

Balancing the Options

Despite their significant differences, both Ayleen and Heidi used radio production and radio journalism as a means to do the real work of RG: calling girls to be public actors weighing in on range of social and political issues and indirectly helping girls rethink their understandings of feminism within and against today's public pedagogies. Within this shared project, the different social practices and identities Ayleen and Heidi fostered offer important lessons about how to develop effective feminist pedagogies. In RG's better attended first phase, Ayleen promoted girls' agendas within embedded feminist frameworks, and the girls came up with their own definitions of social competency. Through their fun, friendships, and focus on social competency as they defined it, girls grew to want this social identity of a RadioGirl, engaging in feminist and activist practices even if many did not adopt this label. In RG's second stage, Heidi promoted overt awareness of feminism as crucial, and she saw radio production as a central means of pursing that goal. With explicit feminist activist frameworks yet diminished logistical support of the workshops, Heidi encouraged a more independent, activist, feminist identity of a RadioGirl. And most RadioGirls stopped coming.

Although it is typical for grassroots projects to emerge when a confluence of factors converge and then to disappear when these factors are no longer pressing, in RG's case, a change in two factors of organizers' pedagogies seemed to decisively shape RG. First was a more overtly feminist agenda. Second was the diminished logistical support. Both could justify the exodus from RG, but when we consider the other long-term projects participants undertook—Miriam learned to write for *The News-Gazette*; Sarah became a debater for the middle school Problem Solvers; and Sophia became a journalist for the IMC and an airshifter at WEFT—we see these required girls to develop specific and individualized expertise with logistical support comparable to what RG offered. The girls' continued energy away from RG suggests it was RG's more overly feminist, activist agenda that seemed to diminish girls' interest in RG.

This conclusion raises a troubling question for feminist pedagogies: if many girls check out of explicitly feminist activist frameworks, how should feminists design their pedagogies while still providing girls with social identities and practices girls want to pursue? Locating this question within national trends raises larger questions about the role of pedagogy within third-wave feminist thought. In the spate of third-wave manifestas and academic collections, there are personal reflections about the need to extend and/or alter this new generation's relationship with the feminist movement, with political engagement, with identity categories. There are detailed analyses of the ways that the socioeconomic changes associated with globalization inform the third-wave issues, alliances, strategies, and activism.[34] Yet scant explicit attention is paid to third-wave classroom pedagogies,[35] a particularly notable gap since many third-wave feminists are consciously influenced by the extensive earlier feminist research about schools and pedagogy.[36]

This diminished attention to school, feminisms, and pedagogy raises a related question: are slow-to-change institutions such as traditional schools the best place to think about what identities are needed in a rapidly changing socioeconomic context? Like the third-wave's attention to out-of-school settings, much current pedagogical research questions how/if traditional school-based pedagogies help people become meaningful social actors. In her chair's address to the Conference on College Composition and Communication, Kathleen Blake Yancey argued that too often writing for and in the classroom seems artificial or irrelevant to our students. Yancey argues that if writing studies scholars want to stay relevant in today's rapid technological and communication changes, we need to better understand the everyday kinds of writings our students engage in or will need to engage in. This issue of relevance indexes larger questions about how people understand writing as a social practice that helps them negotiate their lives.[37] These questions point to out-of-school sites as important on-the-ground think tanks for contemporary feminist pedagogies. Indirectly, they point to the importance of thinking through the lessons that extracurricular sites like GirlZone and RG offer.

The lessons at GirlZone and RG expose a tricky balance. On the one hand, as evident in chapter 4, leaving feminist influences implicit runs the risk of having feminist social identities undermined when girls encounter limiting public pedagogies. On the other hand, RG illustrates that girls reject an overt introduction of feminist frameworks, particularly without scaffolded activities that allow girls to understand feminisms as something other than what many public pedagogies present. As RG's second phase indicates, although girls may come to projects that are both feminist and activist, these girls may stop coming when such influences are overtly foregrounded in the weekly interactions. Therefore, the history of RG argues that to forward a feminist pedagogy successfully, it is wiser to engage girls in feminist-informed if not feminist-identified practices that can help girls investigate how feminist and public pedagogies relate to each other than it is to make understanding feminisms an overt goal of these practices and identities; embedding feminist goals within goals girls already desire can help girls imagine themselves within feminist frames without the knee-jerk reactions public pedagogies often teach.

REPRESENTATIONS AND REDESIGNS OF FEMINIST PEDAGOGIES

In order for people to understand girls as social actors, feminist pedagogies need to help participants counter the public pedagogies that teach girls to be a-political. Because these public pedagogies are powerfully pervasive, feminists cannot simply demonize or avoid them. Instead, feminist pedagogies can encourage people to investigate and possibly interanimate these public pedagogies by locating words such as "girl" in different cultural models. Resonating with multiple valences, "girl" can signify differently, which, in turn, can help girls broaden what they imagine they can do. Before consciously being able to interanimate public pedagogies, however, people need to recognize these public pedagogies and the cultural models they support.

For RadioGirls, the public pedagogies of Champaign-Urbana's newspapers captured and created cultural models that taught their audiences how to understand girls. These newspapers reported on many girls and girls' activities, and generally reported positively on RG itself. Within their affirming reports, these papers operated out of distinct cultural models that provided convergent and divergent public pedagogies about girls, at times supporting and at times challenging Ayleen and Heidi's pedagogies and the social identities these RG facilitators hoped to foster. Within the feminist-informed space of RG, organizers encouraged girls to investigate these representations. Examining how RadioGirls took-up, challenged, and interanimated the public pedagogies found in Champaign-Urbana's newspapers and the more private pedagogies sponsored by RG facilitators highlights how one group of girls negotiated the multiple pedagogies working with and against each other at a space devoted to providing girls with expanded, feminist possibilities.[38]

"Poppy-Girl Punk": The Containing Public Pedagogies of The News-Gazette

Champaign-Urbana's traditional local paper, *The News-Gazette*, featured news about community events such as local festivals, council meetings, and school activities, and relayed how national or international events impacted Champaign-Urbana. Publishing in various forms and under different names since 1852, this independent, locally owned and operated paper has a conservative slant. As stated on its webpage:

> While the *News-Gazette* editorial pages have traditionally reflected conservative viewpoints, we understand our responsibility as the area's leading source of information and news analysis. Therefore, other voices and other views are constantly sought for our opinion pages, through columnists, guest commentaries and letters to the editor.[39]

Although alternative perspectives were invited for balance, *The News-Gazette* forwarded conservative public pedagogies that tended to depict girls in ways that, as detailed below, downplayed girls' disrupting, activist agendas.

Different correspondents wrote several articles about RG and Girl-Zone in *The Gazette*'s Spin Off section, a weekly section devoted to local youth activities. In the breezy style that typifies articles by and about youth, these largely favorable articles limited their references to overtly feminist cultural models or to girls as activists or feminists, a notable absence in a university town with a visible feminist, activist presence and in articles about feminist organizations such as GirlZone and RG. Faith Swords' article about the all-girl band Feaze illustrates this public pedagogy that teaches readers to understand girls as fun-loving, even adventuresome, but still contained.[40]

As referenced in chapter 4, Feaze is the band three GirlZone participants started after taking a GirlZone "Girls Rock!" workshop. Emulating their role models, such as RiotGrrrl-informed national and local bands, Feaze played with the contradictory messages about girls, letting audiences know, as a "Once So Sweet and Innocent" song lyric states, "you don't know what's inside." This song opens with a gentle, melodic voice relaying: "I'm just a little grrrl with a little grudge/I am cute, I am innocent, and I love." Immediately after this sweet sounding introduction, this grrrl relays the "secrets" of her crew. Accompanied by loud, thrashing guitars and frenetic drums, the band screams out the song's chorus:

> Yes we drink/Yes we cuss
> Yes we screw/Yes we fuck
> Yes we smoke/Yes we're sluts
> Yes we have our nice butts . . .[41]

As the chorus makes clear, Feaze often played punk rock music with a disrupting message, a message that let outsiders know these young women were not what they seemed.

The national distributor of independent music Redeye described Feaze and their debut album within a cultural model that acknowledged Feaze's ability to be disruptive:[42]

> FEAZE, three teenage girls, three 15 year old skater chicks who can seriously rock, pop, and pull out a punk rock parlor trick or two when the mood strikes them. FEAZE play grungy, garagy guitar-rock spangled with indie-pop and classic old-school punk change-ups, a blistering set of tunes which will soon find favor with fans of teenage girls, teenage kicks, teenage lusts, and so forth.[43]

Unlike the Redeye description, *The News-Gazette* description of Feaze posits tamer social identities. For example, Swords' opens her article:

> "Feaze: verb to disturb or corrupt." The band's name is a little misleading if you know what it means. Feaze is made up of Kayla [last name] on guitar and lead vocals, Carrie [last name] on bass, and Tonie [last name] on drums and vocals. Playing poppy-girl punk, Feaze is taking Champaign-Urbana by storm.

This supportive, playful, and restrained depiction becomes an unstated support of Swords' claim that the band's title is misleading. Unlike the Redeye description where Feaze provides "blistering" tunes that implicitly infect if not corrupt the everyday order, *The News-Gazette* article makes no mention of Feaze's screaming, disorderly side that challenges stereotypes about girls' anger, innocence, and sexuality. Instead, Swords characterizes Feaze as "poppy-girl punk," a cute, harmless, spunky version of those who wish to disturb or corrupt.

Although Swords' derivation of the band's name highlights Feaze's goal to be disruptive, the article undermines this potential by not pursuing what Feaze wants to unsettle and by depicting Feaze band members as unlikely to be unruly. For example, although Swords emphasizes Feaze's DIY history, the closest the article comes to articulating what Feaze is trying to disturb or combat is in a quote when Kayla comments that Feaze wants to challenge the lack of opportunities and representations of girls in a range of activities. Swords writes:

> Feaze are skaters as well as rockers.
> "There need to be more girl rock bands. There need to be more girl skaters. There just need to be more girls," Kayla said, laughing.
> With upcoming shows Saturday . . .

The inclusion of this quote could indicate that Swords supports Kayla's attempt to interrupt the systems that exclude girls from being in a rock band or being a skater. And yet, Swords does not follow-up on Kayla's comment, a significant omission since Feaze members themselves could redress the lack of female role models for girls in Champaign-Urbana.[44] Instead, Swords describes Kayla by her first name[45] and notes she was laughing, thus weakening Kayla's authority as a speaker and thus disarming the impact of Kayla's questioning the underrepresentation of girls. Despite her band's lyrics and name, and despite Kayla's stated goal of disturbing typical representations that dismiss girls as rockers, Kayla comes off as someone unlikely to challenge the status quo.

Like all representations, this one of Feaze cannot be wholly inscribed within any single cultural model. In some ways, Swords' enthusiastic description does forward RG's project of developing alternative cultural models. When Swords emphasizes the band's unlikely beginnings, current concert commitments, and temporary celebrity status, she depicts these young women as rock stars. Moreover, when Swords focuses on Feaze as a typical band and not as a novelty "girl" band, she normalizes the social identities of girls as rock stars. These representations could and might have fostered Feaze's disrupting agenda. Unfortunately, this possibility was diminished because the *Gazette's* representations were generally inscribed within a cultural model that tended to position girls as depoliticized, as contained, as poppy-girl punk.

Even while being supportive of GirlZone sponsored activities, the public pedagogy of *The News-Gazette* made visible typical social identities that RG organizers aimed to challenge.[46] These generally a-political representations of girls are the highly visible representations that Radio-Girls generally saw available to them, and, at least initially, RadioGirls often represented themselves within these frameworks. This was the case for Miriam when she wrote an article for *The News-Gazette* early in her stint as a RadioGirl.

Miriam was a RG regular whose interest in radio journalism was evident throughout her RG tenure. Her father actively supported Miriam's attendance and frequently offered to help RG in any way he could. As a tween and teen, Miriam was slightly older than the many girls and younger tweens at RG, and she often played a quiet mentoring role to a few girls, from co-writing pieces to paging through tween magazines with a younger girl sitting practically on her lap. Miriam participated in group projects, but generally preferred to write her own pieces on topics ranging from the religious holy days of Ede to, most often, science issues, such as her extended reports on satellites or NASA projects.

In her article, "Want to be on the Air? YOU GO, GIRLS: WEFT Turns over Radio Station for Kids' Show Every Other Sunday,"[47] Miriam proved a competent journalist, providing important background about RG, describing the many activities girls did in planning shows, and quoting the girls and Ayleen. For the bulk of the show Miriam reported on (a show in which she did not participate), the girls chose to read a difficult, extended passage that paid tribute to Martin Luther King. In many ways, this program was a-typical due to the amount of reading of others' writing, writing beyond the reading level of some girls, as illustrated in the mispronunciations of the word "Montgomery" among others. Nonetheless, this program was typical in that it reflected the RadioGirls' desire to comment meaningfully on important social issues; in this case, they wanted to make the life and legacy of King come alive to girls their own age. After this extended segment, music breaks, and public service announcements, the RadioGirls chatted on-air about casual topics to fill the remaining time. This casual conversation, according to Ayleen, offered a nice balance, a playful reprieve from the intensity of their work and the challenging topics of racism and local activism.[48]

For part of her description of what the RadioGirls did, Miriam wrote:

> Chloe announced how girls can get involved in RG . . . Camille did an announcement on art classes for children. And Emma gave the weather report. The girls delivered their announcements well, and none seemed nervous. The theme of this Sunday's show was Martin Luther King, Jr. and the civil rights movement. The girls played songs sung by black artists and aired a pre-recorded piece that they took from a book on King. Their conversation, though, was on tamagotchis, gigapets and Beanie Babies, and it had a spontaneous quality that made it fun to hear.[49]

Miriam clearly appreciates the girls' spontaneity, and she accurately depicts many aspects of this RG show. Nonetheless, she also de-emphasizes their interest in publicizing King's legacy, obscuring how the girls created themselves as actively aware of and honoring King's activism.

The ways Miriam gives short shrift to RadioGirls' activist leanings are apparent in her representations of the on-air speaking roles that RadioGirls selected for themselves.[50] Most of the girls' speaking roles are what Erving Goffman would describe as animators—their reading of things written out for them made the girls "functional nodes in a communication system";[51] when the girls act as principals—a more agentive social identity where girls established themselves as "someone who is committed to what the words say"[52]—the girls are talking about Beanie Babies. Curiously, in a show dominated by both the girls' on-air time and off-air research about Martin Luther King, Jr. and his role as a civil rights leader, this article makes the girls appear competent at mechanical activities (reading announcements and weather reports), but contained—their spontaneity and agency coming from discussions of tamagotchis, gigapets, and Beanie Babies.

One reason for Miriam's construction of the RadioGirls could be that in radio production, agency is often hidden. BBC announcers used to make this explicit when they said, "The news as read by . . ." as if the news were self-evident and radio simply a means to transmit rather than to transform (or even create) knowledge. In this framework, when announcers broke this transparent frame in casual conversation they inserted themselves far more audibly. However, RadioGirls frequently mixed researched segments and casual conversation; they hardly sought to evacuate their presence.[53]

A second reason some may argue that Miriam diminished girls' political activism is the fact that Miriam was barely a teen, and, therefore was presumably too young to participate in such activism. Age may certainly have been a factor in determining Miriam's journalistic perspective, but age alone does not explain why she invoked certain social identities and eschewed others. Instead, a third, even more likely reason Miriam contained the activist impulses of the RadioGirls was that Miriam had a tacit, even unacknowledged, sense of what *The News-Gazette* correspondents should write.[54] Learning to be a journalist for *The News-Gazette* meant learning the conventions of this paper. These conventions are part of cultural models that privilege certain social identities and obscure others. The public pedagogies teaching these cultural models pressure people to conform to these social identities and to recognize the dangers of taking up alternative social identities, such as girls being activists and feminists. As a young new writer, Miriam seemed to have heeded the model *The News-Gazette* presented.

RG organizers challenged these public pedagogies that discourage girls from "finding" and "speaking their voice," potentially leading girls to believe that they do not have one.[55] For example, in an on-air RG debate about how to prevent students from bringing guns to school, six RadioGirls hoped to sway public opinion about the right of youth both to privacy and security.[56] During this debate, RadioGirls did not find 7–11-year-olds advocating school or even national public policy to be exceptional. Rather, they thought their opinions were of interest, as one RadioGirl stated on-air in another context, to "girls just like you and me."[57] Informed by and informing their immediate and imagined audiences,[58] these RadioGirls enacted a public pedagogy that RG facilitators hoped girls would adopt.

For Ayleen, participating in these larger conversations was a success, despite the outcome. In this vein, even though Miriam obscured RadioGirls' social identities as public activists, Ayleen only applauded Miriam for pursuing her journalism. These pursuits, Ayleen hoped, would teach Miriam and other RadioGirls to make their voices heard, a practice that can help girls understand themselves as public actors in a world they can shape.

In addition to the generally contained representations of *The News-Gazette*, representations of RG's alternative public pedagogies were picked up and ratified in the public pedagogies of other newspapers.

"A Responsible Radio Alternative": Alternative Public Pedagogies and the WEFT Revue

During the same month that *The News-Gazette* published Miriam's article, an alternative paper, *WEFT Revue*, published an article that offered different public pedagogies and social identities for RadioGirls. The *WEFT Revue*, like the WEFT radio station, fosters activism and recognizes girls as agents competent in political and social causes. As the name indicates, *WEFT Revue* primarily describes activities of the WEFT radio station, "a non-commercial radio station owned by Prairie Air, Inc., a not-for-profit organization. WEFT is an accessible, responsible and responsive radio alternative, serving the diverse communities of radio listeners in East Central Illinois."[59] WEFT is underwritten by many community organizations, including the AFL-CIO of Champaign County and the Alumni Against Racist Mascots, and is sponsored by and forwards similar public pedagogies as the local "alternative" newspaper, *The Octopus*. While Jazz and Blues are the most prevalent types of music on WEFT, weekly programming includes other music (e.g., world music, local bands, women in rock, soul, hip-hop, rap, and ethnic), and talk shows (e.g., public affairs, labor issues, and poetry). As the community sponsors and diverse programming indicate, the radio station operates out of alternative cultural models.

A WEFT airshifter and community radio supporter who describes WEFT radio and its patrons emphasizes this point:

> I don't subscribe to *The News-Gazette* and I don't watch the evening news. I know that this country's mass media are coming under increasing commodification and control by their corporate owners. That's a polite way of saying that the mainstream news is censored. WEFT is not corporate owned. WEFT is owned by local residents like me. And as long as we own it, we can get the Pacifica Report, Women's International News Gathering Service, This Way Out International Gay & Lesbian News,

Native American News, The Labor Journal, all the information that we can't get anywhere else. Furthermore, I can tune in to John Lee Johnson or Eunice Buckner Boone to hear some voices and perspectives from the black residents of my town. I can go into the studio during Women Making Waves and sing or say what I want people to hear and know. I can catch some slide guitar in the mornings, some Klazmir in the afternoons, some bagpipes in the evenings. I can get news and music from Nigeria, Bulgarian women's choral music, and Salsa. If there is something that I need that I'm not hearing, I can sign up for an airshifter class and put it out there myself. That's power, my friends. That's freedom and creativity and that is democracy.[60]

Reveling in the power of offering alternative public pedagogies, this WEFT patron rejects the representations that "censored" mainstream media provide and seeks to produce the diverse perspectives she finds missing. She and presumably other WEFT patrons value themselves as knowers, able to design news and music coverage that incorporates a fuller range of options, often from groups excluded from mainstream media production—women, minorities based on race or sexuality, and nonmainstream artists. WEFT patrons are highly invested in expanding the range of public pedagogies available, in making their own decisions about what they want to do and hear, and in producing resources that do *not* rely on prevalent cultural models. This RG sponsor encourages others to do the same.

Far more than *The News-Gazette*, the *WEFT Revue* recognizes both RadioGirls' desire to build alternative social identities and RG as a space in which to do so. Although girls were less likely to read the *WEFT Revue*—unlike *The News-Gazette*, it did not circulate widely outside of its local setting—when girls were at RG, when a WEFT patron called into RG, or when girls were shown *WEFT Revue* articles about Ayleen or RG, the RadioGirls saw and heard representations of themselves as public actors. One such example is Melissa Mitchell's "'Radio Girl': Giving Voices to Youths."

Much of this *WEFT Revue* article is about Ayleen, but when correspondent Melissa Mitchell describes the girls, she depicts them as confident producers of messages. In the ten short paragraphs describing RG participants, the girls are the grammatical subjects almost 70 percent of the time, overwhelmingly in active positions; girls pick the topics, research and write the segments, select music, and broadcast live or prerecorded pieces for their biweekly radio program.

By depicting RadioGirls as knowledgeable airshifters who have valuable social and political ideas to share, Mitchell counters cultural models that obscure girls' activism:

[Cyan's last name], a 7-year-old home-schooled vegetarian from Monticello, also is interested in social and political issues that some might think would be reserved for adult concerns.

[Cyan's last name] is so troubled by the [university mascot which depicts a Native American Chief] issue that she wrote a letter to the [university's] Board of Trustees, suggesting that they change the mascot to some type of sports figure. Her idea of a hero, she said, is not someone like John Glenn, "who doesn't think women should be astronauts;" instead, she looks up to Native American activist and artist Charlene Teeters, "because she is a leader in the group against [the university mascot].". . .

[Cyan's mother] said what [Cyan's last name] likes best about "Radio Girl" is "the fact that it allows [the girls] to have voices at this young age. They are tuned in to what's going on in the world, and unless there's a forum to talk about those things, that's quite a wait for these children."[61]

Throughout the article, Mitchell challenges public pedagogies that depict girls as contained. Indeed, in this part of the article, RadioGirls or their ideas are the subject of every sentence in this passage. "Interested in social and political issues that some might think would be reserved for adult concerns," RadioGirls identify problems and actively address them.

The fact that Mitchell challenges contained representations of girls is particularly evident when Mitchell depicts Cyan. Instead of detailing her high-pitched, youthful voice that might diminish Cyan's authority, Mitchell describes Cyan by her last name, by her choices, and by her awareness of current issues. In addition, Mitchell includes quotes by others who portray Cyan as active, even an activist. In the public pedagogies Mitchell offers, Cyan speaks as what Goffman would call a principal, closely linked to what she is saying; by writing a letter to the university Board of Trustees and writing segments for RG about the need to abolish the university mascot, Cyan constructs herself as an activist taking a controversial stand in this university town. This public pedagogy acknowledges Cyan's agency and ratifies a social identity that RG hoped to foster.

These *News-Gazette* and *WEFT Revue* articles forward public pedagogies that support at least partially competing social identities: girls as contained and girls as activists. And yet, the impact of these pedagogies cannot be predetermined. Did *The News-Gazette* deflect fears about RG, thus drawing more people into activities they might not otherwise approach? Did the *WEFT Revue* and *The News-Gazette* attract different types of participants and sponsors, thus broadening RG's appeal or brewing potential problems? There can be no definitive answers, since both people and representations travel and are interpreted differently as they do. Partially aware of these travels, RadioGirls defined themselves and their radio program by drawing on and redesigning the social identities from diverse cultural models.

RADIOGIRLS' INTERANIMATION OF PUBLIC PEDAGOGIES

RG organizers could not hope to overpower the pervasive public pedagogies that tended to offer girls a-political, contained identities. Although organizers might seek to hold these public pedagogies temporarily in abeyance, this organization was simultaneously shot through with them; participants brought in public pedagogies not only in the magazines under their arms or in songs they sang, but also in their internalized ways of understanding their world and their position within the world. Therefore, RG organizers needed to engage and alter these public pedagogies, offering girls new desired identities as girls travel through and beyond feminist spaces. One way to do this is to help girls recognize what public pedagogies encourage. Affirming that girls need not adopt these lessons, RG organizers teach girls to interanimate these public pedagogies, a process many girls may already do implicitly, but one that is less often overtly encouraged.

As a group, RadioGirls tended to be aware of what girls and Radio-Girls are expected to be. Although this awareness was explicit at times, as when several RadioGirls told Sophia they didn't want RG to become so activist, more often these negotiations were implied. For example, the week prior to Valentine's Day, the girls lamented that they were expected to do a show on "mushy kinds of love." Ayleen offered that they need not take up others' expectations. Instead of focusing on romantic love, Ayleen encouraged girls to investigate alternative stories. She was working toward the idea that the girls could investigate family love, friendship love, and homosexual love, but the girls cut her off; seemingly liberated by the permission to rework typical expectations and excited by the idea of an "Alternative Valentine's Program," they focused on violence as much as on love (e.g., the St. Valentine's Day Massacre, mythical gods of war and love).

Throughout this session, girls questioned traditional links between girls, Valentine's Day, and "mushy kinds of love" by not only highlighting, but also playing with, multiple expectations of who RadioGirls can be. At one point in the planning, tween Maddie suggested she research and write a report on honor killings in Jordan and what King Hussein was planning to do about them before he died. Although this topic fit with the theme and many girls felt that discussing this crime against women was important, the girls also felt that their audience might find it "too heavy" to air on Valentine's Day, and this story was indefinitely postponed. In this interaction, RadioGirls simultaneously pushed on what they considered typical expectations of them on Valentine's Day and acknowledged they did not feel free to disregard these expectations completely. Although Radio-Girls ultimately located their radio program on a conservative end of "alternative" cultural models, the girls did make these cultural models a topic to be discussed and a framework to be challenged.

Occasionally, when balancing the multiple, competing expectations of public and RG organizers' pedagogies, RadioGirls' sought to make supposedly typical understandings of the girls themselves resonate a bit differently. Two RadioGirls displayed one enactment of this balancing in their on-air performance of a poem they wrote about what it means to be a RadioGirl. Mudita was a RG regular during Ayleen's tenure who stopped coming shortly after Ayleen's departure. Invested in her tween world as defined by pop culture, Mudita brought in teen magazines, talked extensively about tween star culture, and experimented with more sexualized clothes and makeup. Caley was a more sporadic RG participant. Although she could be happily engaged in the banter about Hollywood representations of what it meant to be a tween, she seldom brought in mass-produced tween accoutrements nor did her style of dress reflect the common tween desire to be years older than she was.

Despite their differences, both clearly desired the RadioGirl social identity, as evident when they playfully composed their "RadioGirl" poem for a prerecorded show to be aired after Ayleen left but before Heidi began.

> "R"   Responsible for everything we do
> "A"   Attitude, strength, and health
> "D"   Determined to reach our goals
> "I"   Intelligent as we come
> "O"   Outstanding, unique, and talented
> "G"   Girls are as equal as anybody
> "I"   Inside and out filled with beauty
> "R"   Respectful to others
> "L"   Living our lives up
> "S"   Sisters with attitude
> And that spells RadioGirls.[62]

According to these middle schoolers, what it means to be a RadioGirl is, among other things, to be full of attitude, talent, and intelligence. These representations challenge the unstated but clearly present pedagogies that imply girls have limited social identities, such as girls are defined by their external beauty (the second letter "I") or that girls are compared to a standard, boys (letter "G").[63] This interanimation of feminist and public pedagogies is further exposed in how Mudita and Caley delivered their poem. The boldness of the girls' voices, the unusually loud volume of much of this poem, and the format of their presentation mark their delivery as that of a cheerleader, a social identity that middle-school girls often see available for themselves. As cheerleaders for RG, Mudita and Caley seem to conform to public pedagogies that teach girls to be ornamental supporters of others' activity, a social identity RG challenged. In their on-air performance, Mudita and Caley reinforce *and undermine* expectations of what it might mean to be a cheerleader. Cheering for themselves, these RadioGirls are both the subject and object of the cheer, challenging public pedagogies about girls and troubling assumptions that cheerleaders function as mere decoration.

By recognizing themselves in the feminist-informed ways the RG community does, these girls interanimated and therefore altered the social identities that public pedagogies seem to sediment into girls' practices, language, and ideas. The power of this sedimentation, however, was evident even as Mudita and Caley performed their "RadioGirls" poem. During the summer when Mudita used "RadioGirls" to talk back to evaluations of girls based on their outward appearance, she began what Sophia implies are the antifeminist gender norms of fifth grade, which for Sophia meant wearing "too much" makeup and overly sexualized clothes.[64]

As "RadioGirl" illustrates, enactments of public and feminist pedagogies are neither static nor singular and the ways these interanimate each other cannot be predetermined. Similarly, although *The News-Gazette* and *WEFT Revue* present pedagogies that typify a variety of cultural models about girls, taken alone they reflect neither the complexity of social identities, nor the potential that interanimation offers in redesigning social identities. RG pushed on this potential. Even as many of the social identities girls see available to them echo or respond to the expectations of powerfully diffuse cultural models that limit girls' agency, RG facilitators hoped to counter these depoliticized public pedagogies. Since these representations pervade girls' lives, facilitators could not avoid them and since girls would tune out if organizers merely denigrated these public pedagogies, organizers put feminist and public pedagogies into conversation so that girls could inflect prevalent social identities within more feminist friendly cultural models. This focus on interanimation— on resituating RadioGirls within feminist cultural models with the hopes of expanding girls' social identities—is a particularly important tactic for communities like RG, communities who meet one hour per week as opposed to the untold hours that girls encounter public pedagogies.

Throughout their tenure, RG facilitators sought systematic ways to expand the identities girls saw available to them, and girls often took up these identities—as middle schooler, activist, or cheerleader—in ways that exceed the boundaries of any one cultural model. As the "RadioGirl" poem illustrates, interanimating familiar public pedagogies is one strategy that acknowledges and works within these ever shifting boundaries, a practice explored at the GirlZone-sponsored GrrrlFest, as the next chapter details.

6

Redesigning Girls' Image Stores

[When I was a girl] I don't remember being able to go out and celebrate girl culture. I mean, there wasn't a concept like that. That was an oxymoron. And so, I think ["girl power"] has given a sense of solidarity to female children. And even if that solidarity is from one perspective based on cosmetics, it's still about more than that to little girls. I think it's about fantasy and imagination and something mythical. Like participating in myth to some degree. . . . Finding your identity through commodity, you can't escape it [but] I think that you have to look beyond the commodity and see what kind of fantasy or what kind of meaning a child intends or what they're looking for and work with that.

—Joni, GrrrlFest workshop facilitator, 2003

According to Joni, girls and young women in the United States simply do not have the opportunity to imagine their identities in contexts free from consumer culture. This creates significant dilemmas for feminists who both celebrate an emerging girl culture and seek to wrest this culture from the indifferent, even hostile, influences of commercialism. Some feminists advocate a *dis*engagement with consumer culture, yet who in the United States can live outside of it? For many girls, the question is who would want to? For those like Joni who see no way out of consumer culture, the question is how can feminists constructively use it to better suit girls' and women's needs when feminists' ideas have so often been emptied of their radical potential in order to sell commodities like "girl power" cosmetics or facial scrub? For feminists of all sorts, the dilemmas center on finding productive ways to help girls engage with today's consumer culture.

These questions have added urgency in recent years as consumer culture has more and more come to define what it means to be a girl. Today, girls (and boys) are exposed daily to over six hours of media (television, music, movies, IM, video games).[1] Despite the proliferation of venues, these media offer generally homogenized images and narratives, constructing a marketplace of childhood that further teaches youth to be active consumers.[2] Barbie brand is a classic example. Mattel has now created several girls' worlds with "lifestyle products" appropriate for the differentiated target audiences of

3–5-year-olds, 5–7-year-olds, and 8–10-year-olds. Doing $3.6 billion in retail sales worldwide,[3] the Barbie brand encourages girls to understand themselves within Barbie's lifestyle of buy, buy, buy. A consequence of this self-understanding, Angela McRobbie argues, is that "the norms governing recognition for the category of girl are now largely and dangerously provided by consumer culture as a regime of truth which has recently supplanted or at least overtaken other truth-dispensing regimes such as those associated with the state including education, family and community."[4]

One tactic feminists can use to help girls mitigate or even redirect this power is to redesign what Anne Haas Dyson calls youth's "image stores," the shared representations that orient how people will interact with others and understand themselves.[5] For example, Dyson noticed how the third grade students she studied redesigned the classroom's image stores (e.g., stories and images about superheroes, Greek gods, and civil rights activists) as ways to broker new social roles and relations in their everyday world

This practice of redesign was evident in third grader Tina's introduction of her character "Venus," a powerful female able to be the sole superhero of a story.

> Venus had entered the classroom image store, along with the Power Rangers, the X-Men, and Rosa Parks. That store held for each child the symbolic means for examining an aspect of themselves. But their use of those symbols was not an act of individual self-expression but of an evolving social response to those around them. . . . In their unofficial play, their official dramatic enactments and follow-up discussions, and in their own individual contributions as writers, the children not only appropriate, or invert, available roles and relations; they could reconstruct them, imagining new choices from expanding possibilities. Through marking, elaborating, and transforming the features, actions, and circumstances of powerful characters, children themselves gained some power—some ability to have a say—in the evolving community dialogue.[6]

Remediating pervasive superhero stories that tend to assign girls pretty, passive, sidekick, or victim roles, Tina introduces her character "Venus" so that girls can imagine themselves as forceful figures. Tina creates a textual resource that expands her classroom's image store. In so doing, Tina challenges limiting practices and identities not only within the classroom, but also on the playground and other extracurricular spaces.

Despite this hopeful example and the recognition that girls have engaged in the process of redesign for a long time,[7] I argue that a project of *feminist* redesign needs to be modeled. In today's media-saturated, market-driven environment, girls see few examples of redesigning beyond what the commercialized image stores make available. The difficulty of modeling a feminist practice of redesign in today's consumerist and antifeminist social climate requires a doubleness in feminist strategies, which both evokes a frequently circulating message and tweaks that message to alter its meaning. Simultaneously safe play to outsiders and provocative references to insiders,

Fig. 6.1. GrrrlFest 2002 Logo. *Note:* Reproduced by permission of Aimee, co-founder of GirlZone.

this doubleness can extend a message within a new context, combine elements to create a new whole, and subvert an intended message by exposing the message's hidden valences. Feminists can use this doubleness to entice people to learn more about the paradoxical pleasures of feminist engagements with consumer culture. Such doubleness, in fact, was a goal of the GrrrlFest logo.

Within the omnipresent consumerist frameworks of capitalistic society, reclaiming a more feminist understanding of girl power was a central project of the GirlZone-sponsored "GrrrlFest: Throw like a girl." Once a year from 2001–2003, this "weekend long celebration of girls and women" featured music showcases and offered girls and women open forums, panel discussions, and hands-on workshops on topics ranging from basic car mechanics to grant writing, and from sewing to claiming your anger. The GrrrlFests were hugely successful, drawing participants from across the country, including musicians from a New York City-based RiotGrrrl chapter. Primarily, however, GrrrlFest retained a local focus. Organizers used local media to blanket the community with information about both the Fest and the need to support girls and women. The organizers fostered community participation by having GrrrlFest events throughout Champaign-Urbana: music showcases were in the street and in local bars; panel presentations were held at the public library and the Independent Media Center; workshops were everywhere from computer centers and Aikido dojos to vegetarian restaurants and skate parks. These workshops combined consciousness raising (e.g., workshops like "Mind your Mind over your Manners"), and skill building (e.g., workshops on knitting or bike repair) so that participants could use their Do-It-Yourself (DIY) skills to imagine and create what they wanted.

Redesigning prevalent images and texts, the GrrrlFest logo is an exemplary microcosm of the cultural work that the Fest as a whole accomplished.

Using multiple modes (i.e., textual and iconic), the logo forwards a "doubled" message. For example, the "grrrl" of the GrrrlFest plays multiple ways, indexing the RiotGrrrl movement to an insider audience while being merely fun wordplay for a general audience. Similarly, in the logo, GrrrlFest organizers combined a cheeky but provocative textual slogan, "Throw like a girl," with a variation of a popular image already circulating in girls' image stores, the Powerpuff Girls. Critical and ironic as well as playful and optimistic, the GrrrlFest logo redesigned these individual components in order to infuse feminist understandings into girls' commercialized image stores.

The way the logo became a gloss for the work of GrrrlFest itself illustrates the central role visual representation plays in today's youth culture, whether in textbooks and news reports or computer games and music videos. Although GrrrlFest workshops were awash in texts (e.g., articles on girls' self-esteem and schooling practices; lists of resources for girls-in-science camps; postcards to politicians that lobbied for halting proposed changes to Title IX), organizers were well aware that visuals were what initially and immediately attracted girls. Years earlier, Gina explained the importance of visual representation for drawing girls to GirlZone: "I think that [girls] don't care about the mission statement. I think the mission statement is more for adults or for maybe a teenager. I think [girls] respond to the activities and probably to visuals."[8] Consequently, when GirlZone and GrrrlFest organizers thought about how to attract girls to participate in feminist-inspired workshops, discussions, and concerts, they chose to focus less on providing girls with persuasive texts and more on providing girls with activities and images that captured who organizers hoped GrrrlFest participants could be. The way GrrrlFest organizers used the logo to broker feminist-informed practices and identities illustrates both GrrrlFests' mission and one model of how to pursue it.

Before evaluating the efficacy of this logo as a project of feminist design, the first half of this chapter examines the complex relationships among feminism, girl culture, and consumer culture. Analyzing the difficulties in countering the pervasive and often damaging effects of consumerism, this first section argues for local interventions that expose and expand today's consumerized girl culture so that girls and women can imagine identities that exceed those of an individualized consumer. After this overview, the second half of this chapter draws on Gunther Kress' theory of design to provide ways to examine the practice of doubleness I have been advocating. In particular, this second section investigates how the logo illustrates a practice of redesign by redirecting the consequences of the trends analyzed in the first part of the chapter. This second section moves from positing an expanded definition of literacy that addresses the multimodal nature of so many contemporary documents to examining how GrrrlFests' multimodal "visual identity"[9] facilitated, with mixed success, the Fests' goals of helping participants understand and challenge the commodification and denigration of girl culture.

FEMINISM, GIRL CULTURE,
AND CONSUMER CULTURE

Sharing buzz words such as "freedom," "choice," and "independence," contemporary discourses of consumer culture overlap with those of the most visible cohort of the previous feminist generation, liberal feminism. And yet, in practice the marketplace drains feminist goals of their activist import. Whereas feminists intertwine individual and collective social action in their work for social change (e.g., the personal is political), consumer culture, in contrast, focuses on an individualistic "I" and commodifies large-scale resistance (e.g., Amazon.com sells Che Guevera T-shirts).[10] Without being anchored in feminist frameworks, "liberated" girls and young women are more likely to understand themselves within prevalent consumerist discourses where people are individual economic actors without concern for social justice.[11] This construction troubles many feminists; despite the marketplace's touting of a world of economic actors with equal buying power, national issues such as affordable day care and the feminization of poverty (let alone the global sex trade and the effects of environmental destruction) challenge the lived reality of this supposed economic equality. In a typical pattern, consumer culture evacuates feminist discourses in order to sell a product.

This "co-opting" of activist feminist agendas is hardly new. Susan Douglass describes how in the 1980s consumerist discourses redeployed liberal feminist discourses so that feminist goals of collective liberation and radical social change became capitalist goals of individualistic liberation and advancement within current the system, generally by consuming certain products. Douglass explains:

> one of capitalism's greatest strengths—perhaps its greatest—is its ability to co-opt and domesticate opposition, to transubstantiate criticism into a host of new, marketable products. Instead of group action, we got escapist solitude. Instead of solidarity, we got female competition over men . . . [N]arcissism as liberation is liberation repackaged, deferred, and denied . . . [o]f all the disfigurements of feminism, this, perhaps, has been the most effective.[12]

Douglass makes clear how capitalism uses the shell of feminism to further ends that feminists oppose. This trend continues, as evident in the discourses surrounding a recent niche market: girls.

Construction of Identity: Girls as Sexualized Economic Actors

Girls learn to take-up their market-defined identities from a variety of media sources found in the mushrooming of tween magazines, television shows, movies, music, and videos.[13] Each pushes consumer culture. Similarly, tweens' everyday geography includes shopping malls, places tween girls are twice as likely as any other demographic to visit on a weekend.[14]

These public spaces construct consumption and girl identities through stores such as the United Kingdom's Girl Heaven, an all pink and glittery store that sells girls what it means to be a girl and what it means to be in heaven (i.e., what girls should desire). According to Girl Heaven, both girls and girls' desires combine leisure, fun, and girl bonding. These desires are mediated through and linked to consumption of hair, nail, and makeup products.[15]

Even childhood toys push consumerism, not merely to sell a product, but also a lifestyle. The recently popular doll series Diva Starz illustrates this lesson. One selling point of these dolls is their ability to hold over ten thousand "conversations" with the target audience of 6–12-year-old girls. Within Diva Starz repertoire, consumer culture plays a prevalent role. For example, Alexa shapes girls' conversations and image stores with these opening lines:

> I just love to go shopping with my friends. It makes me so happy. Do you like shopping for birthday presents? Let's invite a friend to go shopping. Who should we invite? Fabulous. Let's go to the mall with our friends and find something we can wear to parties.
>
> I'm so sad. I *so* need a new outfit. Wanna go to the mall? Let's invite a friend to go shopping! Who should we invite? Fabulous, let's go to the mall with our friends and buy something we can wear to parties. Wanna go to the mall?[16]

Constructing girls' identities within a matrix of friendship, emotions, and the mall, Alexa's messages are similar to those of the other Diva Starz. For example, Summer similarly addresses girls in ways that teach that consumerism should be a central part of their worlds:

> Let's go shopping with some friends. My friends are way into fashion. Are your friends into fashion? Which of your friends has the best fashion style? No way! I love buying presents for my friends. Do you like shopping?
>
> I'm in a bad mood. Let's go shopping. Do you like shopping? What's your favorite kind of clothes? What are you going to wear today?[17]

Like so much of contemporary girl culture, Diva Starz teach girls that girlhood and shopping are inextricably intertwined.

For girls, this consumer identity is frequently associated with the sexualization of younger and younger women and girls, sometimes called "prost-i-tots." Beyond high profile examples (e.g., JonBenet Ramsey),[18] the process of sexualizing young girls has been evident in a range of lower profile trends. For example, packaged as a way to empower girls by helping them improve their self-confidence, a recent trend in high school graduation gifts for young women is breast implants.[19] Instead of a scrapbook for past accomplishments or a computer for future challenges, a growing number of presumably upper- and middle-class young women and their parents (who pay thousands of dollars for this elective surgery) feel augmenting teens' breasts is a better way to prepare young women for the challenges they face. The sexualized environment for girls extends beyond radical surgery into everyday apparel: many young girls wear "sex bracelets," multicolored rubber bands that indicate which sex act the wearer is willing to/has already performed; the newly (again) cool Playboy bunny is prominently emblazoned on shirts, baseball caps and other recently released Playboy products targeted to youth; this bunny, as well as a range of other images—from the childhood icons such as Hello Kitty and the Cookie Monster to racier messages such as "feeling lucky?"—can be found on the $152 million worth of thongs that 13–17-year-olds bought in 2003 alone.[20] And while not apparel, the ever-present cell phone is used by middle and high schoolers to set up sex dates, at times with those they scarcely know and at other times with "friends with benefits," acquaintances or friends with whom they have no-strings-attached sex.[21]

For those who would like girls to find a greater range of opportunities and identities for themselves—beyond linking self-esteem with breast implants and seeing their identity through a prism of sexualized consumerism—it is difficult to imagine how to combat these powerful economic and cultural trends. What, in other words, is an effective way to intervene in a consumerist and sexualized girl culture? And, how can feminists in particular help girls productively redesign their relationship with this problematic consumer culture?

Feminist Strategies of Engaging with Consumer Culture

The media and fashion industries may be constructing girls to be sexualized subjects in ways that make it difficult for girls *not* to be objectified by others. Yet, these constructions and girls' uptake of them are hardly monolithic. Indeed, many girls follow the prevailing fashion choices of wearing thongs or middrifts, but this sexualization does not necessarily mean girls will be sexually active. This place of ambiguity provides feminists with an opening to attend to girls' pleasure and to help girls examine and possibly redesign these pleasures. Girls are already engaged in this work. Girls at Girl Heaven claimed they enjoyed parts of Girl Heaven but resisted the wholesale message; they wanted makeup, not to be made-over.[22] The girls' responses expose the possibilities for helping girls redesign both their image stores and the images marketers attempt to sell them.

Of the varied feminist forays into this project during the 1990s two trends are significant. The first can be called DIY's goal of opting-out of consumerist structures; the second, a desired constructive complicity within these structures. Although very different, both were sparked by the sweeping power consumer culture had in shaping the possibilities girls saw for themselves. Despite this evident problem, both responses ran into trouble, as the following sections explain.

DIY Opting Out

In the early 1990s, the DIY philosophy—a hands-on philosophy where people join together to take care of their own needs through their own collective actions—was made popular again by the punk music and zine influenced RiotGrrrls' movement.[23] Highly visible DIY feminist activists such as the RiotGrrrls offered idealistic but often untenable models for circumventing and even opting-out of consumerist structures. For example, through zines such as *Grrrl Germs*, *Satan Wears a Bra*, and *Quit Whining*, RiotGrrrls fostered local feminist networks that sought to be outside of and critical of consumerist networks. Furthermore, zine authors countered the music industry's widespread commercialization by producing and distributing their own representations of themselves and possible female identities.

Although RiotGrrrl's DIY philosophy was idealistic and although grrrl power energized a new generation of feminists, this form of feminist activism made little headway in productively altering consumerist practices. For example, in her analysis of zines, Third-wave activist Jennifer Bleyer details how the marketplace altered the meaning of grrrl/girl power to such a degree that the DIY inspired girl power became reinflected to mean an individualistic, trendy commodification. Lamenting how consumer culture co-opted this DIY philosophy, Bleyer argues that zines have been

> swallowed up by the great maw of popular culture with dollar signs flashing in its eyes. Like hip-hop, grunge, and punk rock, the language and style of RiotGrrrl were absorbed, repackaged, and marketed back to us in the most superficial form of its origin. Whereas RiotGrrrl's "grrrl power" was about doing it yourself and questioning authority, pop culture appropriated the message to sell a sanitized version of "girl power" that was essentially capitalism dressed up in baby doll dresses, blue nail polish, and mall-bought nose rings. Indeed, the values—fearlessness, independence, daring, and a solid middle finger to the patriarchy—on which many girls zines were built and for which their writers were denigrated as "angry" and "self-indulgent," were flipped upon their heads and used to sell everything from cars and cigarettes to athletic shoes. The selling of girl power illustrated, as Naomi Klein wrote in *No logo*, how "the cool hunters reduce vibrant cultural ideas to the status of archaeological artifacts, and drain away whatever meaning they once held for the people who lived them."[24]

Bleyer's discussion of the commodification of girl power echoes music writer Ann Powers who notes, "at this intersection between the conventional feminine and the evolving Girl [girl power], what's springing up is not a revolution but a mall . . . thus, a genuine movement devolved into a giant shopping spree, where girls are encouraged to purchase whatever identity fits them best off the rack."[25] Unlike the RiotGrrrl agenda of using grrrl power to resist consumer culture, girls became subjects of a commodified girl power by taking up their consumer identities. And, instead of the RiotGrrrl's grrrl power becoming a feminist "Revolution Girl-Style Now!," by decade's end, girl power had become a marketer's gold mine.

Despite these significant distortions, the popularity garnered through the RiotGrrrl's commodification ironically facilitated feminists' attempt to redirect girl culture by providing a "cool" entry point to talk about feminist ideas with girls and young women who were ambivalent about or resistant to claiming a feminist label. This can be seen at GirlZone, where after a few years Aimee publicly aligned GirlZone with the RiotGrrrl tradition of feminist girl power in newsletters, GrrrlFest advertisements, and newspaper articles. For example, in a blurb for the sporadically published *GirlZine*, Aimee describes the GirlZone book club as a project that takes up the RiotGrrrl traditions:

> The name BookGrrrl comes from the RiotGrrrl movement, where girls and women worked together to make space for females in mosh pits at punk concerts, which were usually filled with guys who treated girls pretty nasty. Girls in the RiotGrrrl movement went in to the mosh pits together with arms linked and stood their ground, saying 'We have a right to be here too!' We know girls have a right to have a place in books, and to read about strong, active girls. In GirlZone, we're putting our foot down and claiming our right to have a space for real girls in what we read—not as helpless waifs that need saving—but as cool characters we can respect and relate to. And that's why we called GirlZone's book club "BookGrrrl."[26]

In this text, Aimee articulates both feminist critiques, such as how many cultural practices treat girls "pretty nasty," and feminist tactics, such as how girls can channel their anger into action. Similar to the RiotGrrrls demand of space in mosh pits, BookGrrrls demand discursive space that provides images of girls beyond the diminutive and sidekick "ettes" of pop culture[27] and the waifs needing to be saved. The cache of the RiotGrrrls—developed at the expense of some of their key beliefs—means that years after their decline, feminists such as Aimee can invoke popularized RiotGrrrl representations to help girls expand their image stores and therefore to expand the shared resources girls have for making sense of themselves and their place in the world.

Constructive Complicity

In addition to circumventing consumer culture, some feminists at the turn of the twenty-first century tried to be constructively complicit with it.[28] Feminists in this camp argued that since there was no way out of consumer culture, people should work within available structures and adapt them for feminist ends. This tactic emphasized play, often celebrating the "guilty pleasures" of consumerism.

Initially, feminists felt that the marketplace was responding to their agendas, if only because feminists purchase things too. For example, in women's and girls' magazines, there was an increased attention to what women desire, a freeing of the sexual double standard, and an expanded range of options that exceeded the sappy romance trope,[29] even if unhealthy body images and the push to buy products continued. Beyond magazines, popular culture more generally depicted adventuresome women taking up male action roles, though these women simultaneously retained "safe" female roles. As a sexualized, powerful, but usually dutiful daughter, *Tomb Raider*'s Lara Croft was hugely successful in the traditionally male market of computer games and action movies. Similarly, lead characters Yu Shu Lien and Jen Yu are simultaneously powerful martial artists able to defeat male or female foes and desirable heterosexual love interests in the critically acclaimed and commercially successful motion picture *Crouching Tiger, Hidden Dragon.*

With a slightly different bent, other popular media swarmed with ostensibly humorous and slightly neurotic characters that addressed feminist issues of the day: how to participate in consumer culture; how to balance work and family; how to value their sexuality in the age of sexual freedom. Despite referencing important feminist issues, the representations evident in popular and/or award winning television shows such as *Ally McBeal* and *Sex and the City* and best-selling books (and later movies) such as *Bridget Jones's Diary* portrayed safe, white,[30] economically independent, professional women who typically end in relationships with male characters. Even as the marketplace sold this idea of women's emancipation, these debatably feminist representations offered a highly constrained emancipation that was largely anti- or postfeminist and strongly linked to consumerism. These representations shied away from sustained critique and the "angry feminist" label that brought attention to social injustices and material inequities. As these representations illustrate, consumer culture once again had reinflected common feminist messages, but feminisms' social justice mission had made little headway in productively altering consumerist practices. In the end, the benefits of feminists' complicity could not sufficiently outweigh the ethical and political costs of the intended constructive work.

Within and beyond feminist communities, the Spice Girls represented girl culture's fraught attempt at constructive complicity. Upbeat, infantalizing, highly choreographed, and scantily clad, the Spice Girls sought to expand the mid-1990s boy band phenomenon to include girls and women. With their meteoric rise, the Spice Girls exposed literally millions of girls to their version of girl power. Their evacuation of RiotGrrrl informed girl power made the ideals of female solidarity and racial harmony hip, trendy, and thoroughly commodified.

Despite the potential of popularizing the concept of girl power in ways that, as Joni's opening quote implies, can help children expand what they imagine is possible, GirlZone organizers and facilitators believed the Spice Girls were complicit with consumer culture, but not constructively so. Out of girls' earshot, GirlZone organizers and facilitators frequently lamented how the Spice Girls were emblematic of a commercialized sense of girl power. Nonetheless, the Spice Girls provided an important opportunity for organizers to ask girls to interrogate (paraphrasing a Spice Girls' song) "what they want, what they really really want." Keying in on this hit song, organizers feared that the Spice Girls encouraged girls to want to be objectified, infantalized, and valued for their bodies. To intervene in what girls want, organizers repeatedly attempted to redesign the pervasive commodifying images of women and girls. For example, in a collage workshop on all the "cool" things girls can do, girls flipped through magazines and chatted about which of the Spice Girls each wanted to be, a decision heavily influenced by the revealing outfits each Spice Girl wore.[31] During this workshop, Aimee walked among the girls, talking about their collages and asking both why the Spice Girls seemed so popular and what other images of girls might be good ones to make popular. In doing so, Aimee wanted to highlight the possibility of redesigning the social identities imbricated in the commercialized girl power that the Spice Girls represented.

At one point in the ongoing talk, textual production, and graphic work at the collage workshop, Aimee stopped to chat with eleven-year-old Sage who was discussing the values of Sporty Spice. Sage lived in an economically depressed town outside of Champaign-Urbana, but became a GirlZone regular due to her mom's commitment to Sage's participation. In contrast to her later Goth stage, tween Sage was captivated by this cute, commodified, pop girl group, identifying especially with the powerful, multiracial Sporty Spice. Sage's Spice Girl knowledge garnered Sage clout at GirlZone and eased her social interactions with girls she might not play with under different circumstances. On her rounds during the collage workshop, Aimee complimented Sage on her collage and in particular the picture of an ice-skater. Ice-skaters, noted Aimee, have such control over their bodies; they have bodies that do, that are powerful and graceful. According to Aimee, the ice-skater in the picture looked like a confident person having fun. Sage responded that she liked the ice-skater's pretty costume, drifted back into the contested Spice Girls debate, and eventually wrote "beautiful isn't she" under the picture. Although Sage and Aimee ostensibly tussled over how to make sense of an ice-skater, this interaction more accurately reflected Aimee's desire and Sage's resistance to redesign images of girl power that made girls more likely to value ice-skaters (and perhaps themselves) for their pretty outfits instead of for their athletic abilities.

Despite Aimee's lack of success in this example, GirlZone organizers and workshop facilitators continually focused their activist efforts on challenging and redesigning the consumerist representations of girl power that the Spice Girls embodied. GirlZone organizers and feminists more generally recognized that the very girls they wanted to address flocked to the Spice Girls and their girl power message, which presented girls and women as playful and powerful agents. Even if this message were only the product of a mass-marketing campaign, to dismiss millions of girls from around the world as dupes eliminates the possibility of engaging them; it misses an opportunity to learn about what girls crave, what they are sold, and how feminism can intervene in that equation.

Fig. 6.2. Sage's Image of and Commentary on an Ice-Skater. *Note:* Reproduced by permission of Sage's mother on Informed Consent Sheet.

Catherine Driscoll makes a similar argument about the importance of recognizing and not merely dismissing, the marketed power of the Spice Girls.[32] Reviewing the July 1997 *Rolling Stone* article, "Pop Tarts: Spice Girls Conquer the World," Driscoll warns feminists' that their knee-jerk rejection of the Spice Girls is ill-advised:

> The Spice Girls talk about feminism in a massively popular field. Further, they talk about how what they say and do may or may not be feminism, and about the relations between politics and popular culture. Many people have done this, but not on the terrain of international multiple-platinum-selling pop music articulated as by and for girls. I am not making revolutionary claims for this. I am arguing that this is a shift in the dominant paradigms of cultural production directed to girls which might be indebted to the impact of other girl culture forms, like the riot grrrls and cyber girls, but is also newly inflected by an embracing of popular rather than avant-garde cultural production. It is worth considering the effects of this shift, and what limits those effects.[33]

According to Driscoll, the RiotGrrrls energized and educated girls and women already participating in what *Rolling Stone* describes as the plugged in avant-garde. The Spice Girls broached feminism with those not already plugged in. Effectively using globalized mass-marketing to popularize the idea of girl power in ways feminists have not been able to, the Spice Girls helped girl power enter the lexicon and imagination—the image stores—of girls and boys world wide. Since it is far too late to avoid the mass-marketing of girl power, the question is how to interpret in and possibly mediate the ways girls make sense of this marketing. Thus, Driscoll's analysis and GirlZone participants' experiences return to earlier questions: once girl power has entered girls' image stores, how can feminists make even problematic, consumerist understandings more constructive? How can feminists provide girls with resources and practices to redesign even contested conceptions of girl power prevalent in youth's image stores?

Despite Aimee's concern that marketers exploit girls' cravings at girls' expense, Aimee acknowledges there is much to learn from marketing strategies. For example, she notes that advertising is one of the "few places that allow kids to tinker not with things given but with what they can create. Advertisers help them imagine themselves in control. That's why advertising is so enjoyable, insidious, powerful. It's letting them move beyond this stock thing to this stock thing that includes them."[34] Aimee sought to redesign parts of this advertising philosophy at GirlZone by making girls feel included, heard, and in control in ways that exceeded girls' being sexualized consumers.

THE GRRRLFEST LOGO:
A DOUBLED PROCESS OF REDESIGN

Although both the DIY opting-out strategy and the constructive complicity strategy identified and attempted to counter the pervasive power of consumer culture, neither could overcome its sway; whereas DIY underestimated the power of consumer culture to commodify almost everything, even DIY's most basic tenets, the constructive complicity strategy overestimated its ability to shape consumer culture. An analysis of GrrrlFest's logo highlights a third, more effective response to the commodification of girl power. This third response posits a locally situated redesign of girls' commercialized image stores that foregrounds multiplicity and ambiguity, attends to pleasure and critique, and teaches girls how to read and navigate these multiple meanings. The doubleness of these redesign practices can help girls reimagine the resources at hand and, potentially, use them more to their liking.

Manipulating what is given and what can be imagined, communication theorist Gunther Kress' theory of design offers an important if limited strategy in the project of redesigning girls image stores. As outlined in chapter 4, Kress argues that the rapid social, economic, communication, and technological changes associated with globalization demand a shift where "models of use" make room for "models of design." In Kress' theory, models of use rely on conventions that privilege the practice of critique, whereas models of design focus primarily on designing something new. In the past, structures were more stable so critiquing and modifying these structures was a likely goal. Now, however, globalization of both consumer and popular culture is dramatically altering structures that shape access to the production, reception, and distribution of messages in the public domain. These alterations restructure power in the field of representation and communication and anticipate a shift in social competency from one based on critique to one based on redesigning available resources to create innovative responses that better suit one's needs.[35]

Kress' theory of design can frame the range of youthquake activism that responded to the global structures that supported the ratcheting up of consumer culture. For example, from the mid-1990s to the early 2000s—the same time GirlZone and GrrrlFest were emerging and when antiglobal activists received widespread attention—technological changes associated with the Internet (e.g., the digitization of images; the ease of producing and distributing of redesigned messages) meant that these activists had a new set of tools to alter given messages. Through playful and clever practices such as culture jamming and ad busting,[36] activists reworked the commercial messages around them and encouraged others to recognize that they could too.

Kress' theory clearly locates local literate activities in much larger trends. Acknowledging that literate activities cannot of themselves change these trends, Kress' theory of design can nonetheless provide ways to encourage girls to resee the pervasive images that bombard them everyday as well as the systems of logic that undergird these image stores. This, in fact, was a goal of the GrrrlFest logo.

The Logo as a Multimodal Tactic of Redesign

The 2002 icon of the GrrrlFest logo is a clear derivative of the animated crime-fighting trio, the Powerpuff Girls.[37] The dark hair and furrowed brow evoke Buttercup, who is, according to the Powerpuff Girl theme song, "the toughest fighter" of the three, yet the icon's pigtailed hair is in the style of Bubbles, the sweet one who is "joy and the laughter." This icon flies below the GrrrlFest banner and above the "Throw like a girl" slogan which itself is above the dates for GrrrlFest. Pastel bubbles and star graphics surround this girly superhero. The icon's large eyes make up the 00 part of 2002 and her mouth is in a tight smile, ambiguously invoking both fierce determination and a welcome. Finally, her tiny arms, that do not look like they could throw much of anything, drape over the "Throw like a girl" slogan. Intertwining text and image, fierceness and play, the

GrrrlFest logo indexes the Fests' goal of helping participants understand and expand the available identities they imagine for themselves, in part by modeling how girls can engage with consumer culture in feminist ways.

To make sense of this logo requires attention to the ways multiple modalities (in this case iconic and textual) play with and against each other; in other words, it requires an expanded definition of literacy that attends to this document's multimodality.[38] On one hand, components of this logo seem distinct, and almost to undermine each other. The pastel colors of the free floating bubbles evoke sugar, and spice, and everything nice girlie[39] associations. These associations reverberate against the growling grrrl in GrrrlFest and the angry, furrowed brow of the icon. On the other hand, the logo's multiple modes fully intertwine. The text provides not only the name of GrrrlFest, its slogan, and the Fest's logistical information, but also a visual frame that draws the viewer's eye to the icon. Similarly, the 00 in the 2002 text cannot be separated from large iconic eyes. Although the "2002" text and the Powerpuff Girl icon can be described separately, in the action of the logo their intertwining means that neither text nor icon can be taken alone. In fact, it is their combination that functions as a redesigned resource for GrrrlFest participants. Participants recognized this new possibility: "It's like extracting the good things and creating your own context by putting those images [the Powerpuff Girl and the slogan] in concert with one another and creating a different whole."[40] To analyze what Joni describes as a redesigned "different whole" requires a multimodal definition of literacy that attends to how the logo's text and icon work together and on their own to expose and challenge the sexism that is so normed that is goes unmarked. This definition would provide ways to analyze *how* the logo invokes and talks back to prevalent notions of girl power that inform participants' conceptions of themselves, of feminism, and, for a few participants, of consumer culture.

In such an analysis, text and icon each carry distinct parts of what Kress calls a message's "functional load," or the way a document conveys its meaning.[41] For most participants, the campy and playful slogan carries an overtly challenging message that evokes two related ideas: a reclaiming and revaluing of what a girl is; and, similarly, but more aggressively, a talking back to those people and those systems of knowledge that belittle and demean girls and women. At the turn of the twenty-first century, organizers believed that feminism was a word (though not a concept) that girls fled. Organizers did not want to cede public understandings of feminism to the likes of Rush Limbaugh and his "feminazi" representations, even as organizers recognized his power to malign the feminist movements. The Fests attempted to crack open these public understandings, providing possibilities to create new representations of feminists and of feminisms.

This was apparent in the logo. The creator of this visual image was Aaron, a behind-the-scenes male participant with professional graphic design skills.[42] A strong supporter of GirlZone, Aaron came up with this logo after he and Aimee brainstormed about the goals of GrrrlFest more generally. In creating the logo, Aaron intended for the slogan to talk back to those who dismiss girls.

> We've been taught to think that throwing like a girl is a bad thing, and here it was an invitation to be that way and embrace it. . . . I mean, in the extreme interpretation of that phrase, I've also heard it to mean fighting, like to throw down is to get into a fight with somebody, but I don't think it's necessarily always that extreme. But when I was doing the logo, I did think about it that way as well. It was in itself a provocative phrase.[43]

The provocation of the slogan came from making explicit what Mikhail M. Bakhtin would call the phrase's "hidden dialogicality," the many present but unseen forces that give an utterance its meaning. These are the "deep traces" that have "a determining influence" on the meaning that the interlocutors recognize.[44]

In the case of the GrrrlFest slogan, the hidden dialogicality of you "throw like a girl" is the homophobic and misogynistic forces that make this phrase a taunt. On playgrounds, sports fields, and hazing spaces of all kinds, the phrase "to throw like a girl" is used to demean. This phrase is like so many other cultural messages that, according to Aimee, "demonize," "bastardize" and "trivialize" the idea of being a girl. These messages harm girls, because in their logic, a girl must disown her sex in order to succeed.[45] The logo, however, challenges this teaching. Affirming girls' sense of themselves, whether they throw like a professional pitcher or like they have never thrown before, the logo locates "throw like a girl" within feminist frames that defamiliarize the typical associations of this slogan and interrupt the messages that associate negativity with being a girl.

In an e-mail exchange reproduced on GrrrlFest 2003's website, Aimee makes this textual strategy clear. Responding to an e-mail that asked: "Here's a thought. What if you changed "Throw like a Girl" to "Throw with Accuracy." Aren't we all in this together? Peace," Aimee wrote:

> hey, that's a totally nice thought would be so awesome. the saying, though, reclaims the idea of "throwing like a girl" from an all-too-commonly used derogatory (joke or not) to a place of personal pride, where all accts of individual interest and effort would be. yeah, we wanna be "all in this together," but, to be fair, the concept of "throwing like a girl" first needs some heavy duty thought, challenge, and clarification given to the negative gender associations and implications it holds before we can act from a place where we really are, or claim that we are. that's why we use it.[46]

Like culture jams and ad busting that represented and enacted a textual form of activism, the GrrrlFest logo, Aimee makes clear, wants to turn commonly accepted messages on their head. Through a doubleness that simultaneously exposes and talks back to what Aimee refers to elsewhere as the ubiquitous "systems of domination" that shape what girls can imagine for themselves, the logo changes the slogan's connotations and models an alternative meaning. Ironic and playful, this slogan calls GrrrlFest participants and the local community to embrace the idea of throwing and being like a girl.

The slogan's ability to reclaim this phrase is facilitated by many factors. Extratextually, the fact that this is a slogan for GrrrlFest already locates this phrase in feminist frames that challenge sexist and homophobic messages. In the logo itself, this challenging slogan is paired with the seemingly safe, playful, and pervasive image of a Powerpuff Girl. In other words, GrrrlFest participants could first encounter the commercialized icon to attract those who might tune out when confronted with an overt feminist challenge. After scanning the icon, readers could engage with the slogan that makes visible and challenges the prevalent, everyday sexism girls face.

One reason Aimee valued the Powerpuff Girls' image was because she had repeatedly seen how threatening feminist understandings of girl power can be when embodied in a woman. In 2002 alone, GirlZone had lost a funding opportunity in part, Aimee believes, because of the funders' perception of Aimee as angry (see next chapter). The funding debacle made visible the sociopolitical climate where being a passionate feminist might mean being perceived as angry, perhaps dangerous, or at least something to be dismissed. At GrrrlFest, the Powerpuff-inspired icon *safely* challenged constructions of little girls; girls may be saving the world, but as the Powerpuff Girls' cartoon explains, they do so "before bedtime."

The efficacy of this model of redesign comes through the logo's simultaneous use of many modes to tap and remediate (in a Vygotskian sense) GrrrlFest participants' familiar image stores. Individually, both the text and the icon facilitate feminist messages, temporarily locating GrrrlFest's girl power messages within what organizers felt were productive feminist engagements with consumer culture. And, although the icon's playful image may subvert the text's more radical agenda, this "subversion" seemed a useful softening of the provocative slogan, making the logo as a whole more appealing to people who might have a knee-jerk reaction against overtly feminist messages. Targeting girls and young women in Champaign-Urbana, this redesigned resource used multiple modes to combine feminist frameworks with identities girls would want to pursue.

The Logo as a Broker of New Possibilities

From heady discussions on "What a Girl Wants," "Love Some Body" and "GirlZone Lessons" to hands-on workshops on "Shiny, Slimy Chemical Creations," "Aren't You a Crafty Girl," and "Little Drummer Grrrl," the Fests celebrated girls and women, built communities attentive to systemic obstacles girls and women face, and provided safe spaces and guided opportunities to explore a range of options participants would not normally explore. The girls picked up these practices. For example, in a RadioGirl interview conducted during GrrrlFest, preteen Lillie stated: "My favorite thing to do at GrrrlFest is skateboarding, except maybe it's physics because there's that going on too. . . . Or maybe it's boxing."[47] Seconds later, pre-teen Margot chimed in: "My favorite thing about GrrrlFest so far is that you can do different things that you wouldn't normally be able to do. And it's not like, it's not like cheerleading or something like that; it's different and exciting."[48] Both Lillie and Margot believe GrrrlFest provides a rare opportunity to try new things. Margot in particular recognizes that at GrrrlFest participants are encouraged to redesign typically available identity options; they are encouraged to go beyond cheering from the sidelines, to get in the game, and, as the GrrrlFest logo states, to throw like a girl.

For many GrrrlFest participants, the logo captures this project. As the Fests' visual identity, the logo encouraged participants to play with, celebrate, challenge, and even redesign what it means to "throw like a girl." The logo became a resource participants could draw upon. Once the logo became part of the participants' image stores, they could use it to make sense of themselves and their relations with others at and beyond GrrrlFest.[49] The following sections tellingly detail the possibilities and limits of this sense making.

Sophia: Tuning In to Feminist Possibilities Within Consumer Culture

In order for the Fest's visual identity to get its challenging feminist message out, the logo tied into youth's playful, commercial image stores: *The Powerpuff Girls* was named one of the top ten new children's shows by *TV Guide*, reached up to 2.2 million households per episode, and sold millions of dollars of merchandizing.[50] This popular image could attract participants to a feminist festival during a time when girls and young women were exposed to largely anti- or postfeminist ideas. As Aimee describes:

> For any icon, if it needs to be an image that gives a message, then something from popular culture seems the most direct way to do it, most effective. Perhaps not most profound but . . . . [*The Powerpuff Girls* show] is an awesome idea that being a little girl is a lot more than being sugar and spice and stuff. Tying to that image is a good way of showing what we are trying to do with the Fest, to diversify, to expand on what notions are given to what successful girls could be. And go beyond what traditionally is being forwarded as this crappy girl power.[51]

Aimee didn't just want to tie to girls' image stores; she wanted to re-design them. In particular, Aimee wanted to alter the "crappy girl power" that sells girls middrift shirts and tells them their power comes from being sexualized. Unlike the popular Disney Princesses (Snow White, Aurora, Cinderella, Jasmine) and the fading Spice Girls, the kindergarten-aged Powerpuff Girls in general and certainly the logo (with only the arms of the body represented) excised sexuality.[52] An alternative to prevalent images of girls as passive and/or sexualized, this Powerpuff Girl image playfully alludes to feminist goals of expanding girls' identities.

Helping participants make themselves meaningful within consumerist constructions of girl culture had proven a challenge for some GrrrlFest participants such as Sophia.[53] Years earlier, when Sophia attended Girl-Zone regularly, she was among a minority of girls who spoke of the limitations of the 1990s trendy and commodified girl culture. Unlike the majority of girls who discussed which Spice Girl they wanted to be, Sophia was annoyed by the Spice Girl phenomenon and opted-out of these interactions, generally by disengaging from the common Spice Girl banter. She justified her position when she was thirteen years old, distinguishing between what she called "Spice Girl" girl positive as opposed to "real" girl positive. When pressed as to what she meant by "Spice Girl girl positive" Sophia replied:

> Well, the Spice Girls' slogan was girl power. . . . And as far as I have been able to see, it's like they took this thing, girl power, and they made it as consumerist as everything else. It's girl power, so buy our stuff and make yourself into a sex object. It's not girl positive because it's so objectifying. It looks like girl power, sort of, when you first look at it but when you look closer it's, it's not. It's stuff like that sells itself by looking empowering and then it's not. Fashion magazines are not empowering. Makeup is not empowering despite what they say.[54]

For Sophia, the Spice Girls' version of girl power created limiting configurations of what girls were allowed to do and be. Spice Girls thwart "real" girl power by reinscribing girls' social identities within consumerist social relations. Without explicit awareness, Sophia highlighted how the girl power niche represented by the Spice Girls is situated at the cash nexus that drives so much of contemporary culture. As Sophia noted, girl power lost its "real" girl power meaning of empowerment, but not its commercialized potential to sell stuff that made girl power, as Sophia described elsewhere in this interview, as "icky as everything else." Because Sophia did not want to be part of the "icky" commercialization of girl power, she chose not to participate in the frequent social interactions that were shaped by prevalent image stores of that time.

Two and a half years after these comments about the Spice Girls, Sophia attended GrrrlFest 2002. The ways the GrrrlFest logo redesigned the Powerpuff Girl image helped Sophia imagine how consumer culture can be viewed within feminist frames. Now sixteen-years-old, Sophia described how her involvement with GrrrlFest caused her to rethink the Powerpuff Girls:

> going to the GrrrlFest was the first time that I learned that the Powerpuffs was actually a decent television show. I've never watched it, but it would start to come on TV and I'd be like "oh that's stupid," and I'd

turn it off. I just assumed that it was another silly kids TV show, probably because the girls had names like Puffy [*sic*] and Buttercup and stuff
like that so I went ahead and assumed that it wasn't going to be any
good so I turned it off.[55]

When asked why she no longer thought the show was stupid, Sophia
replied, "I don't think anyone told me anything in particular. It's just
something that I picked up. . . . I just remember that I had to rethink
that."[56] As a self-defined feminist,[57] Sophia felt that she would find shows
that feature girls named "Puffy and Buttercup" to be things to tune out
and turn off. Although Sophia could not identify why she changed her
mind, surely the logo prodded her rethinking. This logo redesigned commercialized images to help celebrate girls and women within GrrrlFest's
feminisms, an idea Sophia "just picked up." When Sophia observed the
explicitly feminist participants at GrrrlFest playfully invoke the slogan
and gush over the image, she found a model for how she could use consumer culture to explore feminist-friendly identities and practices. Regardless of Sophia's final assessment of the actual *The Powerpuff Girls*
programming, the logo modeled a practice of redesign that allowed
Sophia to imagine new ways to participate in consumer culture and to
interact with her peers.

For Sophia and other GrrrlFest participants, the logo temporarily sit-
uates GrrrlFest's meaning of girl power not only within feminist constructions of girl culture, but also within consumer ones. In fact, GrrrlFest
illustrates that the relationships between capitalism and feminism are not
unidirectional. Since feminism and consumer culture are operationalized
in varied practices, GrrrlFest organizers struggled to design possibly productive engagements. One such engagement was to sell GrrrlFests' message. Emblazoned on flyers, T-shirts, and CDs sold at GrrrlFest and other
GirlZone-sponsored events, the logo traveled in undetermined but potentially productive ways. On the 1200 GirlZone and GrrrlFest T-shirts[58] circulating predominantly in this midwestern community, the logos became
communal images that introduced feminist possibilities to those who
might not readily be open to those possibilities. This tactic of using commercialized images and capitalistic structures for feminist purposes
seemed helpful for Sophia and for GrrrlFest itself, but as the next section
details, the efficacy of GrrrlFest's feminist ideas and images lessened the
farther the logo traveled in time and space from GrrrlFest community.

Joni: Circulations of a Safe Feminism

As the visual identity of the Fests, the logo functioned as a material instantiation of organizers' attempts to redesign popular understandings of
feminism. Girls, workshop facilitators, and Fest organizers overwhelmingly described how this instantiation captured something that was im-

portant to them, far beyond the GrrrlFest weekend. Joni, whose quoted words open this chapter, voiced a typical sentiment.

Joni was among the group of facilitators who stayed in Champaign-Urbana for a few years after graduating from the state university before moving on. While living in Urbana, Joni worked in the female-owned, Girl-Zone friendly coffee shop and took improvisation lessons to help her enter the thriving but male-dominated local jazz scene. As facilitator of the 2002 Fest's Jazz Singing workshop, Joni initially performed a short jazz set and then called the thirty girls and women in the audience to join her on stage. Despite the fact that workshop participants had just completed a full day of new and affirming activities, their anxiety was palpable. Joni eased the group into scat sing before she encouraged each person to approach the microphone, whether or not she spoke into it. As Joni allayed people's fears about appearing foolish or unworthy of being on stage, a fear she struggled to vanquish in her nights at the jazz clubs, she simultaneously pushed participants to analyze how their internalized discomfort with assuming center stage thwarted their creativity and freedom to pursue their interests.

When reflecting on GrrrlFest a year after this workshop, Joni fondly revealed that she calls the shirt with the GrrrlFest logo on it her "blankey." This metaphor links GrrrlFest to a comfort that envelops Joni within an imagined, safe, feminist community that was very present during the Fest. Despite a blankey's associations with childhood, Joni relies on her GrrrlFest shirt to feel supported by the GrrrlFest community in very adult settings, such as her interactions with the people at what she calls the "bottom of the barrel" bar where she worked in 2003, almost two hundred miles away from GrrrlFest. Describing how she uses the shirt to do so, Joni states:

> I'm in a very middle American town right now and I've never heard anybody make a connection between Powerpuff Girls and the changing roles of women and things like that. It's not threatening to them because it's a cartoon. So, many people asked me about [the logo on my shirt]. It was cool because I got to have these completely different interactions. I was normally prepared to just put up a wall, just prepared to be defensive, to deflect their jokes, try to figure out how to turn [their sexualized comments] around on them or give it back to them.
>
> And, so many people asked me about this shirt, and that the grrrl itself has three r's. That's another thing that's pretty cool about [the multiple interpretations of "grrrl"]. So I found myself being in these conversations, telling people about [GrrrlFest], "well I participated in this thing." And I was really proud to have participated in it and it was really cool that a lot of these guys were asking me about it. And I would tell them, "well it's this program for girls that encourages them to do things they normally wouldn't be encouraged to do, like skateboarding and drumming." And they'd be like, "cool." So instead of, so the program is really accessible to people. Its mission is acceptable to people. Because, who could find fault, well some people could, well what average person could find fault with teaching girls to play the drums or skateboard?[59]

Joni was clearly enthusiastic about how the logo encouraged people to talk about accessible feminist activity. This discussion temporarily replaced the tired, daily interactions that made Joni defensive. Nonetheless, Joni's un-acknowledged ambivalence about the logo's effectiveness can be seen when she started, stopped and then redirected her thoughts: "And I would tell them, 'well it's this program for girls that encourages them to do things they normally wouldn't be encouraged to do, like skateboarding and drumming.' And they'd be like 'cool.' *So instead of, so the program is really accessible to people*" (emphasis mine).[60] What Joni would have said after "so instead of" is unknowable, but her story seems to build toward claiming a tangible change in gendered social relations. Joni, however, did not or could not make that claim. Instead, she redirected her conclusion to focus on a safer feminist message: the *acceptability* of GirlZone's mission. This acceptability invited GrrrlFest participants as well as remote and unanticipated audiences into conversations about what it means to celebrate girls and women. Yet, this accessibility shied away from explicitly challenging the unjust structural forces that limit this power.

This tension is captured in the logo. Ambiguous enough to prompt discussion, the playful icon facilitated feminist goals. The fact that the icon was not threatening helped Joni posit expanded identities and activities for girls and women (e.g., drumming and skateboarding) and helped men who make sexist comments claim that girls venturing into these male dominated activities was "cool." And yet, this safe representation masked the difficult work needed to achieve a *sustained* expansion of girls and women's power. Joni obliquely but knowingly references this more challenging feminist agenda when she mentions "grrrl." As Joni was well aware, grrrl comes from the RiotGrrrl movement that seeks to intervene in the everyday of girls and women. As noted earlier, GrrrlFest explicitly claimed its allegiance with the RiotGrrrls in internal e-mails and community-wide flyers for the GrrrlFest Concert Series. Even so, organizers recognized the work of the actual RiotGrrrls was playful, but also more threatening than the cartoon Powerpuff Girls. The RiotGrrrls swore; they yelled, growled, and ranted. This might scare people,[61] which may explain why the logo did not make this linking explicit for those outside of a sympathetic audience who could understand the grrrl references.

While Joni used the logo as an opening, a space through which she could alter the social relations at the bar, Joni's working conditions coupled with the perceived need for "safe" feminist messages makes clear how redesigning popular image stores is *one part* of a more encompassing project. Not surprisingly, when Aaron created the logo, he never intended that by itself it could overturn sexual harassment at a bar hundreds of miles away. Indeed, the fact that Joni was able to use this logo to broker even temporary benefits is an important local accomplishment. Yet, the logo hardly created a space where sexual harassment ceases. Joni's economic realities, her choices, and her options meant that Joni was not working at a supportive feminist collective but rather at this often sexist bar. Here she could use the logo for temporary, individual ends, but what she really needed were systemic changes.

Joni's experiences demonstrate the potential of a feminist project of redesign. At the same time, however, Joni's experiences expose the need for more sustained feminist action and the difficulty of that action; as the logo illustrates, the perceived need to present a safe feminist representation foregrounds the negative associations surrounding the term and the values of an imagined feminism. Joni's and Sophia's experiences also highlight how the invocation of consumer culture is a fraught one, with the potential of being used for feminist goals and, as noted earlier, with the potential of emptying feminist goals for commercial ends. In local contexts like GrrrlFest, participants can initially shape the distribution and contexts for understanding these messages. The contexts shift, however, when the messages travel. As illustrated in Joni's unsuccessful attempt to have others acknowledge her expanded image stores, the difficulty of redesigning consumerist systems of meaning in order to make material change highlights the difficulty of the feminist project.

LESSONS FROM THE FEST

The tensions surrounding the logo expose once again a central dilemma feminists face: the need to be safe in order to be heard in today's supposedly postfeminist world and the need to help girls and women redesign the image stores and material conditions prevalent in today's socioeconomic climate. Even without knowing how best to negotiate this dilemma, feminists recognize they need to find ways to intervene in consumer culture. This powerful force saturates contemporary girl culture, a fraught nexus where various constituencies (e.g., girls, feminists, marketers) struggle to achieve often contradictory goals. For activists seeking to help girls and young women find feminist values in today's commercialized celebration and exploitation of girl culture, one tactic is to redesign the available image stores girls and young women draw upon, providing a doubleness needed to popularize feminist messages in a consumerist climate.

The GrrrlFest logo illustrates that the process of design can be part of a successful, albeit a qualified, way to achieve this doubleness. This logo uses multiple modes to offer a double message. Both safe and provocative, the logo combines the available resources of a playful, commercial girl power image with a slogan that evokes girls' ability to claim their own sense of power. Optimistically and ironically tapping into the paradoxical pleasures of girls' and feminists' engagement with consumer culture, the logo illustrates the messiness of redesigning available image stores. It highlights the unstable, contested circulation of meaning that both helps and hinders GrrlFest participants broker new possibilities in their everyday. As a first step, the logo attracts participants to learn more about GrrlFests' mission and workshops. Paired with a focus on how to encourage new possibilities for material change, the logo's process of redesign is a useful but partial tactic.

The fact that this tactic is limited does not invalidate it. Local achievements are valuable both in the moment and in future possibilities, possibilities that can come together in unexpected ways. As the next chapter explores, however, as valuable as these local achievements can be, they need to be linked to larger structural changes for grassroots activism to be sustained.

7

The Economics of Activism

We never started GirlZone for a business so it feels a little wrong to think of it as a business, but I think it is for the best. We have gotten lots of signs that GirlZone is important, but we need to start thinking of economic realities.

Now I'm thinking [about] what do we need to do, what do I need to do, what does GirlZone need to do so that energy still exists. But it can't just be about making money, but it does need backing. Especially now that I need to have a full time job to live in this town and pay a mortgage. So now GirlZone is in a space of re-assessing where that energy is going so that we continue to do the programming that is important for the girls and the adults. GirlZone is wild right now. It is always on the brink of becoming amazing and not becoming at all. But it's like a ball of energy that needs to be re-shaped.

—Aimee, 2002

For Aimee, grassroots feminist activists must balance the need to remain economically viable and the need to not "sell out" in the current sink or swim business environment. Aimee's repeated use of the word "but" constructs this balance as an implicit dichotomy. On the one hand, activism is valued, apparently outside of economic realities, and cannot be limited to market forces. In this view, grassroots feminists fear that the energy activists need to channel into local programs is being diluted by business concerns. On the other hand, market forces reflect economic realities. Since grassroots organizations need backing, they need to engage these forces. In practice, as in Aimee's description above, business practices and grassroots activism are deeply intertwined, exposing both fissures with profound disconnections and important points of overlap about what is possible and what is likely. The problem for Aimee is how/if she can make these points of overlap productive for grassroots feminists at GirlZone.[1]

Aimee's struggle to locate her activism within the changing market forces parallels the struggles many feminists and activists faced at the turn of the twenty-first century. As a new generation of feminist activists navigated ongoing socioeconomic trends during the 1990s, the term "entrepreneurial feminism" became increasingly popular. Initially, entrepreneurial feminism was predominantly used in technological or business fields, as women in these areas responded to the rapidly changing technological and economic conditions that helped make the 1980s the "decade of the entrepreneur."[2] More recently, however, a range of feminists invoke the term to mean a more general partnering with or even explicit forays into the market forces shaping all aspects of society. I use entrepreneurial feminism to reflect diverse feminist responses within this latter project.

From the outset, entrepreneurial feminism has been a lightening rod within feminist circles, largely because it exposes feminists' conflicted ability and desire to engage with and intervene in capitalism. For example, when Elaine Showalter deplores feminists' "lack of enterprise in politics and popular culture,"[3] she means feminists have been slow to create newly appropriate solutions within today's hyper-capitalized world: "Instead of insisting that all personal problems are political and need to be met by legal change, women can be encouraged to be more entrepreneurial and resourceful, and to take responsibility for coming up with exemplary solutions." She continues: "Even that anathema of the left, free enterprise, could solve some unfinished business of the last women's movement."[4] Although feminists agree that they need to be responsive to the times, they disagree on whether entrepreneurial feminism is the answer. To some feminists, entrepreneurial feminism either uncritically justifies women's participation in capitalistic expansion without the added component of social justice or, as Teresa Ebert claims, entrepreneurial feminism could be merely "a legitimisation of the class politics of an 'upper-middle class' Euroamerican feminism."[5]

These tensions played out in social justice movements beyond feminism. For example, during the 1990s J. Gregory Dees popularized the term "social entrepreneur" to marry what he considered the determined, innovative, and resourceful spirit of entrepreneurialism with a focus on social change.[6] Not surprisingly, activists are divided about this. Some feel social entrepreneurs provide a useful and adaptive response to the changing needs of local communities and the possibilities in today's global climate; others want to halt the naturalization of the market metaphor and argue instead for social activity and responsibility to be the supra category with economic frameworks as a subset.[7] For feminist and other activists, these debates exposed the dilemmas about how best to participate in contemporary capitalistic frameworks.

Examining the literate activities of grassroots organizations can help activists both understand and develop tactics to address these dilemmas. According to feminist sociologist Dorothy E. Smith, in today's increasingly bureaucratic society, texts mediate social practices and relations.[8] Those who control these texts shape the ways people come to know how to make sense of their experiences. By examining how texts work, we can see the metadiscourses and material, socioeconomic conditions that make these texts meaningful. With this understanding, grassroots feminists can better articulate strategies to challenge, alter, or gain access to this power.

The literate activities surrounding GirlZone's first and last grant proposals are examples of how texts make visible the ways large-scale socioeconomic trends (e.g., the changing nature of feminist sponsorship) mediate micro practices (e.g., grassroots activists seeking funds). As discussed in chapter 4, Aimee's first grant proposal to the Girl's Best Friend Foundation highlights the power of literacy; through her grant proposals Aimee garnered institutional resources and a sense of legitimacy for this fledgling organization. Literacy's power, however, did not work only in ways Aimee had imagined. For example, the organizational activities elicited by this grant proposal pulled GirlZone into a more business-type model. And while Girl's Best Friend encouraged this pull as one way to help GirlZone focus on sustainability—a goal GirlZone appreciated even if it could not meet—Aimee feared that framing GirlZone activists' commitment to social justice within a business model is, as Aimee described in another context, just "a little wrong." In GirlZone's last grant proposal to the United Way, Aimee learned another import lesson: without the support of funding organizations, feminists will lack the contexts and resources to make their texts effective. In particular, without frameworks and foundations that validate grassroots feminist activism in nonurban areas, even eloquent arguments will be read as *un*-fund worthy.

The conflicted value of literate activities in today's funding climate—where literate activities are simultaneously powerful enough to pull people into models they may resist yet impotent against the socioeconomic conditions that work against grassroots feminist activism in nonurban America—speaks both to the necessity of learning how to court sponsors and to the lack of feminist sponsors that activists currently have. Although literate activities surrounding grant proposals are key to grassroots organizations' economic survival, the experiences at GirlZone make clear that too often activists suspect their proposals can bear a greater burden of organizational representation than is the case. In practice, all documents are located in larger socioeconomic contexts, contexts informed by the choices these funding bodies make. When determining what is of value, funders may ignore actual proposals, while favoring other information.

This chapter explores the challenges GirlZone experienced in this funding environment as a way to examine the potential and the problems that feminists face when they seek foundation monies. After providing a history of grassroots feminist organizations' recent sponsors, this chapter analyzes the activities surrounding GirlZone's grant proposals not only as examples of what is possible, but also what can go wrong when activists must adapt to emerging forms of sponsorship made available in changing socioeconomic conditions. Based on this analysis, this chapter articulates potential strategies for grassroots feminist activism and concludes by considering the evanescence of grassroots projects such as GirlZone.

THE LEGACY OF RECENT SPONSORSHIP
ON GRASSROOTS FEMINIST ORGANIZATIONS

Like all generations of feminists, the one that became active in the mid-1990s had multiple and diverse sponsors whose influences accumulated and mutated during this generation's lifetime. Sponsors, according to Deborah Brandt's definition of sponsors of literacy, are those agents who make large-scale socioeconomic forces present on a local level.[9] Although typically sponsors are individuals, sponsors can also include groups and even institutions. For grassroots activists in the 1990s, the legacy of changing sponsors shaped the resources activists had for imagining their work.

During the 1960s–1970s, the government was a perhaps surprising sponsor of the emergence of activist networks through its (albeit uneven) financial and structural support. For example, through John F. Kennedy's focus on national service and Lyndon B. Johnson's "War on Poverty," the government funded and supported domestic service programs that encouraged community activism.[10] Government funded programs such as Volunteers in Service to America (VISTA) merged local leadership and knowledge with expertise from people outside the community in order to help community groups empower themselves to change their neighborhoods. In addition to addressing poverty and other intractable problems within the United States, these programs fostered thick activist networks where people were mentored, pursued paid career opportunities, and built alliances.

With the 1980s came the ascendancy of New Right policies. Government sponsorship shifted away from a broad funding of the welfare of citizens and toward a neoconservative market-driven policy. This defunding of what key New Right policy makers considered "Left" programs broke liberal activist networks, requiring groups such as grassroots feminists to scramble for support.[11] Consequently, by the 1990s, many feminist activists working on immigration, legal assistance, food banks, or other ventures adjusted their priorities from political organizing and developing structures to sheer survival.[12] Many organizations did not survive. Activists who endured latched onto or aligned with amenable organizations, exemplifying how the withdrawal of government support made the 1980s a time of what Myra Marx Ferree and Beth B. Hess call "defensive consolidation."[13]

Due to this consolidation, feminists sought new sponsors such as the academy and its newly formed women's studies departments. Universities, colleges, and community colleges hired faculty to teach "women's" courses and these feminists often maintained strong links with activists in the community. When women's studies became more established, however, these links were harder to sustain. With the formation of minors, majors, and even departments, academic feminists focused their attention on institutional activism: there were sexual harassment policies to create, courses to design, and many, many committees that needed (and even wanted) feminist input.[14] Although the consequences of the institutionalization of women's studies are contested,[15] women's studies departments provided time and space for groups of feminists to become aware of and/or theorize feminist issues, models for action, and networks of like-minded activists. Despite the very real academic-activist tensions, academic feminists used at least some of their resources to partner with the community and to sponsor university activist projects (e.g., Take Back the Night marches, task forces to address a range of diversity issues, rape crises lines). Academic sponsorship, therefore, facilitated the rebuilding of activist networks able to pursue a range of social justice causes.

By the 1990s, with the government's continual underfunding of higher education, feminists within the academy joined feminist activists outside this institutional space in their dual project of courting alternative funding sources, such as foundation monies, and of creating alternative funding sources, such as feminist foundations. Unfortunately for feminists, few national funding bodies had feminists on their "must fund" list in the 1990s. In fact, although there were a sprinkling of feminist foundations on the national and local levels during the early 1990s,[16] the vast majority of foundations have generally been slow to fund women and girls' organizations. Jung-Rin Kim points out that: "For every four private foundation grants to boys' groups, only one is given for girls. For example, YMCAs receive $106 million of these supposedly general funds, while YWCAs received only $66 million. Similarly, while the Boy Scouts received $88 million, the Girl Scouts received only $56 million. Even though women constitute half of the total population, their issues, organizations and needs have received much less attention than those of their male counterparts."[17]

In addition to the fact that boys' and men's organizations receive more funding than girls' and women's organizations, the distribution of so-called generic (or gender blind) monies such as those devoted to youth seem to disproportionately benefit boys. Of the monies devoted to special populations, a sizable 22 percent of foundation funding goes to youth programs,[18] yet much of this money favors male youth, especially as youth get older. For example, programs may devote significant resources to offering youth open gym nights that overwhelmingly serve boys and young men. This attention to male youth reflects, at least partially, funders' assessment that boys are a greater threat to society.[19] The outcome of this practice is that during the intense gender norming phase of adolescence, youth organizations disproportionately target boys and give girls who want to join the obligation of defying these gender-norming pressures. Some may read this as an opportunity, but more likely it is funders giving girls a less attractive option of *having* to defy gender norms if they want to participate.

This argument has been raised for decades by women's groups, often to the anger of philanthropic organizations that claim that general youth funding addresses girls' needs. The debate has at times been contentious.

Even so, in research sponsored by the Global Fund for Women, Michigan Women's Foundation, Resourceful Women, Women and Philanthropy, and the Women's Funding Network, Mary Ellen S. Capek argues that there are few studies that comprehensively examine this question.[20] What research there is generally supports the claims that generic funding does not serve girls' and women's needs in the ways funders might assume.[21] The tentative consensus, as summed up by Molly Mead, is that generic giving disproportionately benefits boys and men. According to Mead, this finding highlights a "lack of understanding both of gender as a relevant category in grant-making and of the role of programs for women and gender."[22] The importance of gender, it seems, is not infused throughout foundation culture.

Aside from generic youth funding projects, only about 6 percent of foundation grants designated for special populations goes to specifically girls' and women's organizations.[23] Of the money devoted to girls, trends in the 1990s favored inner city problems, especially teen pregnancy. Pregnancy prevention is a very real concern, yet this practice makes girls visible and valued (in terms of resources devoted to them) largely based on their reproductive capacity. Although advocates for girls' organizations want girls' needs to be recognized, they do not want girls' needs and therefore girls themselves to be conflated with their fertility potential. Girls and their needs falling outside this priority are too seldom afforded funded programs that deem them socially important. With the withdrawal of government sponsorship that fostered community activism and with the scarce foundational resources devoted to girls, what are feminist and girls' organizations to do?

Navigating the ebb and flow of sponsorship, grassroots feminists alternatively adapted to the resources offered and scrambled to pursue additional sponsors (such as foundations) when traditional sponsors (such as the government) withdrew their resources. This shift has pushed grassroots feminist activists who seek to create enduring organizational structures—a goal not all activists shared—to learn the skills that sponsors demand if these activists want to gain the sponsorship they so desperately need. This was the case at GirlZone, even if organizers did not yet fully grasp this complex relationship between grassroots activism and funding organizations. GirlZone's first and last grant proposals—texts that called GirlZone into existence and eventually made clear to Aimee that GirlZone was no longer viable—are two examples that illustrate what can happen without this awareness.

THE STORY OF TWO GRANTS

As noted earlier, GirlZone organizers struggled constantly to make GirlZone an economically viable organization. Despite the stated sliding fee, volunteer workshop leaders were either too uncomfortable or too busy to collect money. Consequently, Aimee and Gina financially supported Girl-

Zone out of their own pockets. To remedy this problem, Aimee wrote many, many grants,[24] an idea she learned in part from her work on a grant during her Master's program in Instructional Evaluation. This university grant assessed how youth's engagement with science can be enhanced through hands-on activities, an approach that directly affected how Aimee designed GirlZone workshops. Moreover, because Aimee was out of the country working on this project when GirlZone's resubmission to the Girl's Best Friend was due, Gina and others at GirlZone (indirectly me as well) learned to appreciate grant writing as necessary to grassroots activism. For these feminists, the resubmission highlighted the importance of developing professionalized skills in order to garner scarce foundation monies.

The success of this first grant proposal reinforced the idea that if organizers could master this genre, they could at least partially alleviate their economic worries, making grant writing an important element for GirlZone's sustained feminist activism in the 1990s. Despite this awareness, however, the activities surrounding these grant proposals illustrated how even powerfully written grant proposals could not overcome the biases that limit what foundation resources are offered to a girls' organization outside of an urban area that does not focus on pregnancy prevention. On one level, GirlZone organizers knew that literacy could not overcome the opposition feminist activists faced; Aimee's life experiences as a passionate feminist ensured she was not this naive. Yet, on another level, organizers had few other options for raising funds for this all-volunteer feminist organization made up largely of young girls, college students, and overstretched grassroots activists. Without good options and reluctant to acknowledge that this activity was not as powerful as they hoped, GirlZone organizers continued writing grant proposals that were repeatedly rejected. It took the United Way's response to Aimee's grant—the last grant proposal Aimee wrote at GirlZone—to make perfectly clear that she could not write Girl-Zone into continued existence. The activities surrounding this grant proposal highlight how the failure of this grant proposal had more to do with GirlZone's and Aimee's mis-match with foundation culture than to do with GirlZone's texts themselves.

The following sections investigate these contradictions, focusing on the vagaries of literacy's power and on who controls that power. Examining the literate activities surrounding GirlZone's first and last grant proposals, these investigations expose how fully texts, grassroots activism, and feminist tactics roil about.

The Proleptic Power of the Girl's Best Friend Grant

Within the first year of offering workshops, Aimee applied to the Chicago-based Girl's Best Friend Foundation.[25] Much to Aimee and Gina's surprise, this foundation awarded GirlZone one of their few fully funded $10,000 grants. In a bitter dispute, however, the Disciples' Foundation—the local sponsoring organization that offered GirlZone a home office and a non-profit tax ID number—wanted a percentage of the grant for administrative costs. Since paying for operating expenses went against the preconditions of the Girl's Best Friend grant, GirlZone lost the grant monies. After changing local sponsoring organizations, GirlZone organizers reapplied the following year and were again awarded a $10,000 grant for operating expenses (not staff lines), renewable for two years. Although GirlZone organizers were ecstatic both about the money and about the sense of legitimacy this money conferred, they quickly realized the money was less important than they initially thought. Since their new local sponsoring organization afforded free photocopying and meeting space, GirlZone's two greatest coverable expenses, what GirlZone most needed was help in managing this grassroots feminist experiment; they needed mentoring, activist frameworks, and the business savvy of the foundation staff—all things the money could not be used to address.[26] Surprising GirlZone organizers, Girl's Best Friend greatest service was its attempt to help GirlZone combine the "rightness" GirlZone organizers felt about their activism with a more business-like approach that focused on sustainability. In particular, Girl's Best Friend called on GirlZone to recognize the economic realities and organizational practices needed for ongoing activism, a lesson that would become increasingly apparent.

To help GirlZone become more than a committed but ephemeral group of activists, Girl's Best Friend provided a carrot and stick approach that prodded GirlZone to change its structures. The obvious carrot was the money and the legitimacy this money potentially conveyed to future funders. An additional reward, which Aimee and Gina initially felt to be a stick, was that the foundation required Aimee and Gina to attend training workshops. These workshops were designed to teach aspects of assessment and structural survival, in part by encouraging participants to form partnerships with both the foundation and other girls' organizations. As the guidelines make clear, in addition to awarding money, Girl's Best Friend "want[s] grantees to think of us as a partner working collectively to improve the lives of girls."[27] Aimee and Gina did benefit not only from these partnerships, primarily from the foundation's direct guidance, but also by gaining access to research and people who could provide models or sounding boards for future problems.

This focus on partnership justified the foundation's most obvious stick: internal reviews administered by GirlZone and external reviews administered by Girl's Best Friend. Texts were a central mediator in these reviews, detailing actual and wished-for social practices and social relations. For example, writing the self-assessments for these reviews productively forced GirlZone's organizers to break from the everyday demands of running an organization and to work on long-term strategic planning. This was evident in a 1999 internal review report to the Girl's Best Friend where Aimee wrote about the persistent problems of moving people into leadership positions:

The coordinators became personally invested in not allowing the ball to drop within GirlZone—they had spent too much of their passions to allow the "volunteer-run" organization to take the hits that might typically knock about an organization with weekly programming run by volunteers. There is a good chance that "super-coordinator" appearance of the coordinators allowed others within the organization to see themselves as not so essential to the programs existence . . . [Almost 30 months later] the coordinator is still at the center of the organization, and is still unable to let the ball drop. Not yet. This experience [Gina leaving and Aimee putting in 40+ hours/week] has reaffirmed two dire structural needs of GirlZone: (1) The convening of a Steering Committee of women serving year terms for organizational vision, continuity and program oversight. To date, eight women have taken on roles within GirlZone, awaiting the commencement of the Steering Committee in February 2000; (2) Paid positions for those tending of [sic] day-to-day organizational programming and delegation of tasks.[28]

Obligated to write a follow-up report to Girl's Best Friend, Aimee reflected on GirlZone's current state of affairs. Assessing what had been and what would continue to be GirlZone's greatest concerns, Aimee acknowledges two "dire structural needs" and begins planning for how to meet these needs. This text provides an artifact, a road map organizers would reference in planning GirlZone's future. As we'll see below, following this roadmap, particularly getting funding for staff lines, proved critical, and elusive.

GirlZone organizers generally assessed the proleptic power of the grant proposal as decidedly positive, especially on a structural level. Writing to and interacting with Girl's Best Friend helped organizers think through economic and organizational realities that could help GirlZone become more sustainable. Organizers felt that these grant proposals and the activities surrounding them both helped GirlZone survive its early days and shaped what GirlZone would become in the future.[29] In addition, Girl's Best Friend's influence informed how GirlZone organizers negotiated their feminist activism within an organizational model that Aimee felt was in service of her activism, a beneficial model that proved rare. More common, as the next section describes, is how Aimee felt grassroots feminist activism suffered when in service of a business model that did not value this work.

The United Way's Dismissal

After its two-year grant expired and as Girl's Best Friend refocused its efforts on girls in urban areas, GirlZone was largely without a financial sponsor. During this time, GirlZone's structural needs were proving greater than drop-in volunteers could accommodate and more overwhelming than Aimee could do on her own. As the sole organizer at this point, Aimee could no longer keep GirlZone running and maintain a life away from GirlZone that paid the bills and forwarded her interests. Once again, Aimee wrote and oversaw grants on and off for years, with the particular goal of securing funds for staff lines. Unfortunately, few funding agencies support staff lines. Near the end of GirlZone's financial rope, Aimee actively pursued the United Way, the one funding organization in central Illinois that Aimee believed could fund this need.

The United Way of Champaign County has a strong presence in nonurban areas in downstate Illinois. Through their "Youth Focus" funding, for example, the United Way supported a variety of programs, such as those affiliated with the Boys Scouts, the Champaign County YMCA, Big Brothers Big Sisters, and the Don Moyer Boys & Girls Club. It also offered scarce funds to what would generally be considered established feminist organizations, such as shelters for women in transition, rape crises centers, and Planned Parenthood.[30] GirlZone, however, was not so fortunate.

After the United Way's official letter of rejection and, more telling to Aimee, unofficial reasons for their rejection of GirlZone's grant proposal, Aimee struggled to make sense of what to do next. In her verbalization of this struggle, Aimee broached a range of issues about the economics of activism: the conservative nature of funding organizations in relation to feminism and youth activism; the bind of grassroots feminist organizations without other forms of obvious sponsorship; and the tension between the energizing Do-It-Yourself philosophy and the business of grassroots activism.

To see how conflated these issues are in practice, it is worth quoting from a brief part of a larger interview that happened after Aimee learned of the United Way's response but before she decided to close GirlZone. Her comments precede those of this chapter's epigraph when, at least initially, Aimee responded to my asking if the United Way's rejection of the grant indicated anything about their funding of emerging feminist organizations:

> [The foundation representative] didn't go as far as to say that they had a problem with feminism. But that they had a problem with me. This was a grant meeting. They came in and it was a very corporate meeting. I mean this is the United Way, a conservative group. I remember focusing on not that word [feminism] or challenging the dominant paradigm but that we do workshops for girls, but that we encourage them to see how they are talented in areas they may not think of themselves as talented or interested.
>
> But [their rejection] was really telling, and it hit harder than I thought it would. Because, an active, passionate woman being called "angry" is a common thing. But to have it be called to me by the United Way that is the main funding source in this community, to dismiss the whole program because of something they perceive about me is so offensive, so offensive. And then later I heard from one of the people who was on the on-site interview, [that person] was working with the United Way, and if you want I can give you [that] contact information, but they also thought that I smoked pot. [And] I'm a huge opponent, I mean I hate pot more than anybody in this town. I say that because I think it might dullen out all the active, the passion that anybody who's thinking of doing anything not along the traditional lines could have. It just kills

all the potential movers and shakers off from any action. So the fact that I hate it and don't do it means so much less than this is how funding is made. [Imitating a distant, authoritative voice] "We think you might smoke pot so your organization won't get any money."

And to an extent I am an angry woman and I'm going to claim that. It has been a productive anger. It's not a festering anger; it's an anger to action. I have a right to be angry; girls have a right to be angry; this community has a right to be angry, but not to stay angry. Do something about it. So, coming off of a couple years like that, it's been pretty frustrating. And right now GirlZone is more dispassionate than it has ever been. But dispassionate in sort of a business way. We never started GirlZone for a business so it feels a little wrong to think of it as a business, but I think it is for the best. We have gotten lots of signs that GirlZone is important, but we need to start thinking of economic realities.[31]

In her response, Aimee describes a bias against feminist organizations from the conservative sponsors of contemporary community activism; the lack of alternative models in grassroots feminist activism in the mid 1990s; and most fundamentally, a need to rethink feminist grassroots activism within current economic realities. As Aimee asked in the chapter's epigraph, What is this ball of energy? Who has the resources that activists need in order to think about how it should be reshaped?

Aimee found it particularly difficult to think through these questions without detailed feedback from the United Way. While she did receive an official letter, she described her thwarted attempts for more substantive feedback in ways that paralleled my experiences in gathering the United Way's perspective. In 2005, I contacted the United Way for their official reasons and any other information that may explain their decision to reject GirlZone's grant proposal. Despite a warm e-mail stating they would address my query in the next few months, it took multiple months and e-mails before the United Way CEO encouragingly relayed that she could release this information if the YMCA—GirlZone's sponsoring organization—gave its consent. Stating that he agreed with the United Way's decision but did not want to actively participate in any study, the Executive Director of the YMCA nonetheless gave his unqualified consent that the United Way could release any information to me. Unfortunately, my follow-up e-mails to the United Way for these documents have not been returned, and I never received the requested information.

Like Aimee, I was unable to gather the official perspective of either the United Way or the YMCA, so I pursued other avenues to gather more information about this decision. Two separate sources confirmed Aimee's explanation of the rejection of GirlZone's grant. One source received funding from the United Way, had informal links to Aimee, and felt confident that he was expected to relay the unofficial justifications to her. According to this source, a United Way board member found Aimee to be "angry" in an implicitly problematic way. A second source learned from a United Way employee that a board member thought he smelled pot on a GirlZone member.

Although this source could not confirm that this GirlZone member was Aimee, Aimee herself relayed she was the only GrilZone person at both the site visit and follow-up meeting with the United Way.

In the absence of an extended United Way official narrative and in the presence of troubling unofficial reports, Aimee's understanding shaped how the grassroots activists at GirlZone made sense of this moment of profound disappointment. In addition to her incredulity, Aimee's narrative hinges on her struggles to situate her passion to make social change within economic frames that do not value this passion. Although activists need financial support, the organizations in positions to offer that support readily dismiss feminists like Aimee as angry. And, without the resources these decision makers withhold, how are young feminist activists able to forge the necessary but underdeveloped social structures that might enable them to gain access to existing networks of power?

This dilemma seems most evident in an interestingly jumbled part of this excerpt that exposes Aimee's assessment of the fraught relationship between grassroots activism and business: "We never started GirlZone for a business so it feels a little wrong to think of it as a business, but I think it is for the best. We have gotten lots of signs that GirlZone is important, but we need to start thinking of economic realities." When Aimee says that thinking of GirlZone as a business "is for the best," she does not mean this is something she is happy about. Nonetheless, she sees the necessity, perhaps the inevitability, of addressing the economics of activism in this way.

Of course, grassroots activists address the economics of activism on a regular basis. On a programmatic level, for example, GirlZone offered several workshops directly addressing economic issues, such as a four session series of workshops on "Money Matters" that taught girls how to become entrepreneurs, among other things. On an institutional level, GirlZone organizers also dealt with the economic factors. As Aimee noted above, GirlZone, like other girl-centered grassroots activist organizations in the turn of the century youthquake, relied heavily on young activists who volunteer their time and talents to meet the many needs of girls and women. Yet, when this younger cohort ages and acquires increased financial and time obligations, such as a mortgage or a family, they feel spread thin, generating problems for grassroots organizations like GirlZone that cannot offer full-time paid positions and cannot survive with only part-time oversight. Clearly, grassroots feminists recognize the importance of balancing their activism and their economic needs.[32] It is not economics, then, but rather the privileging of the economic system over other values that organizers like Aimee struggle with. In particular, it is the elision between addressing economic issues and the reframing of grassroots activism as primarily an economic issue (and not one of social justice) that Aimee finds problematic.

This problem refers to the ways that women and girls, especially outside of urban areas, can be ill-served in these economic frameworks. Obviously, it would be foolish for funding organizations to disregard how potential recipients acknowledge fiscal realities. And yet for Aimee, the United Way's decision made clear that GirlZone's fiscal realities were bleak, particularly, as she assessed it, because conservative funding organizations withhold potential resources due to dubious decision-making practices.

Although Aimee was not so explicit, the compromises Aimee felt forced to make come at a significant personal cost. For example, as described in the above quote, Aimee tried to obfuscate her feminism; she focused on empowering girls by fostering their talents and she diminished feminist analyses that might "challenge the dominant paradigm." Yet even when using empowerment frames, Aimee could neither mask the constitutive feminist elements of her activism nor could she control how "feminist" gets coded as "angry," a damaging characteristic at least to one Board Member. Forced to adopt new frameworks but with little to show for it, Aimee felt powerless in a system that did not value her grassroots feminist activism.[33] This powerlessness, these compromises, this lack of funding made Aimee feel she had little choice but to end this grassroots feminist foray into sustained local activism. As Aimee pointed out, "We've tried everything to get this organization funded. . . . We ran out of ideas and we ran out of hope, which is no way to run an organization like GirlZone."[34]

The fact that the United Way rejected GirlZone's grant proposal, and in particular the reasons circulating for this rejection, speak to the difficulty that grassroots girls' activists face, especially those in Middle America who are even less present on national funding radars. It also speaks to the large-scale socioeconomic forces, namely, the lack of alternative funding options, that make activists hope their arguments can break into the conservative funding priorities of foundation culture. Without alternatives, grassroots organizations return to potential sponsors who have repeatedly declined to support these feminist projects in the past, causing those without other resources to cling to narratives about the importance of literacy, which generally imply if not claim that being rhetorically persuasive will lead to a changed world.

Contrary to such messages about the power of literacy, Aimee's story indicates that feminist arguments cannot break the tight circle of funding that denies girls as a priority. And yet, despite overwhelming rejection, organizers like Aimee may continue to write grants, demonstrating perhaps their ingrained notion that literate activity is central to economic viability and perhaps their lack of other options.[35]

STRATEGIES FOR CONTINUED
GRASSROOTS FEMINIST ACTIVISM

The lessons from GirlZone's bookend grant proposals expose the significant power funding organizations have on contemporary grassroots activism and the material costs of the dearth of sponsors for girls' organizations in nonurban America. To be successful in this context, these girls' organizations must both understand how their texts are read in the current funding climate and alter this climate to make it friendlier to their agendas. As Girl-Zone's grant proposals illustrate, grassroots feminist activists need to design new strategies and create new sponsors.

Design New Strategies: How to Change Traditional Foundation Culture

For grassroots feminist activists, working to change traditional foundation culture that still controls the purse strings is both important and tricky. In "The Winnowing of Organizations," Thomas James argues that part of the challenge is that funding for youth programs is guided by tight networks of social and economic elites, largely "men of wealth and high social standing."[36] Their sponsorship exerts a strong influence not only on foundation funding, but also on public policy by shaping who and what are "acceptable" (fundable) in youth-based settings. Because it is difficult to alter this tight circle, it is difficult to re-direct funding priorities to sustain innovative community organizations.

Even though more women have become influential in philanthropic giving in the decade since James' research, philanthropic organizations tend to be reluctant to address uncomfortable issues such as those surrounding race, ethnicity, and gender,[37] as corroborated by Mary Ellen S. Capek in her three volume monograph series entitled *Women and Philanthropy: Old Stereotypes, New Challenges.* In the second of these monographs, *Foundation Support for Women and Girls: "Special Interest" Funding or Effective Philanthropy?*, Capek argues that there are "few real spurs" that could force a change in this foundation culture: "Most foundations are small institutions, with little turnover in personnel or board positions, and because of the power dynamics built into the giving away of money, foundation executives seldom get honest feedback from outside constituencies."[38] This partially explains a long-standing conservative history of foundation culture that has been slow to advance programs that challenge traditional constructions of gender and other "discomfort issues." When this explanation is paired with the increasing sponsorship role foundations play since the government has defunded existing activism, it becomes clear that activists addressing issues of race, ethnicity, and gender are in a tenuous position.

To note these difficulties, however, is not to give up. In fact, in the third monograph in her series, Capek offers strategies to break into and/or alter philanthropic giving: find allies; influence public policy; mentor women and minority board members; collaborate with other organizations; become more media savvy; and strengthen grassroots organizations.[39] In addition to these suggestions to alter the conditions of foundation culture, another practice is explicitly and implicitly foregrounded: strategic rhetoric.[40] Generally, Capek posits this as a hopeful practice, encouraging girls and women's organizations to ask "what would sell, what would be of interest, what gets us in the door?" To achieve this goal, Capek encourages women and girls' organizations to change from the moral imperative language (often framed as social responsibilities) to the language of effective grant making, namely, framing women's issues less as women's social problems and more as funding the "low-skilled" and "unemployed." As GirlZone's history illustrates, central to negotiating these choices is how grantees retain a sense of self.

The shift in strategic rhetoric that Capek describes extends far beyond the United States. In her research on grassroots feminist activism in South Africa during the mid-1990s, Deborah Mindry examines how agencies funding South African women's grassroots activists shifted their discursive register with significant material consequences. Although funders desired similar skills (e.g., gardening, sewing, candle making), funders responded more favorably if these formerly dubbed "self-help" skills framed in "civilizing" and "uplifting" discourses were reframed as "microenterprise" and "entrepreneurship" skills within what Mindry calls "development" and "enterprise" discourses.[41] In other words, without necessarily changing their practices, those seeking foundation money had to change their textual representations of themselves and of their relations with the funders away from relations based on moral uplift and toward relations based on economic enterprise. These strategic shifts in language respond to the shift in funding organizations and society more generally away from a social and moral responsibility of citizens to a privatization of the social sector and an individualization of responsibility, largely within an entrepreneurial or at least economic realm.

Two aspects to this rhetoric are particularly instructive. First, although moral and economic discourses clearly overlap, this shift in privileging reflects how work and economic discourses rather than moral discourses have become the coin of the realm in granting circles. To engage with contemporary philanthropic organizations, feminists need to learn the discourses of enterprise. These discourses alternatively reference "the new economy," "the knowledge society," or "the new work order," frameworks that privilege economic values of contemporary society. Instead of focusing on government's responsibilities or on rights owed to girls and women, feminists seeking funds have correspondingly focused on critiquing and redressing the deleterious effects of globalization, often by foregrounding the economic and social conditions that lead women into danger, debt, and under- and unemployment. These discursive shifts expose feminisms' multiple relations to the changing conditions associated with global capitalism. As many feminists have pointed out, globalization is hardly monolithic. Rather, global capitalism benefits the powerful, who are disproportionately men, and hurts the poor, who are disproportionately women. In addition, globalization is not operationalized on a homogenous gender line; many

U.S. women benefit from increased material and cultural capital at the expense of women in developing nations. As has always been the case, in global capitalism, gender, power, and privilege intersect in various ways.

For years, feminists have sought to understand feminisms within the frameworks of the globalized new work order not merely for funding, but also to articulate today's feminist agendas. As Michelle Sidler argues, a new generation of feminists "must overhaul feminism to operate within this 'new world order.'"[42] What this overhaul means for feminisms is still an open question and leaves unresolved the conflict between critiquing the globalization often supported by the elites who are so important to philanthropic giving on the one hand and acquiring funding from these same sources on the other hand.[43] What is not an open question, however, is the importance for feminists to pursue the discursive and material power of global capitalism. Entrepreneurial feminism is one prevalent if troubled model.

For those who still want to foreground gender concerns, a second aspect of Mary Ellen S. Capek's strategy on how to alter foundation culture is more significant. In her encouragement to reframe feminist concerns, Capek leaves an impression that an alteration of rhetoric can break into the slow-to-change, tight-knit circles of the funding elite. In her report for the Center on Philanthropy and Civil Society, Elsa M. Davidson describes how other strategists for women and girls' organizations offer similar advice.[44] One person Davidson highlights is Susan Ostrander, co-founder of the National Board of Directors of the Women's Funding Network. While Ostrander opposes Capek's goal of toning down the feminist vocabulary—Ostrander argues instead for making clear the range of women's issues—Ostrander and Capek share the idea that a central challenge is getting mainstream foundations to appreciate how women's issues are the same issues that matter to these foundations.

Certainly feminists need to frame their goals to better account for the economic, social, and political realities that shape feminism (and funding) in today's globalized new work order. And, in this new work order, grassroots organizations are generally the marginalized ones seeking money and support from more centralized sources of power, such as foundations. Because grant proposals mediate the initial and the majority of foundation–grant seeker interactions, becoming rhetorically savvy seems an important way for feminists to make their arguments. Nonetheless, rhetorically placing girls and women's issues on the map *as* girls and women's issues needs to be recognized as a limited strategy within current funding frameworks. Representations of the girl crisis—which publicized how schools, the media, and other powerful socializing forces provided insufficient institutional resources and harmful media representations that silenced girls or encouraged them to pursue dangerous behaviors[45]—sparked extensive feminist activism during the 1990s, including the creation of GirlZone. Despite this fact, grassroots community organizations focusing on these crises received disappointingly little financial sponsorship from traditional foundations.

Capek herself points out the limitations of a focus on rhetorical strategies. Capek notes that CEOs and board members—in other words those making the funding decisions—often live in what she calls an "insular world"[46] displaying what I would call anti- or postfeminist sentiments, sentiments either overtly antagonistic to feminism or covertly antagonistic to feminism by believing feminism has already accomplished its goals and therefore is no longer needed. As Capek reports: "one senior foundation male executive noted that 'we *don't* discriminate against women; that's why we make 'generic' grants. This is 1997. Women are equally considered in every way. We *don't* need a special program to make sure women get their fair share."[47] In this postfeminist sentiment where feminist successes would appear to have made feminism irrelevant, this foundation executive believes that the foundation money women receive is their fair share. If redressing gender inequities is the focus, there seems little space to challenge that assumption overtly. In fact, according to Capek's research, there is difficulty raising issues addressing the needs of girls and women since they are not on the funding agenda, and "'if you do raise issues not on the agenda, especially as regards women and girls, you're seen as a feminist, and that's a 'bad thing'." Another quipped sarcastically, 'We *did* women in the eighties; let's move on.'"[48] With issues relating to girls and women seen as so passé, so 1980s, it seems questionable if issues that disproportionately impact girls and women are still salient for foundation funders.

For feminist grassroots activists, a dilemma of the 1990s was how to foster feminist activism that enabled them to be both fundable and committed to their mission. For those courting foundations as sponsors, writing grants meant focusing on how to intertwine literacy, feminism, and economic realities to forward their activism. Most seeking grant money know the importance of this rhetorical task, yet institutional survival is far more than rhetorical. Within this funding climate, the constraints surrounding the literate activities of grant writing should cause feminist activists to focus on altering the terms of the struggle (e.g., providing additional/alternative sponsorship possibilities) as much as if not more than on the rhetorical strategies themselves. Without this, feminist texts may not have a chance, as was evident in Aimee's understanding of GirlZone's grant to the United Way.

Aimee's assessment reinforces James' notion that the viability of grassroots activism is heavily dependent on a tight-knit group of conservative philanthropic elite. For example, years after GirlZone closed, Aimee responded to a local reporter's questions about why GirlZone would not reconstitute by stating:

Local social service funding, like a lot of life, is not a meritocracy. The way military contracts are granted is depressing and daunting, but take a look at [local foundation funding structures] for an extra dollop of unmonitored nepotism in our own backyard. Lots of work needs to be done addressing the crony-ism, insiderness, and agendas of our local social service funding circles before orgs and efforts appreciated by and benefiting the community that are outside of these circles will be able to even come close to having a piece of the pie. Discussion on the unjust status of local social service funding has not even begun.[49]

Similarly, Aimee's self-monitoring reinforces Capek's perceptions that issues framed as feminist are problematic, especially to these powerful conservative elites. However, the United Way's response also challenges, or at least qualifies, two of Capek's other notions: first, that there is a shift from moral issues to economic ones;[50] and second, that a change in rhetoric can break into this elite world. If Aimee's description is accurate, the United Way funders disapproved of what they thought were Aimee's values and this played a significant role in why GirlZone lost the grant. Although those giving money should expect those seeking funds to share their agenda, Aimee felt her grant proposal made clear how GirlZone met the United Way's stated agenda of addressing the needs of underserved youth in Champaign County. In addition, despite Aimee's current or future rhetorical shifts, she could not control or even respond to the board member's profound misreading of her—that during the site visit Aimee was angry and smelled like pot—because these readings were not officially made. This misreading raises concerns about whether alternative, grassroots activists can make their projects and themselves fundable. The values and practices of the philanthropic elite also profoundly challenge the belief that a persuasively written proposal can succeed; until board members' assumptions change, literate activities cannot overcome the very real biases that do not recognize the needs of many feminist organizations.

These conclusions raise several questions: Are there any issues that would have motivated funders to sponsor girls' organizations in significant ways? For feminist, activist, rural grassroots organizations devoted to girls during the 1990s, what literate activities could have garnered sponsors? How do girls and feminist organizations bear the ideological freight for access to funders' resources[51] while simultaneously maintaining their own agenda? For composition scholars as well as feminist activists, these questions foreground a teaching moment of a very real kind: How does this funding reality shape an effective pedagogy for feminist activists seeking to forward an alternative education? Based on the narrative Aimee constructs and in the absence of the United Way's response, the story of GirlZone's two grants indicates that the answer to the funding problem lies less in better-crafted texts and more in either altering constructions of feminism (see previous chapters), or in creating alternative material conditions that can make these texts meaningful, such as creating new funding sources, perhaps within the convoluted world of entrepreneurial feminism.

Create New Sponsors: Entrepreneurship and Activist Organizations

For a new generation of grassroots activists who seek to make their feminism responsive to the changing socioeconomic, global trends so evident by the 1990s, economic entrepreneurialism has become a central framework to engage. As GirlZone's grant proposal to the United Way illustrates, however, adopting this framework with traditional foundations may be necessary but it is hardly sufficient. Consequently, entrepreneurial feminism also seeks to create new sponsors, such as feminist philanthropic organizations that might better align with feminist and girls' organizations.

This project has been ongoing and in the last two decades there has been an impressive increase in the number of feminist foundations. According to the National Committee for Responsive Philanthropy, the change for women's foundations has been dramatic: In 1985, feminist foundations raised about $4.8 million dollars while in 1994 they raised $25 million; in 1985, the ten largest feminist foundations distributed $1.2 million in grants while in 1994 that number had jumped to $9 million.[52] This is a fraction of all philanthropic money given out, but it is an important trend.

Another trend, as outlined in a 2004–2005 report sponsored by Women and Philanthropy, is that there are more private grant making foundations: In 2003, "more than one-third of all private grant making foundations in the U.S. have been created since 1996." These new foundations are "key catalysts for change" and offer important (potential) resources for feminist activists.[53] These new foundations have appeared on a variety of local and national levels. Local foundations are responsive to the community's needs and therefore may be more likely to fund local feminist organizations addressing those needs. Feminist activist Jung-Rin Kim encourages girls and women's organizations to create or seek out the increasing numbers of community-based organizations as a way to solve what she considers the "uneven allocation of social attention and funding."[54] New forms of national organizations are also attempting to address this uneven allocation of funding. For example, in the mid-1990s, the Third Wave Foundation was established, initially with an annual budget of under $10,000 though by 2004 it had an annual budget of over $800,000.[55] This U.S. foundation specifically sponsors activism by and for young people under the age of thirty-five, with a particular attention to gender issues. This foundation offers financial resources, generally small grants or scholarships, not the scarce staff lines organizations like GirlZone so desperately need. Nonetheless, the Third Wave Foundation has participated in and fueled what is a hopeful recent trend to provide leadership training and ongoing networking possibilities, possibilities that may eventually fund these lines in the future.

The Third Wave Foundation is a particularly successful model of entrepreneurial feminism that exposes how feminists have worked their fraught but necessary relations with capitalism to their advantage. Instead of shying away from capitalism's sources of power, such as money and the media, this foundation's co-founder Rebecca Walker encourages feminists to seek these out. To do this, the Third Wave reframed feminists' understandable distrust of capitalistic power. As Walker argues, although capitalism can co-opt feminist messages, grassroots activists need to pursue capitalism's power in order to both survive and thrive:

> We don't want to be exploited in the name of social change, and so we vow to factor salaries for ourselves into our budgets and call ourselves a corporation. We do not want to be marginalized as we have seen so many activist groups become, and so we vow, too, to be unafraid of both large sums of money and the media, and aggressively seek both out, determined to market our empowerment message. . . . I speak of marketing social change.[56]

Walker's comfort in adopting the capitalistic frameworks operative today is a productive trend for many grassroots organizations. As Walker notes, this sort of entrepreneurial feminism encourages grassroots activists to view their social activism partly as a "business of direct action" that is "into the business of redistributing wealth."[57] Although Walker is hardly the first to conclude that feminists need to court power, media, and money, her explicit embrace of entrepreneurial business practices and her stature among third wave feminist activists model the viability of these practices for a new generation of feminists.

Despite the Third Wave Foundation's success, GirlZone shows the on-the-ground difficulties many grassroots feminists have in taking up entrepreneurial feminism. Tellingly, GirlZone closed just when Aimee decided to more fully endorse an entrepreneurial model. Perhaps this reflects that Aimee's implementation of this philosophy was too late. More likely, Aimee still found it too dissonant to imagine her quest for social justice as an entrepreneurial project. For Aimee, social justice is not a business. This was made clear years earlier when Aimee left her newly permanent job with Girl's Best Friend after just one summer. In spite of believing in this foundation's mission, valuing its everyday activist networks, and appreciating both regular paychecks and health insurance, Aimee felt that this business model of sustainable activism was sucking the activist passion out of her.

Even so, just prior to her decision to close GirlZone, Aimee claimed that she needed to run GirlZone more like a business, the same conclusion Walker advocates in an entrepreneurial feminist tradition:

> I'm tired of volunteer-run programs. It's such an effort. It's not that people aren't interested in it, but it's so hard to create those structures for people to get involved and stay involved. And we do it, and it's good, but I don't want volunteers running this program. Because it's not reliable. It's a lot of ongoing training. It's a lot of ongoing scrapping. So we don't take as many volunteers anymore. . . . It's moved beyond that "do whatever dinner parties." . . . It's my business now. And I don't have a problem saying that now. I had a problem saying that for a long time.[58]

Aimee's reference to "do whatever dinner parties" nods to a belief that sustained grassroots feminist activism has moved beyond merely bringing what you have to offer to a local get-together. That is not enough. Just as the change in governmental support of community organizations during the 1980s led to a professionalization of community programs, ongoing grassroots feminist activism in today's global capitalism may mean grassroots activists learn to think like entrepreneurs. To be an entrepreneur generally means a heavy, often unpaid investment of resources up-front in order to illustrate or create a niche or need. This strategy will eventually pay off when others recognize and value your niche. If people only pay lip service, however, then those initial investments are lost, as GirlZone experienced first hand.

GirlZone proved itself a valuable resource to at least the one thousand plus participants who attended GirlZone and GrrrlFest activities. Nevertheless, Aimee could not get the necessary investment. Rather, she felt exploited by a system that stated the labor of meeting girls and women's needs was important and should be continued, but was not worth funding. Unable to figure out how to buck current foundation trends, Aimee felt she had to close GirlZone. She ended her stint with the following description, posted on the GrrrlFest website and circulated to media, participants, and supporters:

We've done as much as we can do with what we've got.
It's been such a good run.

After more than 1,000 girl participants, 400 workshops, three festivals, and endless hours of far-reaching, unsuccessful, simply heartbreaking efforts to secure local funding to support our extensive volunteer-run operations, GirlZone is throwing in the hat [at] the close of GrrrlFest III, September 14, 2003, marks the end of an amazing eight year stint within Champaign-Urbana for GirlZone. During this time, GirlZone was voted C-U's "Best Workshop" and "Best Non-Profit," received acclaim from local media, as well as from national sources such as The Chicago Tribune, Rockrgrl Magazine, Mary Engelbreit's Home Companion, and NPR, and was given "Trailblazer" honors by the Illinois State Treasurer, as well as an honorary "GirlZone Day" by the cities of Champaign and Urbana.

We are immensely proud of the work we have done in our community mobilizing resources to encourage girls and young women to explore, challenge, and celebrate their individual abilities and interests. We are proud of the economic policies we created for our programs to be accessible to all girls in our community, and of our decision to direct our efforts elsewhere so as not to perpetuate the damaging notion that women who work hard and do important work in the market should do so without concern for just compensation. We are proud of the thoughtfully inspiring organization that we have built, and of what we have all become while we were focusing in on our passions.

We are so very inspired by some of the product of our efforts seen in the abundance of GirlZone folk out there doing it, be it our girls on their

way to the skatepark, heading up veggie restaurants and school news-
papers, going off to Yale, knitting on park benches, booking and start-
ing up bands and running sound, getting their voices out as organizers
and leaders in all kinds of spaces, fixing bikes and computers, support-
ing each other, and our women learning to tap dance at 30, starting their
own businesses, showing up at open stages for the first time, changing
jobs and majors, trusting their thoughts and putting them into zines and
letters to editors, skipping out early to head to the batting cages, self-
reflecting and self-directing, being gentle to themselves and letting them-
selves marvel at other females' strengths.

We greatly appreciate all of the wonderful support given to us by our
girls, our parents, local business leaders, and community members over
the years. We are excited about the great things that will continue to
come from our many, many GirlZone girls and volunteers, and look for-
ward to a wealth of projects, agencies, efforts, and actions following in
our proud, joyful footsteps.

aimee[59]

THE EVANESCENCE OF GRASSROOTS ACTIVISM

The lessons of GirlZone expose the importance of rethinking the ways
grassroots feminists recognize and participate in the socioeconomic contexts that motivate their activism. Today's era of global capitalism provides
new sponsors of feminist activism as well as shapes the need for feminist activism (e.g., the ratcheting-up of sexualized, commodified, and a-political
"girl" identities). These conditions have also fostered the perception that
grassroots feminists should embrace entrepreneurial feminism. Although
grassroots feminists may be troubled by this perception, they recognize that
these conditions are not going away. Therefore, the question is not whether
to engage these increasingly powerful capitalistic networks but rather
how.[60] Analyzing literate activities provides grassroots feminists with both
a way to understand and to create tactics for this engagement.

As mediators of social relations, the literate activities surrounding
GirlZone's bookend grant proposals illustrate the conflicted responses
that the grassroots feminist activists at GirlZone had when pushed to
think of activism in an entrepreneurial, business model. On the one hand,
if GirlZone were to be sustainable, then organizers would need to acquire
competency in the entrepreneurial realm. Without these skills, organizations like GirlZone close. On the other hand, locating activism as *in the*
business of direct action may work against the deep investments that motivated participants in the first place. The personal costs of "selling out"
or even being complicit with this entrepreneurial business model may feel
too high. In this case, too, GirlZone closes. This conundrum plagued
Aimee long after GirlZone's closing. Yet, the following coda explores
how assessments of GirlZone and its afterlife point to some possibilities.

Coda

Success and Sustainability

I think it's a shame that GirlZone never got much funding; it's sad that there is so little funding available for so many great services and organizations, and it's sad that very few people determine where that money goes. I do agree that as long as we were there to provide girls programming for free, there was little incentive for anybody to fund dedicated girl-centered programming. It's sort of the same story girls are told in different contexts—why buy the cow when you can get the milk for free? Why pay for milk when you can get an organization of women working in their free time to raise the cows, milk the cows, train the cows to give really good milk, put the milk in a glass, print and hang flyers advertising the availability of said glass . . . and then give you the milk for free if you're not able or willing to pay?

For that reason, and a number of others, GirlZone *can't* reconstitute. I would love to see public institutions and services take up the challenge and come up with their own programming, and we certainly listed some places that have—the Douglas Branch of the CPL, the parks district, and so on—at the meeting. GirlZone should not have to be "The Place For Girls To Do Stuff"; there should be lots of places for girls—and boys, and men, and women—to do stuff without being an insider, or affluent, or able to attend by invitation only. Regrouping GirlZone, were such a thing even possible, would be saying "okay, you didn't bother, so I guess we'll keep being the one to do it."

—Ali, GirlZone and GrrrlFest facilitator, 2006

Any final assessment of GirlZone needs to address the fact that GirlZone closed, unable to secure funds to underwrite staff positions and support the professionalization of this grassroots organization. This closing could be read as failure. Yet, for reasons that go beyond my affective attachment to the mission and participants of GirlZone, I want to hold that conclusion in abeyance. Calling GirlZone a failure begs the question of what is success. And, although GirlZone organizers and facilitators wanted a self-sustaining organization, they did not want it at all costs, a fact that complicates an a-contextual use of sustainability as a primary criterion for success.

As the epigraph details, some GirlZone participants challenged this a-contextual criterion by de-coupling the commonly yoked pair of success and sustainability. Responding to a reporter's question about whether GirlZone might reconstitute, perhaps as a renewed bid for success, facilitator Ali makes this clear. This core facilitator for GrrrlFest 2003 was developing her feminist roots in Champaign-Urbana, in part by playing in a punk band with other GirlZone facilitators, by learning to tap dance as an adult, and by advancing in her workplace hierarchy. Loosely, GirlZone was successful in helping Ali in these accomplishments; as she notes elsewhere, GirlZone achieved its stated goal of nudging her to expand her expectations about what girls and women do. Despite this success, GirlZone was not sustainable. Ali links this unsustainability to a devaluing of girls' programming by foundations and public institutions. Sustaining GirlZone in this climate, according to Ali, would require participating in this structural devaluation. Therefore, Ali argues not only that sustainability is not the primary marker of GirlZone's successes, but also more provocatively, that GirlZone's successes would be undermined if linked to sustainability in the current conditions.

From the outset, organizers were aware of the difficulty of tracking GirlZone's success, a project far more complex than tracking the numbers of girls attending workshops or than collecting anecdotal stories of praise relayed by participants. Early in GirlZone's history, founding organizer Gina articulated one assessment of success by imagining, hopefully, GirlZone's impact on a hypothetical girl. According to Gina, GirlZone would be a success if a girl who took a bike repair project became a girl who took a predominantly male-dominated physics class, and became a girl who grew confident enough in her abilities to end an abusive relationship.[1] Although this image of success discounts the material conditions that make it more or less feasible for a person to leave an abusive relationship, it illustrates how Gina's definition of success far exceeds the specific goals of each three-hour GirlZone workshop. For Gina, success was about facilitating a sense of empowerment in a girl's life, a definition that makes it difficult to pinpoint GirlZone's direct influence. And indeed, for many girls, GirlZone's direct influence was difficult to trace. GirlZone workshops offered both fun and a respite from what the frequent attendees described as the sexist, homophobic, body-image obsessed, conformist environments of middle school. As a community and a concept, GirlZone became a location from which girls could explore ways to deal with these challenges. This can be seen with Sophia, who explicitly credits GirlZone and Radio-Girl with fostering her belief in herself and encouraging her to pursue interests not necessarily validated in middle school settings, such as traveling to the Southern Feminist Conference several states away; being arrested for supporting protesters agitating for gay and lesbian rights; and becoming involved with the radical schooling movement. GirlZone provided

Sophia with individual mentors and an introduction to collective groups who valued and learned from her participation. Moreover, Sophia's Radio-Girl and Independent Media Center (IMC) reporting on issues including presidential politics, genetically modified food, and youthquake protests inspired a reporter in the IMC Colorado Springs bureau to forward Sophia as a model of how local community members can be "radio active."[2] That report explicitly cites GirlZone and RadioGirl as critical sponsors for Sophia's radio activity.

Beyond showcasing a success story of one individual, which in itself could not justify the time and effort of GirlZone, I argue that to deem GirlZone a failure is to misunderstand the uneven ways that institutional and social change happens. Like the influence GirlZone had on most participants, the impact of institutional and social change is seldom evident in a direct line. Instead, these changes happen in what Cynthia Kaufman calls the "micro-politics of subtle transformation;"[3] their impact may not be seen until years later, long after the source has disappeared, when many factors come together to highlight networks formed, ideas made popular, and experiences that shaped life trajectories.

As GirlZone institutionally aged, organizers more overtly wrestled with the relationships between success and sustainability. This struggle was apparent in a "postmortem" discussion Aimee and I had a few months after GirlZone closed, when Aimee had moved to New York City to care for her terminally ill sister and subsequently worked to develop and oversee outcomes evaluations for the Girl Scouts of America.[4] In this new physical and mental space, Aimee and I considered what it would have taken to make GirlZone institutionally viable. I asked if in retrospect she would have represented GirlZone as a way to prevent girls from getting pregnant in order to garner scarce foundation resources. After all, I posited, if girls see themselves as social agents beyond the highly sexualized options most readily available to them—a goal GirlZone did have—then girls may be less likely to take-up these sexualized identities. For Aimee, however, GirlZone was about defining girls without defaulting to considerations of their reproductive status. Girls and women are more than walking wombs and to construct the goals of GirlZone within these frameworks would have gone against what Aimee was creating GirlZone and GirlZone girls to be.

This exchange highlights the tensions between success and sustainability. To Aimee, my suggested bid for institutional success meant undermining the ideals that motivated her activism and compromising her understandings of herself and of GirlZone. And yet, the cost of *not* "selling out" was that GirlZone closed, and the girls and women of GirlZone as well as the community of Champaign-Urbana paid this price. As chapter 7 describes, this conundrum raised a seemingly irresolvable tension: at the time of GirlZone's closing, Aimee realized that what motivated GirlZone could not be sacrificed and had to be sacrificed at the same time.

Finding a way out of this tension and of balancing success and sustainability remained a focus in our discussions of how grassroots activists should proceed. Moving from national funding trends to local community support, I joked that I secretly wished that GirlZone could have been like the 1940s or 1950s musicals. We, who were willing to put in the time to meet a community-recognized need, would be able to pool our talents and hard work to rally the community to ratify an important resource that girls had validated through their enthusiasm and attendance. We could sing and dance, "build the barn," and "save the school," or at least this one grassroots community organization. Taking up my 1940–50s musical frame, Aimee located GirlZone's demise within the general decline in civic and community participation, commenting that "GirlZone was beautiful at singing and dancing and building the barn, but we had not realized that everybody had given up on the barn a long time ago."[5] For Aimee, if grassroots activist organizations like GirlZone are to be sustainable, then they need to build multiple local and national connections to funders and foundations, and have individuals and institutions tangibly value what these grassroots communities try to create.

Aimee's comments obliquely reference the professionalization of contemporary grassroots activism, a professionalization that seems only temporarily challenged by the youthquake eruptions. For example, when a group of central Illinois women initially decided to start GirlZone, they knew they would need to find workshop facilitators, market to a range of girls and parents, and persuade businesses to donate materials and space. These women had a sense of organizational needs, such as creating and maintaining contact information, and getting tax exempt status. On this level, they could draw upon their community's volunteer resources. These grassroots activists were *un*aware, however, that two of them, in their spare time and without financial compensation, had to do all of this as well as learn to motivate and manage, write business documents, meet with prospective donors, and become skilled at a whole host of other professional skills. As a telling case, GirlZone highlights how contemporary grassroots feminist activism requires training to be a professional. And, as chapter 5 argues in relation to feminist pedagogies developing desired social identities, grassroots feminist activists need to find ways to construct these professionalized identities as in the service (and not a selling out) of their activist projects.

Toward the end of our conversation that night, Aimee indicated she had become more comfortable situating her activism within business models. In fact, Aimee commented that running GirlZone had been like running her own small business and that she had been reading on business practices, especially books targeted to female business owners. Even while combining her activism and her imagined small-business practices, Aimee continued to struggle with how to sustain a local DIY business in a climate where national and multinational businesses are taking over mom and pop operations that might share this DIY mentality.

Less than a year after our postmortem discussions, GirlZone participants again reflected on the relationship between success and sustainability. In March 2006, thirty months after GirlZone closed and just three months after Aimee returned to Champaign-Urbana from her time in New York City, Aimee invited former GirlZone girls and those who had supported GirlZone (parents, volunteers, counselors, community members, business community, etc.) to an informational/brainstorming meeting. The purpose of this meeting was to examine the resources Champaign-Urbana provides girls to "lead healthy lives." According to Aimee:

> This [meeting] is not about what to start. It is about what to address so that things can start and stay. There is a different investment and timeline required to think beyond creating supportive programs to thinking what it will take to create a supportive culture—particularly within communities where primary funding agencies discredit the work of meaningful feminist groups with casual labels of "angry woman" and "pot smoker."[6]

Aimee once again raises the tensions between success and sustainability. In longevity, GirlZone had exceeded typical expectations. According to Myra Marx Ferree and Beth B. Hess, "Very few [feminist] local action groups have been able to survive and maintain their original goals for as long as five years."[7] GirlZone survived for almost seven. But Aimee, Ali and other GirlZone participants wanted more. In this 2006 moment, Aimee offered a layered definition of success that included how girls engage with local communities and national trends, such as those associated with the economics of activism and with negative feminist identities. Aimee's new definition of success included building a sustainable, supportive culture that can foster subtle transformations in and beyond girls' organizations.

Aimee's statements about this final meeting, or perhaps the first of future activist meetings, expresses despair about the forces behind Girl-Zone's closing; grassroots organizations are by their nature evanescent things, sparked by creative thinking and local possibilities, but difficult to sustain. And yet, the fact that Aimee called this meeting, and that so many people showed up, also speaks to the hope of grassroots activism. This hope motivates people to contribute to the uneven ways social change occurs, whether or not the sources of these contributions institutionally survive. This hope is made compelling, even successful, when community members and activists—and I would add researchers, cultural critics and feminists—understand the powerful forces shaping local action, and can find ways to be effective within these forces.

Notes

CHAPTER 1. THE TELLING CASE OF GIRLZONE

1. Anne Ruggles Gere, "Kitchen Tables and Rented Rooms: The Extracurriculum of Composition," *College Composition and Communication* 45 (1994): 75–92.

2. For a similar argument, see James E. Porter, Patricia Sullivan, Jeff T. Grabill, Stuart Blythe, and Libby Miles, "Institutional Critique: A Rhetorical Methodology for Change," *College Composition and Communication* 51 (2000): 610–42.

3. See, for example, foundational work in this tradition by Sylvia Scribner and Michael Cole from psychology, Shirley Brice Heath in sociocultural anthropology and Brian Street from Education. These early articulations described literacy as one among many social practices through which people act in the world. These theorists are also key representatives from the three primary out-of-school literacy research traditions that Glynda Hull and Katherine Schultz note: Ethnography of Communication (Heath); Sociohistoric Theory (Cole); and New Literacy Studies (Street). Sylvia Scribner and Michael Cole, *The Psychology of Literacy* (Cambridge, MA: Harvard University Press, 1981); Shirley Brice Heath, *Ways with Words: Language, Life and Work in Communities and Classrooms* (Cambridge, England: Cambridge University Press, 1983); Brian Street, *Literacy in Theory and Practice* (Cambridge, England: Cambridge University Press, 1984); Michael Cole, *Cultural Psychology: A Once and Future Discipline* (Cambridge, MA: Belknap Press of Harvard University Press, 1996); Brian Street, *Cross-Cultural Approaches to Literacy* (Cambridge, England: Cambridge University Press. 1993); Glynda Hull and Katherine Schultz, *School's Out! Bridging Out-of-School Literacies with Classroom Practice* (New York: Teachers College Press, 2002).

4. See Heath's use of "literate events" and Street's use "literate practices." Shirley Brice Heath. "What No Bedtime Story Means," *Language and Society* 11 (1982): 49–76; Street, *Cross Cultural Approaches*, 1993.

5. Paul A. Prior, *Writing/Disciplinarity: A Sociohistoric Account of Literate Activity in the Academy* (Mahwah, NJ: Lawrence Erlbaum, 1998), xi.

6. David Barton and Mary Hamilton, *Local Literacies: Reading and Writing in One Community* (New York: Routledge, 1998).

7. Gunther Kress, *Literacy in the New Media Age* (New York: Routledge, 2003).

8. Anne Ruggles Gere, *Intimate Practices: Literacy and Cultural Work in U.S. Women's Clubs, 1880–1920* (Urbana, IL: University of Illinois Press, 1997).

9. Margaret J. Finders, *Just Girls: Hidden Literacies and Life in Junior High* (New York: Teachers College Press, 1997).

10. Dorothy Smith, *The Conceptual Practices of Power: A Feminist Sociology of Knowledge*, (Boston, MA: Northeastern University Press, 1990).

11. Examples of recent books and films include: Rachel Simmons, *Odd Girl Out: The Hidden Culture of Aggression in Girls*, (New York: Harcourt, 2002); Rosalyn Wiseman, *Queen Bees & Wannabes: Helping Your Daughter Survive Cliques, Gossip, Boyfriends, and Other Realities of Adolescence* (New York: Crown Publishers, 2002); Catherine Hardwicke (Director), *Thirteen* [DVD] (USA and Canada: Twentieth Century Fox Home Video, 2003); Mark Waters. (Director), *Mean Girls* [DVD] (USA and Canada: Paramount Home Video, 2004). *Mean Girls* is a fictional film adaptation of Wiseman's *Queen Bees & Wannabes*.

12. Girls and women actively embracing accoutrements of girlhood while still working for feminist change called themselves "girlies"; those working on the web adopted the moniker "gURLS" (or cybergrrrls); activists following the punk bands and zine writers of the RiotGrrrls called themselves grrrls. Grrrls and cybergrrrls share a DIY mentality of taking care of their own needs with a defiant transgression of stereotypical girlish stereotypes. For an early representation of many of these monikers see: Kathy Bail, ed., *DIY Feminism* (Sydney, Australia: Allen & Unwin, 1996).

13. For oft-cited psychological work on this topic, see Carol Gilligan, *In a Different Voice: Psychological Theory and Women's Development* (Cambridge, MA: Harvard University Press, 1982); Lyn Mikel Brown and Carol Gilligan, *Meeting at the Crossroads: Women's Psychology and Girls' Development* (New York: Random House, 1992); Mary Pipher, *Reviving Ophelia: Saving the Selves of Adolescent Girls* (New York: Putnam, 1994).

14. Lev Grossman, Nadia Mustafa, Diedre van Dyk, Kristin Kloberdanz and Marc Schultz, "Grow Up? Not so fast," *Time* 165 (January 24, 2005): 42–54.

15. American Association of University Women (AAUW), *Hostile Hallways: The AAUW Survey on Sexual Harassment in America's Schools* (Washington, DC: AAUW Educational Foundation, 1993); Mary Pipher, *Reviewing Ophelia*, 1994.

16. Angela McRobbie, *Feminism and Youth Culture*, rev. 2d ed. (New York: Routledge, 2000).

17. Angela McRobbie and Jenny Garber, "Girls and Subcultures," *Feminism and Youth Culture*, rev 2d ed., ed. Angela McRobbie, 12–25 (New York: Routledge, 2000). First published in Stuart Hall and Tony Jefferson, ed., *Resistance through Rituals* (London: Hutchinson, 1976).

18. Dorothy Sheridan, Brian V. Street, and David Bloom, *Writing Ourselves: Mass Observation and Literacy Practices* (Cresskill, NJ: Hampton Press, 2000).

19. For a newer line of critique of Heath's analysis, for example, see Catherine Prendergast, *Literacy and Racial Justice: The Politics of Learning after Brown v. Board of Education* (Carbondale, IL: Southern Illinois University Press, 2003).

20. Heather Bruce, *Literacies, Lies, and Silences: Girls Writing Lives in the Classroom* (New York: Peter Lang, 2003); Margaret Finders, *Just Girls* (New York: Teachers College Press, 1997; Carolyn Steedman, *The Tidy House: Little Girls Writing* (London, UK: Virago Press, 1981).

21. Anne Ruggles Gere, *Intimate Practices: Literacy and Cultural Work in U.S. Women's Clubs, 1880–1920* (Urbana, IL: University of Illinois Press, 1997); Jacqueline Jones Royster, *Traces of a Stream: Literacy and Social Change among African American Women* (Pittsburgh, PA: University of Pittsburgh Press, 2000); Shirley Logan, *We are Coming: The Persuasive Discourse of Nineteenth-Century Black Women* (Carbondale, IL: Southern Illinois University Press, 1999); Nan Johnson, *Gender and Rhetorical Space in American Life, 1866–1910* (Carbondale, IL: Southern Illinois University Press, 2002); Susan Miller, *Assuming the Positions: Cultural Pedagogy and the Politics of Commonplace Writing* (Pittsburgh, PA: University of Pittsburgh Press, 1997).

22. Cf Jacobi Mahiri, *Shooting for Excellence: African American and Youth Culture in New Century Schools* (New York: Teachers College Press, 1998).

23. Catherine Driscoll, *Girls: Feminine Adolescence in Popular Culture and Cultural Theory* (New York: Columbia University Press, 2002); Anita Harris, *Future Girl: Young Women in the 21st Century* (London: Routledge, 2004); Michelle Fine, ed. *All About the Girl: Culture, Power, Identity* (New York: Routledge, 2004).

24. Rachel Simmons, *Odd Girls Out* (New York: Harcourt, 2002); Rosalyn Wiseman, *Queen Bees and Wannabees*, 2002; Sharon Lamb, *The Secret Lives of Girls: What Good Girls Really Do—Sex Play, Aggression, and Their Guilt* (New York: Free Press, 2001).

25. This research may be of particular interest to sociologists and social movement theorists and to feminist activists who are increasingly studying and writing about grassroots activism. See, for example: Dorothy Smith, *Institutional Ethnography: A Sociology for People* (Walnut Creek, CA: AltaMira Press, 2005); Myra Marx Ferree and Patricia Yancey Martin, eds., *Feminist Organizations: Harvest of the New Women's Movement* (Philadelphia, PA: Temple University Press, 1995); Jennifer Baumgardner and Amy Richards, *Grassroots: A Field Guide for Feminist Activism* (New York: Farrar, Straus, and Giroux, 2005).

26. For a successful example, see Deborah Brandt, *Literacy in American Lives* (Cambridge, MA: Cambridge University Press, 2001).

27. Anne Haas Dyson, *Writing Superheroes: Contemporary Childhood, Popular Culture, and Classroom Literacy* (New York: Teachers College Press, 1997). Dyson draws on Marina Warner for the term "image stores." Marina Warner, *From the Beast to the Blonde: On Fairy Tales and Their Tellers* (London: Chatto & Windus, 1994).

28. The Foundation Center, "Foundation Grants Designed for Special Population Groups, circa 2003" (FC Stats: The Foundation Center's Statistical Information Service, posted 2005). http://fdncenter.org/fd_stats/pdf/08_fund_pop/2003/16_03.pdr (accessed May 13, 2006).

CHAPTER 2. BUILDING A YOUTHQUAKE

Aimee, interview with author, November 6, 1998.

1. "The League of Pissed off Voters and You (Your Town, USA)," in *How to Get the Stupid White Men Out of Office: The Anti-politics, Un-boring Guide to Power*, ed. Adrienne Maree Brown & William Upski Wimsatt (Brooklyn: Soft Skull Press, 2004), 186.

2. This problem is not new. As Rosalyn Baxandall and Linda Gordon note in relation to grassroots activism prevalent in second-wave women's health histories, "The largest part of the women's movement is difficult to study precisely because it was so big, so decentralized, so varied, and often left few records. It is hardly surprising that most of what has been written has focused on the main national feminist organization, the National Organization for Women, because this aspect of the movement was more centralized, less outrageous, more focused. . . . By contrast, the larger, mass women's liberation movement has been less studied and more misrepresented." Rosalyn Baxandall and Linda Gordon, "Introduction," in *Dear Sisters: Dispatches From the Women's Liberation Movement*, eds. Rosalyn Baxandall and Linda Gordon (New York: Basic Books, 2000), 2.

3. When I solicited participants' choice for pseudonyms, a few participants used their own names. For the adults, I honored that request. Consequently, although most participants' names have been changed and I do not use last names, a few first names are the same.

4. Aimee, 1998.

5. See any number of AAUW studies, most notably *Hostile Hallways: The AAUW Survey on Sexual Harassment in America's Schools* (Washington, DC: AAUW Educational Foundation, 1993). In addition, see Mary Sadker and David Sadker, *Failing at Fairness: How Our Schools Cheat Girls* (New York: Touchstone, 1995).

6. GirlZone, fall 1997 schedule.

7. See chapter 3 for fuller discussion of the 1990s girl crises (e.g., anorexia; mean girls) and girl power movements (e.g., RiotGrrrls, Spice Girls).

8. Verta Taylor, "Watching for Vibes: Bringing Emotions Into the Study of Feminist Organizations," in *Feminist Organizations: Harvest of the New Women's Movement*, eds. Myra Marx Feree and Patricia Yancey Martin, 223–233 (Philadelphia: Temple University Press, 1995).

9. Mary Ellen S. Capek, *Women and Philanthropy: Old Stereotypes, New Challenges* (Battle Creek, MI: The W. K. Kellogg Foundation, 1998), 2. See chapter 7 for further disucssion of foundation support.

10. Aimee, e-mail to author, "success," August 8, 2003.

11. Eric Schragge, *Activism and Social Change: Lessons for Community and Local Organizing* (Ontario, Canada: Broadview Press, 2003).

12. For results from Illinois elections during the two presidential elections when GirlZone was operating (1996 and 2000), see "S2445–1 State of Illinois Official Vote Cast at the General Elections on November 5, 1996," *Illinois Board of Election* (Fiche 1 1 4/97), 92; "State of Illinois Official Vote Cast at the General Elections on November 7, 2000," *Illinois Board of Election* (Fiche 1 2/01), 92.

13. University YMCA Board of Governors, "University YMCA Vision Statement" Champaign, IL: University YMCA (Adopted February 27, 2003). http://www.universityymca.org/vision.html (accessed 12 May 2006).

14. For a more detailed account of the rhetoric surrounding California's Proposition 187, see Kent A. Ono and John M. Sloop, *Shifting Borders: Rhetoric, Immigration, and California's Proposition 187* (Philadelphia, PA: Temple University Press, 2002).

15. For an oft-cited mid-1990s representation of this assessment, see Rebecca Walker's edited collection, especially her introduction. Rebecca Walker, ed.

To Be Real: Telling the Truth and Changing the Face of Feminism (New York: Anchor Books, 1995).

16. When discussing RadioGirl (see chapter 5), a GirlZone spin-off project, I also consider Ayleen and Heidi organizers, since they either created and/or ran this weekly radio program.

17. Gina, Field Notes, February 15, 1999.

18. Here I am evoking Benedict Anderson's work in *Imagined Communities* (London: Verso, 1983), where Anderson argues, in part, that texts construct an imagined community's understanding of itself as part of a nation. Instead of a nationalistic context, however, I use imagined community to refer to how texts, such as Friedan's, shaped the burgeoning second-wave feminist community.

19. Gina, 1998.

20. Ibid.

21. Aimee, interview with author, 1998.

22. Aimee, 1998; Aimee, interview with author, December 30, 2002.

23. See The White House Project website, http://www.TheWhiteHouse Project.org.

24. Erica Gilbert-Levin, "Class Feminist," in *Listen Up: Voices From the Next Feminist Generation*, 2d ed., ed. Barbara Findlen (Seattle, WA: Seal Press, 2001), 168.

25. For a fuller discussion, see Nancy A. Naples, "Women's Community Activism and Feminist Activist Research," in *Community Activism and Feminist Politics: Organizing Across Race, Class, and Gende*, ed. Nancy A. Naples (New York: Routledge, 1998), 22.

26. Jean Lave and Etienne Wenger, *Situated Learning: Legitimate Peripheral Participation*, (Cambridge, UK: Cambridge University Press, 1991). Although the ideas are similar, Lave and Wenger use the term "legitimate peripheral participation," as their title indicates.

27. Although a bit older than many in this group, Gina felt that this appearance reinforced GirlZone's message that there was no one way to be a woman or a girl. As illustrated in chapter 4's analyses of a GirlZone girl's suggestion to have a make-over workshop, dress and discourses of dress sometimes index deep tensions—often along generational lines—among GirlZone participants.

28. Despite persuasive writings about how contemporary activism often uses different leadership styles than those of a generation ago, GirlZone organizers tried to involve people in leadership positions through conventional and alternative means. Organizers lack of success in this project, therefore, marks a problem and not just a difference, as organizers themselves acknowledged. For an analysis of the organization of high profile youthquake events, see Naomi Klein, "The Vision Thing: Were the DC and Seattle Protests Unfocused, or are Critics Missing the Point?", *The Nation* 7 (July 2000): 18–22 http://web23.epnet.com/ DeliveryPrintSave.asp?tb=1&_ug=sid+019377EF52–4814–83E (accessed January 19, 2005).

29. For example, some girls were involved in seasonal activities (e.g., speed skating; swim team) that competed with the times GirlZone met. In these cases, GirlZone's feminist activism was ironically diminished and arguably less needed because of the success of previous feminist activism, such as Title IX's impact on girls' participation in sports.

30. For similar representations of and dilemmas in libratory teaching, see bell hooks, *Teaching to Transgress: Education as the Practice of Freedom* (New York: Routledge, 1994) [drawing on Friere]; Peter Elbow, *Writing Without Teachers* (New York: Oxford University Press, 1973); Ira Shor and Paulo Freire, *A Pedagogy: Dialogues on Transforming Education* (South Hadley, MA: Bergin & Garvey Publishers, 1987).

31. "GirlZone Participant Expectations," *GirlZine* (2000): 6.

32. Initially, GirlZone organizers planned to work with 6–12-year-olds since contemporary research advocated strengthening girls' sense of self before the intensive gender norming hit in adolescence. Yet, when a group of older girls heard about GirlZone, they asked organizers to reconsider the upper end of the age range. The organizers complied. And yet, within eighteen months, the older girls gradually stopped attending most GirlZone workshops, perhaps because looking awkward when trying new things or merely going to GirlZone was deemed "uncool" during this high norming time. At the other end of the age range, younger sisters not yet six attended workshops, and the organizers encouraged their participation.

33. GirlZone did not ask for data on girls' economic or ethnic/racial backgrounds, nor did I. Consequently, my assessment of participants' class and race reflects my conversations and observations at GirlZone.

34. For example, the language of the Informed Consent forms necessary to receive university approval to conduct research sounds quite ominous, and I feared this language could frighten some parents who did not see me regularly interacting with their daughters. Fortunately, these fears of alienating participants and their parents did not materialize and all of the core girls chose to participate in my research. Additionally, I feared the Internal Review Board's restrictions on my research could make me a disaffecting presence at GirlZone. To be less intrusive, in my research I drew heavily on public domain information the girls produced, such as information they wrote for *The GirlZone Times*, or for the radio broadcasts from GirlZone's biweekly RadioGirl program.

35. GirlZone participants came with a range of motivations. The organizers hoped it would be a space to build a feminist community for girls and women where participants could mix fun with work toward social justice in the local and broader contexts. Organizers feared parents would think of GirlZone as cheap day care, a fear that did not materialize. Rather, parents generally imagined GirlZone as a place for their daughters to get access to resources they could not provide, a place to provide girls experiences they wish they had been afforded, and/or a place for home schooled girls to meet other like-minded girls. Girls' motivations also ranged, from a fun Saturday outing, to learning "cool stuff," to meeting up with friends.

36. See AAUW, *Hostile Hallways*, 1993.

37. School for Designing Society, Home, http://www.designingasociety.org/ (accessed June 5, 2006).

38. See chapters 3 and 4 for an examination of academic and popular representations where girls are generally relegated to what Barrie Thorne calls the "domestic realm of privatization." Barrie Thorne, "Re-Visioning Women and Social Change: Where are the Children?", *Gender and Society* 1, no. 1 (1987): 85–109.

39. For discussions about academics' responsibilities in this area, see, for example, Dwight Conquergood, "Performing as a Moral Act: Ethical Dimensions of

the Ethnography of Performance" *Literature in Performance* 5 (1985): 1–13; Ellen Cushman, "The Rhetorician as and Agent of Social Change," *College Composition and Communication* 47, no. 1 (1996): 7–28; Ellen Cushman, "The Public Intellectual, Service Learning, and Activist Research," *College English* 61, no. 3 (1999): 328–336.

40. Lila Abu-Lughod, *Writing Women's Worlds: Bedouin Stories* (Berkeley, CA: University of California Press, 1993).

41. Cf, Naomi Klein, *No Logo* (New York: Picador, 2000/2002).

42. Putnam pointed to a variety of reasons, from increased television viewing to a changing work structure (e.g., increased mobility, more mothers working outside the home, longer hours), for why people are having fewer hours to participate in community organizations where they would build connections, learn cooperative habits and increase their civic participation. Robert Putnam, *Bowling Alone: The Collapse and Revival of American Community* (New York: Simon & Schuster, 2000); Steven Mintz, *Huck's Raft: A History of American Childhood* (Cambridge, MA: Bellknap Press of Harvard University Press, 2004).

CHAPTER 3. REPRESENTATIONS OF GIRL CULTURE, REALITIES OF FEMINIST ACTIVISM

Gina, interview with author, September 25, 1998.

1. Anita Harris has a related categorization of "can–do" girls and "at risk" girls; see Anita Harris, *Future Girl: Young Women in the 21st Century* (London: Routledge, 2004).

2. Mary Pipher, *Reviving Ophelia: Saving the Selves of Adolescent Girls* (New York: Putnam, 1994).

3. Barrie Thorne, "Re-Visioning Women And Social Change: Where Are The Children?", *Gender and Society* 1, no. 1 (1987): 85–109.

4. Defining when girls' culture began is tricky since girlhood has not always been distinct from adulthood. Even so, girlhood has been an important concept in Anglo cultures for at least the last hundred and fifty years. For an analysis of girlhood in the eighteenth and nineteenth centuries, see Lynne Vallone, *Disciplines of Virtue: Girls' Culture in the Eighteenth and Nineteenth Centuries* (New Haven, CT: Yale University Press, 1995); Claudia Nelson and Lynne Vallone, eds., *The Girl's Own: Cultural Histories of the Anglo-American Girl, 1830–1915* (Athens: University of Georgia Press, 1994). For an analysis of girlhood at the turn of the twentieth century, see Sally Mitchell, *The New Girl: Girls' Culture in England, 1880–1915* (New York: Columbia University Press, 1995). In the twentieth century, girl culture particularly flourished, due largely to media's ability to readily reach all U.S. girls and make them consumers. See Sherrie Inness, *Tough Girls: Women Warriors and Wonder Women in Popular Culture* (Philadelphia, PA: University of Pennsylvania Press, 1998).

5. Inness, *Tough Girls*, 1.

6. These include the killings in Perl, Mississippi (1997); West Paducah, KY (1997); Jonesboro, AK (1998); Edinboro, PA (1998); Springfield, OR (1998); and Littleton, CO (1999). The bloodiest of these, the massacre at Columbine (1999), so traumatized the nation that it continues to receive national attention years after the event. See for example, Michael Moore's 2001 documentary film *Bowling for*

Columbine; Gus Van Sant's 2003 fictional film, *Elephant*; Douglas Coupland's 2003 book *Hey Nostradamus!*; and, a series of "Five years after the massacre" news shows such as those on *Nightline* and *20/20*.

7. For a representative example of this latter trend, see Susannah Meadows, Dirk Johnson, and Sarah Downey, "Girl Fight: Savagery in the Chicago Suburbs," *Newsweek* 19 (May 2003): 37.

8. Tweens are those between being a child (girl) and an adolescent (teen). This age differs depending on who is doing the defining, but generally ranges from 8–12.

9. Estimates range, but most find, "the teen market is estimated to be worth $140 billion" (Girls, Inc., *Girls and Economic Literacy*, 3, http://www.girlsinc. org/ic/page.php?id=3.1 (accessed February 9, 2006).

10. For example, in the humanities such as English, feminist tended to pay attention to girls primarily in relation to an increased attention to mothering and motherhood, which then might reach down to address issues of girlhood. See, for example, Carolyn Steedman, *Landscape for a Good Woman: A Story of Two Lives* (New Brunswick, NJ: Rutgers University Press, 1986).

11. For a brief overview of why U.S. feminists seldom use human rights discourses prevalent in global or transnational feminist frameworks, see Dorothy Q. Thomas, "We Are Not The World: U.S. Activism And Human Rights In The Twenty-First Century," *Signs* 25, no. 4 (2000): 1121–1125.

12. The sciences and math also increasingly attended to college women, with Women in Science type mentoring programs. A few universities began to target younger women and girls through summer camps, yet these exceptions focused more on the "add women and stir" model as opposed to addressing deep-seated overt and covert forces keeping women from pursuing these fields. This is changing.

13. Many presentations from the first international girls' studies conference, "Alice in Wonderland" in Amsterdam (June 1992), were published in an edited collection: Marion de Ras and Mieke Lunenberg, eds., *Girls, Girlhood and Girls' Studies in Transition* (Amsterdam: Het Spinhuis, 1993). This collection provides an interesting benchmark of the early international research occurring in girls' studies.

14. American Association of University Women (AAUW), *Shortchanging Girls, Shortchanging America* (Washington, DC: Greenberg Lake Analysis Group, 1991); AAUW, *How Schools Shortchange Girls: A Study of the Major Findings of Girls and Education* (Washington, DC: AAUW Educational Foundation, 1992); AAUW, *Shortchanging Girls, Shortchanging America* (Washington, DC: Greenberg Lake Analysis Group, 1994); AAUW (Peggy Ornstein), *Schoolgirls: Young Women, Self-esteem, and the Confidence Gap* (New York: Doubleday, 1994).

15. Carol Gilligan, *In a Different Voice: Psychological Theory and Women's Development* (Cambridge, MA: Harvard University Press, 1982).

16. These representations are more apparent in Gilligan's later work, such as Lyn Mikel Brown and Carol Gilligan, *Meeting At The Crossroads: Women's Psychology And Girls' Development* (Cambridge, MA: Harvard University Press, 1992).

17. Pipher, *Reviving Ophelia*, 13.

18. Mary Pipher, "Mary Pipher, Ph.D," www.marypipher.net (accessed December 18, 2005).

19. Pipher, *Reviving Ophelia*, 13; AAUW, *Hostile Hallways, How Schools Shortchange Girls*, 1992.

20. Much of this work built on the scholarship of the Finnish scholar Kaj Björkqvist, notably Kaj Björkqvist & Pirkko Niemelä, (Eds.), *Of Mice and Women: Aspects of Female Aggression* (San Diego, CA: Academic Press, 1992).

21. Rachel Simmons, *Odd Girl Out: The Hidden Culture of Aggression in Girls* (New York: Harcourt, 2002); Emily White, *Fast Girls: Teenage Tribes and the Myth of the Slut* (New York: Scribner, 2002); Rosalind Wiseman, *Queen Bees & Wannabes: Helping Your Daughter Survive Cliques, Gossip, Boyfriends, And Other Realities Of Adolescence* (New York: Crown Publishers, 2002).

22. Margaret Talbot, "Girls Just Want to Be Mean," *The New York Times Magazine* 24 (February 2002): 24+. These texts spawned countless discussions throughout popular culture. See, for example, *Newsweek*'s series "In Defense of Teen Girls," "They're Not All 'Mean Girls' and 'Ophelias'; and, "How to Raise a Well-Balanced 'Gamma' Girl," *Newsweek*, June 3, 2002.

23. In just a few week period in the spring of 2002, reports appeared in a range of papers (*The New York Times, The Chicago Tribune, USA Today*) as well as a host of other media: Maureen Dowd, "Mean, Nasty, and Missing," *New York Times*, February 27, 2002, A, 21; Talbot, "Girls Just Want to Be Mean," February 24, 2002; Rachel Simmons, "Aggressive Girls: Interview by Neil Connan," *Talk of the Nation*, National Public Radio, February 27, 2002; Rachel Simmons, "Wild Things: Interview with Rachel Simmons, author of *Odd Girl Out: The Hidden Culture of Aggression in Girls*," *Dateline* NBC, National Broadcasting Company, April 9, 2002; Suzanne Fields, "Mean Girls In The Mean Streets Of Middle School," *The Washington Times*, March 4, 2002; Margaret Littman, "Sugar, Spice And Not Very Nice: Girls' Cruelty to Girls may be Very Old-School, but Experts say it's Time to Start Taking these Mean Streaks Seriously," *The Chicago Tribune*, May 8, 2002; Nancy Hellmich, "Girls Friendships Show Aggression At Younger Ages," *USA Today*, April 9, 2002. For television shows, see *Oprah*, April 24, 2002; "Mean," *Law and Order: SVU*, National Broadcasting Company, February 24, 2004. For films, *Mean Girls* (2004).

24. Frequently cited examples include: legislation on Title IX; American Association of University Women, *Voices of a Generation: Teenage Girls on Sex, School, and Self* (Washington, DC: AAUW Educational Foundation, 1999); Piper, *Reviving Ophelia*, 1994; Myra Sadker and David Sadker, *Failing at Fairness: How America's Schools Cheat Girls* (New York: Scribner and Sons, 1994).

25. Pipher, *Reviving Ophelia*, 12.

26. Pipher mentions other important areas for change, including alternative school settings, more inclusive language, and new definitions of manhood without violence and with caring. GirlZone organizers seconded these calls as well.

27. Talbot, "Girls Just Want to Be Mean," 27.

28. Girls' and young women's textually mediated activism was perhaps most apparent in zines and websites.

29. Sara Shandler, *Ophelia Speaks: Adolescent Girls Write About Their Search For Self* (New York: Harper Perrenial, 1999), xiii.

30. Ibid., xvi.

31. The idea of any oppressed group being able to speak for themselves, if given the chance, is debatable. See for example, Rey Chow, "Gender and Representation," in *Feminist Consequences: Theory for the New Century*, eds. Elisabeth

Bronfen and Misha Kavka (New York: Columbia University Press, 2001), 38–57; or the now classic Gayatri Spivak, "Can the Subaltern Speak," in *Marxism and the Interpretation of Culture*, eds. Cary Nelson and Lawrence Grossberg (Macmillan Education: Bassingoke, 1998), 271–313.

32. Henry A. Giroux, "Teen Girls' Resistance and the Disappearing Social in *Ghost World*," *The Review of Education, Pedagogy, and Cultural Studies* 24 (2002): 283–304.

33. Angela McRobbie and Jennifer Garber, "Girls and Subcultures," reprinted in *Feminism and Youth Culture*, rev. 2d ed., ed. Angela McRobbie (New York: Routledge, 2000), 12–25. Originally published in *Resistance through Rituals*, ed. Stuart Hall and Tony Jefferson, 209–222 (London: Hutchinson, 1976).

34. Much of this work was influenced by scholarship out of the Birmingham School. For references on magazines, see: Angela McRobbie, "Jackie: An Ideology of Adolescent Femininity" (Birmingham: CCCS Stenciled Paper, 1978); Angela McRobbie, *Feminism And Youth Culture: From 'Jackie' To 'Just Seventeen'* (Boston, MA: Unwin Hyman, 1991); Valerie Walkerdine, "Some day my prince will come: Young girls and the preparation for adolescent sexuality," in *Gender and Generation*, eds. Angela McRobbie and Mica Nava (London: Macmillan, 1984); and Elizabeth Frazer, "Teenage Girls Reading Jackie," *Media, Culture And Society* 9 (1987): 407–25. For 1980s analysis of girls' consumption of music, see work by Simon Frith, in particular, *Sound Effects: Youth, Leisure, and the Politics Of Rock'n'Roll* (New York: Pantheon, 1981).

35. See, for example, Morag Shiach, ed., *Feminism and Cultural Studies* (Oxford: Oxford University Press, 1999) for attention to girls in cultural studies, and special editions of feminist journals, such as "Special Issue: Feminism and Youth Culture" of *Signs: Journal of Women in Culture and Society* 23, no. 3 (1998), and *Hypatia: A Journal of Feminist Philosophy* 12, no. 3 (1997) for attention on third-wave feminism.

36. While RiotGrrrls chapters still exist, when people speak of the RiotGrrrls, they generally mean those from this early 1990s moment. For a quick overview of the RiotGrrrl movement, see The Experience Music Project, "Riot Grrrl Retrospective." http://www.emplive.com/explore/riot_grrrl/index.asp (accessed January 18, 2004).

37. Quoted in Mary Celeste Kearney, "Producing Girls: Rethinking the Study of Female Youth Culture," in *Delinquents And Debutantes: Twentieth-Century American Girls' Cultures*, ed. Sherrie Inness (New York: New York University Press, 1998), 298.

38. See Gayle Wald, "Just a Girl? Rock Music, Feminism, and the Cultural Construction of Female Youth," *Signs: Journal of Women in Culture and Society* 23, no. 3 (1998): 585–610.

39. For a sympathetic read about the Spice Girls' contributions to feminism, see Sheila Whitely, *Women and Popular Music: Sexuality, Identity, and Subjectivity* (London: Routledge, 2000).

40. Gold, "Sex Sells Tween Fashion," *Vancouever Sun*, June 19, 2004, D4.

41. In *Writing Superheroes: Contemporary Childhood, Popular Culture, and Classroom Literacy* (New York: Teachers College, 1997), Anne Haas Dyson draws on Marina Warner, *From the Beast to the Blonde: On Fairy Tales and Their Tellers* (London: Chatto and Windus, 1994) to forward this concept of youth's image store. See chapter 6 for a more detailed examination of girls' image stores.

42. The Cartoon Network offered initial shows in 1995 ("Meet Fuzzy Lumpkin") and 1996 ("Crime 101"), with the series debuting in 1998.

43. Creator Craig McCracken's initial idea for The Powerpuff Girls came from an earlier project (Whoopass Stew) where a can of Whoopass was added to the sugar, and spice, and everything nice concoction. This Whoopass turned into Chemical X as the ingredient that transformed the perfect little girls into what would become the Powerpuff Girls.

44. Of course, if the Powerpuff Girls misbehaved, then adults kept them in line.

45. Thorne's descriptions are of sociologists' representations of youth, but these extend to broader representations as well. Thorne, "Re-visioning Women," 1987.

46. For academic work, see Angela McRobbie's work on girls wanting to stay/act young as a response to the dangers of contemporary culture, such as AIDS and the sexual abuse of women, "Shut Up And Dance: Youth Culture And Changing Modes Of Femininity," in *Postmodernism And Popular Culture*, ed. Angela McRobbie (London: Routledge, 1994). For popular representations addressing why youth are altering, if not refusing, traditional markers of adulthood, see *Time*'s series of articles (2005).

CHAPTER 4. FOUNDING DOCUMENTS, FOUNDING FEMINISM

Gina, interview with author, September 25, 1998.

1. Gina, 1998.

2. James Paul Gee, *What Video Games Have to Teach Us About Literacy and Learning* (New York: Palgrave Macmillan, 2003).

3. Nancy Whittier, *Feminist Generations: The Persistence of the Radical Women's Movement* (Philadelphia, PA: Temple University Press, 1995). While appreciating Whittier's work to historicize feminist activism, I join Leslie Heywood and Jennifer Drake in noting that Whittier's general framework, like the "waves" metaphor, problematically diminishes the impact of women-of-color who were so influential to the political generation many call third-wave. See Leslie Heywood and Jennifer Drake, eds., *Third Wave Agenda: Being Feminist, Doing Feminism* (Minneapolis: University of Minnesota Press, 1997), 19 (footnote 19).

4. Rebecca Munford, "'Wake Up and Smell the Lip Gloss': Gender, Generation, and the (A)politics of Girl Power," in *Third Wave Feminism: A Critical Exploration*, eds. Stacey Gillis, Gillian Howie, and Rebecca Munford (New York: Palgrave Macmillan, 2004), 142–153.

5. Williams, Raymond, *Problems in Materialism and Culture* (London: Verso, 1980).

6. Clearly, many legislative victories did indeed codify changes, and the equality sought by ERA was often enshrined by Supreme Court cases, citing equality clauses codified in Title VII. Even so, ERA represents the face of this generation's hopes, both those met and those unrealized.

7. See, for example, Hazel Carby, "White Women Listen! Black Feminism and the Boundaries of Sisterhood," in *The Empire Strikes Back: Race and Racism in 70s Britain*, ed. Centre for Contemporary Cultural Studies (London: Hutchison, 1982), 212–35; Bonnie Thornton Dill, "Race, Class, And Gender: Prospects

For An All-Inclusive Sisterhood," *Feminist Studies* 9, no.1 (1983): 131–50; Cherrie Moraga and Gloria Anzaldua, *This Bridge Called My Back: Writings By Radical Women Of Color* (Watertown, MA: Persephone, 1981); Katheryn M. Fong, "Feminism Is Fine, But What's It Done for Asia America?", *Bridge: An Asian American Perspective* 6, no. 1 (1978): 21–22; Alma M. Garcia, "The Development Of Chicana Feminist Discourse, 1970–1980," *Gender and Society* 3, no. 2 (1989): 217–238.

    8. Myra Marx Ferree and Beth B. Hess, *Controversy And Coalition: The New Feminist Movement Across Four Decades Of Change* (New York: Routledge, 2000).

    9. Misha Kavka, "Introduction," in *Feminist Consequences: Theory For The New Century*, eds. Elisabeth Bronfen and Misha Kavka (New York: Columbia University Press, 2001), ix–xxvi.

    10. Susan Faludi, *Backlash: The Undeclared War Against American Women* (New York: Crown, 1991).

    11. Feminist victories were also evident in international arenas as well. For example, the 1995 United Nations-sponsored Beijing Conference sparked hope for national and international feminist activism. The fact that participation in Non Governmental Organizations (NGOs)—sites outside the male-dominated United Nations—increased more than tenfold from those who attended the 1985 Nairobi Forward-looking Strategies for the Advancement of Women Conference highlighted the increasing role women and women's issues played in local and international activism. "NGOs score victories at Beijing Women's Conference," *Interaction: American Council for Voluntary International Action*, http://www.interaction.org/library/mdbeiji1.html (May 26, 1996) [cited June 2, 2004].

    12. U.S. third world feminists during the second-wave foregrounded these issues of multiplicity, which became foundational for third-wave feminists.

    13. The label "post-feminist" itself means different things to different groups. For some, postfeminist means the work of feminism is over while for others postfeminism implies a feminism based on poststructuralist, postmodern, or postcolonial theories. "Do-Me feminist" is an oft-cited term taken from Tad Friend's (1994) *Esquire* article, "Yes," *Esquire Magazine for Men* 121, no. 2: 48–57.

    14. For a representation of feminist activism at the turn of the century, see Vivien Labaton and Dawn Lundy Martin, eds., *The Fire This Time: Young Activists And The New Feminism* (New York: Anchor Books, 2004).

    15. Jennifer Baumgardner and Amy Richards, *Manifesta: Young Women, Feminism, and the Future* (New York: Farrar, Straus and Giroux, 2000), 17.

    16. Mary Hawkesworth, "The Semiotics Of Premature Burial: Feminism In A Postfeminist Age," *Signs: Journal Of Women In Culture And Society* 29, no. 4: 962–963.

    17. In fact, many feminist organizations used the phrases "girls' and women's empowerment" as a way to avoid the feminist label. While understanding and supporting the ideas behind this move, third-wave feminist Rebecca Walker argues that moves like this leave this generation of feminists with a movement without a name; see Rebecca Walker, "Foreword : We Are Using This Power To Resist," in *The Fire This Time: Young Activists and The New Feminism*, eds. Vivien Labaton and Dawn Lundy Martin (New York: Anchor Books, 2004), xiv.

18. Rebecca Walker, *To Be Real: Telling the Truth and Changing the Face of Feminism* (New York: Anchor, 1995), xxxii–xxxiii.

19. Baumgarden and Richards, *Manifesta*, 36.

20. Walker, "Foreward," 2004, xiv.

21. See Stephen Doheny-Farina, "Writing in an Emerging Organization: An Ethnographic Study," *Written Communication* 3, no. 2 (1986): 158–185; and Stephen Doheny-Farina, "Creating a Text/Creating a Company: The Role of a Text in the Rise and Decline of a New Organization," in *Textual Dynamics of the Professions: Historical and Professional Studies of Writing in Professional Communities*, eds. Charles Bazerman and James Paradis (Madison: University of Wisconsin Press, 1991), 306–335.

22. Aimee, Field Notes, February 15, 1999.

23. See Alison M. Jaggar, *Feminist Politics and Human Nature* (Totowa, NJ: Rowman & Littlefield, 1983).

24. GirlZone, Girl's Best Friend Foundation grant application.

25. Ibid., 3–4.

26. Aimee, interview with author, May 26, 2000.

27. GirlZone, Girl's Best Friend Foundation grant application, 1998, 1; 2–3, 3, 3.

28. Ibid., 2.

29. Ibid., 4.

30. Ibid., 3.

31. According to the grant proposal, these "truisms" include discouraging girls' confidence, self-esteem, and competence and portraying women as "primarily submissive, polite, passive figures whose duty lies in supporting, rather than in doing" (Ibid., 3).

32. For a fuller discussion about misalignments within institutional contexts, see Michael Cole and Yrjo Engestrom, "A Cultural-Historical Approach to Distributed Cognition," in *Distributed Cognitions: Psychological and Educational Considerations*, ed. Gavriel Salomon (New York: Cambridge University Press, 1993).

33. Gina, September 1998.

34. Ibid.

35. Aimee, interview by author, November 6, 1998.

36. Gina, 1998.

37. Shauna Pomerantz, "Grinding the Concrete (Third) Wave," *Sexing the Political: A Journal of Third Wave Feminists on Sexuality* 2, no. 2 (2002), paragraphs 4–6, http://www.iiav.nl/ezines/web/SexingThePolitical/2002/No2.PDF.

38. As is clear throughout *Girls, Feminism, and Grassroots Literacies*, GirlZone would continually struggle to determine how best to balance their implicit and explicit feminist frameworks, but increasingly organizers would locate their desired feminist social competencies within third-wave frames.

39. Gunther Kress, *Literacy in the New Media Age* (New York: Routledge, 2003).

40. See American Association of University Women (AAUW), "Hostile Hallways: Bullying, Teasing, And Sexual Harassment In School," http://www.aauw.org/research/girls_education/hostile.cfm; American Association of University Women

(AAUW), *Hostile Hallways: The AAUW Survey on Sexual Harassment in America's Schools* (Washington, DC: AAUW Educational Foundation, 1993).

41. In follow-up interviews after Aimee and Gina read my analysis, Aimee noted that she struggled with which discourse to use and thought this should be discussed by other GirlZone facilitators, such as the Steering Committee, whenever that became operational. Until then, Aimee felt pressed by GirlZone's daily operating activities, so she anticipated continuing with these safer, coded descriptions (interview by author, August 1, 1999).

42. Gina, Field Notes, February 15, 1999. Gina's comment could be read as a jab at academia and even a jab at me, an academic. In practice, however, it did not feel that way, especially since Gina aligned me with the activists doing the feminist work at GirlZone. Rather, for Gina, who thought of herself as a doer and not a writer or a talker, feminism is *action*. In the feminist academic-activist debates so acrimonious in the 1980 and early 1990s, debates essentially among second-wave cohorts, Gina's assessment reflects the view that academic feminists spend too much time talking/writing and too little time doing the work of feminist activism.

43. GirlZone, Girl's Best Friend Foundation grant application, 1999, p. 5–6.

44. Gina, 1998.

45. Wilma Mankiller, "Coda," in *The Fire This Time*, 291.

46. For more on feminist analyses of the "role of the critic," see Elspeth Probyn, *Sexing the Self: Gendered Positions in Cultural Studies* (London: Routledge, 1993).

47. Aimee, 1998.

48. GirlZone, Girl's Best Friend Foundation grant application, 1998, p. 2.

49. For a range of third-wave insider perspectives on the fashion industry, see "How does a supermodel do feminism? An interview with Veronica Webb" in Rebecca Walker, "Being Real: An Introduction," in *To Be Real: Telling the Truth and Changing the Face of Feminism*, ed. Rebecca Walker (New York: Anchor Books, 1995), 209–218; and Tali Edut, with Dyann Logwood and Ophira Edut, "*HUES* Magazine: The Making of a Movement," in *Third Wave Agenda: Being Feminist, Doing Feminism*, eds. Heywood and Drake, 83–98 (Minneapolis, MN: University of Minnesota Press, 1997).

50. See chapter 6 for more about GirlZone participants' engagement with what Gunther Kress calls the "practices of design." Kress, *Literacy in The New Media Age* (New York: Routledge, 2003).

51. Margaret J. Finders, *Just Girls: Hidden Literacies and Life in Junior High* (New York: Teachers College Press, 1997).

52. The role that fashion magazines play in girls' identities has been explored in several oft cited texts, perhaps most notably throughout Angela McRobbie's career. Angela McRobbie, *Feminism And Youth Culture: From "Jackie" To "Just Seventeen"* (Boston, MA: Unwin Hyman, 1991).

CHAPTER 5. CIRCULATIONS OF A FEMINIST PEDAGOGY

Ayleen, *RadioGirl*, WEFT, July 4, 1999.

1. The participants of RadioGirl call themselves RadioGirls. For clarity and to avoid excessive repetition, "RG" will refer to the radio program and "RadioGirls" to the participants.

2. On a day-to-day basis RG and GirlZone operated independently, but in practice RG shared many of GirlZone's participants, such as Sophia, Cyan, and Ayleen, and practices, such as the pedagogies described in this chapter.

3. See chapter 4 for discussion of anti- and postfeminist discourses that alternatively malign feminisms and paint them as irrelevant.

4. Henry A. Giroux, "Teen Girls' Resistance and the Disappearing Social in *Ghost World*," *The Review of Education, Pedagogy, and Cultural Studies* 24 (2002): 283–304.

5. See Anita Harris, "Revisiting Bedroom Culture: New Spaces for Young Women's Politics," *Hecate* 27, no. 1 (2001): 128–139.

6. James Paul Gee, *What Video Games Have to Teach Us About Learning and Literacy* (New York: Palgrave Macmillan, 2003), 143.

7. Harris, "Revisiting Bedroom Culture."

8. Jessica K. Taft, "Girl Power Politics: Barriers and Organization Resistance," in *All about the Girl: Culture, Power, and Identity*, ed. Anita Harris (New York: Routledge, 2004), 69–78.

9. Taft, "Girl Power Politics," p. 71.

10. Ibid., p. 69.

11. For examples of how people in community spaces use literate activities to help them alter their social identities, see Anne Ruggles Gere, *Intimate Practices: Literacy and Cultural Work in U.S. Women's Clubs, 1880–1920* (Urbana, IL: University of Illinois Press, 1997).

12. American Association of University Women, *Under the Microscope: A Decade of Gender Equity Projects in the Sciences* (Washington, DC: AAUW Educational Foundation, 2004) (available online at http://www.aauw.org/research/microscope.cfm); Katherine Darke, Beatriz Clewell, and Ruta Sevo, "Meeting the Challenge: The Impact of the National Science Foundation's Program for Women and Girls," *The Journal of Women and Minorities in Science and Engineering* 8, no. 3–4: 286–287.

13. These organizations could be loosely associated with the turn of the century youthquake. See chapter 2 for more on this youthquake.

14. Bikes Not Bombs, "Bikes Not Bombs Youth Services," http://www.bikesnotbombs.org/youth-prog.htm (accessed December 9, 2005).

15. The Freechild Project. "Home." http://www.freechild.org/index.htm (accessed December 9, 2005).

16. Chapter 3 points out that the degree to which any marginalized group can speak for themselves is at best debatable. As this chapter explores, however, that hardly means these marginalized groups should accept dominant representations of them.

17. Specifically, Ayleen feared she would force girls to "talk about gay, lesbian, transgender issues" and "scrutinize makeup and fashions." Ayleen, interview with author, May 26, 1999.

18. Ayleen, *RadioGirl* (Pledge Drive), WEFT, October 1998.

19. Ibid.

20. GirlZone, Grant Proposal to Girls' Best Friend Foundation, 1998, 6.

21. Miriam, *Best of RadioGirl*, WEFT, August 29, 1999.

22. *RadioGirl*, WEFT, January 31, 1999.

23. *RadioGirl*, WEFT, December, 6 1998.

24. Field Notes, March 22, 1999.

25. Ayleen, 1999.

26. Sophia, interview with author, July 10, 2000.

27. See Congressional Commission on the Advancement of Women and Minorities in Science, Engineering and Technology Development (CAWMSET), *Land of Plenty: Diversity as America's Competitive Edge in Science, Engineering and* Technology (Arlington, VA: September 1, 2000), 59. Drawn from Shireen Lee, "The New Girls Network: Women Technology, and Feminism," in *The Fire This Time: Young Activists and the New Feminism*, eds. Vivien Labaton and Dawn Lundy Martin (New York: Anchor Books, 2004): 89.

28. American Association of University Women (AAUW), "Tech Savvy: Educating Girls in the New Computer Age" (Washington, DC: AAUW Educational Foundation, 2000) (available on-line at http://www.aauw.org/research/girls_education/techsavvy.cfm).

29. Heidi, *RadioGirl*, WEFT, August 29, 1999.

30. Sophia, interview with author, July 10, 2000.

31. Sophia had recently attended the local public school and a local private school; she had been home-schooled (what she calls "unschooled"), and, eventually found the School for Designing Society (SDS) where she saw Heidi most weeks. Sophia prefers the term "unschoolers" to home schooled, because she associates school with worksheets while she associates her unschooling with projects where she can learn more about what she thinks and has to learn less what the school thinks.

32. Sophia, interview with author, July 10, 2000.

33. Ibid.

34. For foundational third wave texts, see: Barbara Findlen, ed., *Listen Up: Voices from the Next Feminist Generation* (Seattle, WA: Seal, 2002/1995); Rebecca Walker, ed., *To be Real: Telling the Truth and Changing the Face of Feminism* (New York: Anchor Books, 1995); Leslie Heywood and Jennifer Drake, eds., *Third wave agenda: Being feminist, Doing Feminism* (Minneapolis, MN: University of Minnesota Press, 1997); Jennifer Baumgardner and Amy Richards. *Manifesta: Young Women, Feminism, and the Future* (New York: Farrar, Straus & Giroux, 2000). For more recent work, see: Stacy Gillis, Gillian Howe, and Rebecca Munford, *Third Wave Feminism* (New York: Palmgrave, 2004). For recent work addressing activism, see: Vivien Labaton and Martin Dawn Lundy, *The Fire This Time: Young Activists and the New Feminism* (New York: Anchor Books, 2004); and Jennifer Baumgardner and Amy Richards, *Grassroots: A Field Guide for Feminist Activism* (New York: Farrar, Straus & Giroux, 2005).

35. Although third-wave feminists give little heed to classrooms, they give a nod to extracurricular spaces. For an example on the college level, see Sarah Boonin, "Please—Stop Thinking about Tomorrow: Building a Feminist Movement on College Campuses for Today," in *Catching a Wave: Reclaiming Feminism for the 21st Century*, eds. Rory Dicker and Alison Piepmeier (Boston, MA: Northeastern Univerty Press, 2003), 138–156. For an example on the high school level, see Erica Gilbert-Levin, "Class Feminist," in *Listen up: Voices from the next feminist generation*, 2d ed., ed. Barbara Findlen (Seattle, WA: Seal, 2002), 165–172.

36. This can be seen in the second-wave focus on equal access to education and opportunities (e.g., any number of AAUW studies) as well as through feminists cited as direct influences on this movement's attention to multiplicity, hybridity and

fluidity. For example, bell hooks, *Teaching to Transgress: Education as the Practice of Freedom* (New York: Routledge, 1994).

37. Yancey calls for composition research in increasingly diverse settings, such as in the community, in cyberspace, and in workplaces. Composition's new methods and sites of research, according to Gesa E. Kirsch, are "nothing short of a redefinition, a reshaping, a transformation of our discipline." As the field of composition studies reimagines itself, there are dangers to shifting attention toward how people use writing beyond the classroom. As Todd Taylor argues, universities value compositionists because we are "educating an increasingly heterogeneous population with vast differences in educational and cultural backgrounds." In an increasingly globalized world, this educational project is all the more necessary. If compositionists shift away from that goal, we may lose the university clout that has helped us increase the number composition job postings on the MLA list, develop PhD programs, and create free-standing writing programs with vertical curriculum. Beyond the material institutional benefits, the classroom has its research benefits. Not only is there clear institutional backing, as Todd Taylor notes, but also ready-to-hand literate artifacts, and, despite some recent Internal Review Board issues, a readily accessed research site. And yet, there are costs to *not* changing, most significantly of the field becoming irrelevant. This irrelevance is not about the education of today's heterogeneous students; that, I argue, is a major institutional role composition studies plays. Rather, the problem is how or what we are educating them for. Kathleen Blake Yancey, "Made Not Only in Words: Composition in a New Key," *College Composition and Communication 56*, no. 2 (2004): 297–328; Gesa E. Kirsch, "Ethics and the future of composition research," in *Composition Studies in the New Millenium: Rereading the Past, Rewriting the Future*, ed. Lynn Z. Bloom, Donald A. Daiker, and Edward M. White (Carbondale, IL; Southern Illinois University Press, 2003), 131; Todd Taylor, "A Methodology of Our Own," in Bloom et al, 2003, 145.

38. To examine these tensions, this section focuses on RG programs written about in the local media and the ones that were prerecorded (e.g., July 4, 1999; August 28, 1999). The media presentations provided girls with a depiction of how others made sense of RadioGirls. Prerecorded programs allowed for more than one take and involved an atypical amount of forethought—girls did less off-the-cuff commentary and more written-out preparation. The structure of these shows, therefore, encouraged RadioGirls to be more reflective about their public presentation.

39. *The News-Gazette*, History Page. http:/www.news-gazette.com/service/history (accessed June 15, 2006).

40. Faith Swords. "These Girls Rock: Nothin' Fazes Feaze," *The News-Gazette* (Champaign, IL), October 15, 1998, B–8.

41. Feaze, "Once So Sweet and Innocent" on *Feaze: Morning Wood* (Urbana, IL: Mud Records, 1999).

42. See chapter 6 for analysis of the complicated relationships between feminist and capitalistic constructions of girls.

43. Redeye Catalogue. http://www.redeyeusa.com/item.php?item_num=CD-MUD–039 (accessed May 24, 2006).

44. In fact, photos from their *Feaze: Morning Wood* CD show band members acting as role models, as when they sign autographs for girls, including Cyan from GirlZone.

45. While I, too, refer to participants by their first name, the naming practices in my research are the same all GirlZone participants regardless of their age.

46. The organizers repeatedly struggled with this issue. Early on, for example, Aimee believed all press was good press. Later, however, the organizers revisited this, believing they needed to highlight GirlZone's feminist agendas.

47. Miriam, "Want to be on the Air? YOU GO GIRLS: WEFT Turns over Radio Station for Kids' Show Every Other Sunday," *The News-Gazette* (Champaign, IL) February 11, 1998, B–8.

48. Ayleen, 1999.

49. Miriam, B–8.

50. In these varying roles, speakers demonstrate their alignment to what they are saying. And yet, assessing a girls' alignment based on the text she chose is too simple. For example, reading the weather might indicate girls imagining themselves as meteorologists, as active in science, or as meaning makers and not merely meaning readers. More typically, however, girls chose to read the weather report because they were nervous and felt they could read a short text with words they were likely to know. In any assessment, reading the weather report did not indicate a Radio-Girl's taking-up feminist, activist social identities in the same way that reading a two-line "plug" for GirlZone would or that reading an independently researched and written report about women role models in Champaign-Urbana might.

51. Erving Goffman, *Forms of Talk* (Philadelphia, PA: University of Pennsylvania Press, 1981), 144. In social interactions, Goffman describes three main roles speakers can hold. In between animators and principals are "authors," those who actively "selected the sentiments that are being expressed and the words in which they are encoded."

52. Ibid.

53. Clearly "shock jocks" offer an alternative model of radio, and Radio-Girls themselves played with several radio formats (e.g., radio plays, op-ed pieces, news reports). In none of these cases, however, did they aspire to the shock jock genre; indeed, they generally viewed themselves as journalists, often of underreported stories, as seemed the case in this instance.

54. I could not determine whether Miriam was aware of her audience. In my conversations with her, Miriam gave vague answers about her sense of audience (Field Notes, June 27, 1999), but on-air she noted she was aware of her RG audience: "For ideas, I try to do current topics and topics that I think might interest other teenagers and kids," *Best of RadioGirl*, WEFT, August 29, 1999. Her sense of audience for her newspaper reporting seemed similar.

55. Although these representations came from GirlZone's grant proposal to the Girl's Best Friend foundation, Ayleen echoed similar sentiments. Ayleen, 1999.

56. Field Notes, May 23, 1999.

57. RadioGirl, WEFT, January 31, 1999.

58. RadioGirls were aware (if abstractly) that there were hundreds of people listening. Ayleen, interview with author, 1999.

59. *WEFT Revue*, Jan–Feb 1999, 2.

60. *RadioGirl* (Pledge Drive), WEFT, October 1998.

61. Melissa Mitchell, "Radio Girl: Giving Voices to Youths," *WEFT Revue*, Jan–Feb 1999, 3.

62. *RadioGirl*, WEFT, August 29, 1999.

63. This emphasis on equality locates (implicitly at least) RadioGirls within a gender binary. Alternatively, this line can be read as comparing girls to adults. Based on Mudita and Caley's apparent lack of adult responsibilities and their frequent talk of boys, it seems the former.

64. Sophia, interview with author, July, 10, 2000.

CHAPTER 6. REDESIGNING GIRLS' IMAGE STORES

Joni, interview with author, 17 January 2003.

1. Girls Inc. "Girls Inc. Media Literacy," Posted February 1, 2002, http://www.girlsinc.org/ic/ page.php?id=1.2.3

2. New London Group, "A Pedagogy of Multiliteracies: Designing Social Futures," *Harvard Educational Review* 66, no.1 (1996): 70.

3. "Brand Strategy Briefing: No More Growing Pains," *Brand Strategy*, February 7, 2005. Lexis-Nexis.

4. Angela McRobbie, "Young Women and the Consumer Citizenship: The Danger of Too Much Pleasure," paper delivered as part of the AHRC Cultures of Consumption Programme, 2004, para 1, http://www.goldsmiths.ac.uk/departments/media-communications/staff/mcrobbie.php (accessed October 17, 2005).

5. Anne Haas Dyson, *Writing Superheroes: Contemporary Childhood, Popular Culture, and Classroom Literacy* (New York: Teachers College Press, 1997). For this term, Dyson draws on Marina Warner, *From the Beast to the Blonde: On Fairy Tales and Their Tellers* (London: Chatto & Windus, 1994).

6. Dyson, *Writing Suprerheroes* (1997), 143–144.

7. Research into girls and women's reading practices as well as their participation with fan culture highlights the sophisticated ways women and girls have negotiated popular representations of them. Perhaps the most central recent work on reading practices is Janice A. Radway, *Reading the Romance: Women, Patriarch, and Popular Literature* (Chapel Hill, NC: University of North Carolina Press, 1984). The fan culture literature is extensive, including L.E. Lewis, ed., *Adoring Audience: Fan Culture and Popular Media* (London: Routledge, 1992); for girls, see, any number of articles by Angela McRobbie. For a recent example of research on Spice Girl fan culture, see Bettina Fritzsch, "Spice Strategies: Pop Feminist and Other Empowerments in Girl Culture," in *All about the Girl: Culture, Power, and Identity*, ed. Anita Harris (New York: Routledge, 2004), 155–162.

8. Gina, interview with author, September 25, 1998.

9. Aaron, the creator of the logo, called the logo the "funky," "celebratory," "youthful," "visual identity" of the Fests. Aaron, interview with author, December 20, 2002.

10. For a selection of Amazon's Che shirts, see http://www.amazon.com/gp/search//104-2613468-0829540?&node=1036682&keywords=che%20shirts (accessed July 23, 2006). For a recent article describing the commodification of Che Guevera, see David Segal, "The Che Cachet: An Exhibition Traces How the Marxist Revolutionary's Photo Inspired an Army of Capitalists," *The Washington Post*, February 7, 2006. C01 http://www.washingtonpost.com/wp-dyn/content/article/2006/02/06/AR2006020601950.html?sub=AR (accessed July 23, 2006)

11. Now that more women are marrying later, having children later, and working outside the home, they see themselves less in the traditional roles of mothers and caregivers, within a network of responsibility for others, and more in the roles of individuals with increased disposable income. These facts illustrate how young women and girls (of a certain economic class) are more fully embracing the identity of an economic actor, buying material goods, and pursuing pleasure. As citizens, young women are voting less within women's historic focus on family, education, and welfare concerns and more with an eye toward themselves as individuals with economic buying power. See Angela McRobbie, "Shut Up and Dance: Youth Culture and Changing Modes of Femininity," in *Feminism and Cultural Studies*, ed. Morgan Shiach (Oxford: Oxford University Press, 1994), 65–88.

12. Susan Douglass, *Where the Girls Are: Growing Up Female in the Mass Media* (New York: Random House, 1995), 260, 268, quoted in "Introduction," in *Third Wave Agenda: Being Feminist, Doing Feminism*, eds. Leslie Heywood and Jennifer Drake (Minneapolis, MN: University of Minnesota Press, 1997).

13. Frequently, these media outlets converge, bombarding tweens with an ever-changing expert of the moment. For example, Hilary Duff graces the cover of untold teen magazines, is a musician and a movie star, and has teamed up with Mattel to brand Barbie's Fashion Fever Barbie Dolls.

14. Rachel Russell and Melissa Tyler, "Thank Heaven for Little Girls: 'Girl Heaven' and the Commercial Context of Feminine Childhood," *Sociology* 36, no. 3 (2002): 625. For support, Russell and Tyler draw on Jill Brooke. "Girl Power," *Adweek* 39, no. 5 (1998): 18–19; Joanne Cleaver, "Girl Power," *Working Woman* 24 no. 9 (1999): 14.

15. Russell and Tyler, "Thank Heaven for Little Girls," 2002.

16. Victoria Carrington, "I'm in a Bad Mood. Let's go Shopping": Interactive Dolls, Consumer Culture and a 'Glocalized' Model of Literacy," *Journal of Early Childhood Literacy* 3, no. 1 (2003): 89.

17. Ibid., 90.

18. See chapter 1 for more on these high profiles examples.

19. The pervasiveness of this practice was highlighted when teen breast implants became the "hot topic" of the morning television shows. See, for example, "Breast Implants: High School Graduation Gifts?" *Good Morning America*, American Broadcasting Company, June 15, 2004.

20. Kerry Gold, "Sex Sells Tween Fashion," *Vancouver Sun*, June 19, 2004, D4.

21. Benoit Denizet-Lewis, "Friends, Friends with Benefits and the Benefits of the Local Mall," *The New York Times Magazine* (May 30, 2005): 30.

22. Russell and Tyler, "Thank Heaven for Little Girls," 2002.

23. Monikers that highlight the RiotGrrrls influence on punk music, zines, and cyberspace include: grrrls, grrls, gURLs. For more, see Kathy Bail's early DIY feminist collection. Kathy Bail, ed. *DIY Feminism* (Sydney, Australia: Allen & Unwin, 1996).

24. Jennifer Bleyer, "Cut-and-Paste Revolution: Notes from the Girl Zine Explosion," *The Fire This Time: Young Activists and the New Feminism*, ed. Vivien Labaton and Dawn Lundy Martin (New York: Anchor Books, 2004), 51.

25. Quoted in Naomi Klein, *No Logo* (New York: Picador, 2000/2002), 114.

26. Aimee, *GirlZine*, 2000.

27. For an analysis of girls' "ette" status in pop culture, see Katha Pollit, "The Smurfette Principle," *New York Times Magazine* (April 7, 1991): 22.

28. Linda Hutcheon uses the term "complicetous critique" to make a similar critique. Her work has significantly shaped postmodern discussions about this concept. Linda Hutcheon. *The Politics of the Postmodern*, 2d ed. (London: Rutledge, 2002).

29. See Angela McRobbie, *Feminism and Youth Culture*, 2d ed. (Basingstoke, Hampshire: Macmillan, 2000).

30. Increasingly television shows, such as *Girlfriends* (1999–present), or movies, such as *How Stella Got Her Groove Back* (1998) or *Waiting to Exhale* (1995), took up similar representations with African-American women.

31. Field Notes, November 21, 1998; Field Notes, December 5, 1998.

32. Catherine Driscoll, "Girl Culture, Revenge and Global Capitalism: Cybergirls, Riot Grrrls, Spice Girls," *Australian Feminist Studies* 14, no. 2 (1999): 173–193.

33. Driscoll, "Girl Culture," 186.

34. Aimee, interview with author, August 22, 2005.

35. Gunther Kress, *Literacy in the New Media Age* (New York: Routledge, 2003). While accurately critiqued for making this shift seem too rigid, as Kress himself acknowledges, looser versions of Kress' ideas have found parallels in diverse quarters throughout writing studies. See the March 2005 special edition of *Computers & Composition* (22, no. 1) devoted to the impact Gunther Kress has had on this field.

36. Culture jamming and ad busting redesign a company's own messages while still using the company's communication devices to send a subversive message that counters the intended message. For example, "citizen artists" would add the word "Kids" to a Camel cigarette bulletin board to highlight how cigarette companies target youth in their advertising—a message Camel cigarettes would not officially endorse. See, Klein, *No Logo*, 2000/2002, with particular attention to "Culture Jamming," 278–309, especially the quote on 290.

37. The logo changed slightly over the years, primarily to ensure the organizers were adhering to copyright laws. For example, the 2003 logo more dramatically changes the hair so that it is unlike any Powerpuff Girl, though the allusion is still present.

38. For examples of such definitions, see Jay Lemke, "Multimedia Genres in Science: Visual and Verbal Semiotics in Scientific Text," in *Reading Science: Critical and Functional Perspectives of Science*, ed. J. R. Martin (London: Routledge, 1998), 87–113; and Gunther Kress and Theo van Leeuwen, *Reading Images: The Grammar of Visual Design* (London: Routledge, 1996).

39. According to Jennifer Baumgarden and Amy Richards, "girlies" are generally younger feminists seeking to revalue typically feminine, often youthful, accoutrements. Jennifer Baumgarden and Amy Richards, *Manifesta: Young Women, Feminism, and the Future* (New York: Farrar, Straus and Giroux, 2000).

40. Joni, 2003.

41. Kress, *Literacy in New Media Age*, 2003.

42. At GirlZone, men were welcomed to help in many behind-the-scenes ways (e.g., setting up workshops, though not leading them). This was even more the case at GrrrlFests, such as when Aaron agreed to do the logo. Furthermore,

while GrrrlFests workshops were female only, some musical showcases and Fest openings were for all GrrrlFest supporters, regardless of gender. As Aimee described in regard to the musical line-up, GrrrlFest was a local, feminist project and she wanted to send out "props" to support local and female bands. Aimee, "Support those home-grown and female bands," GrrrlFest 2003 website (accessed February 2, 2004).

43. Aaron, 2002.

44. Mikhail M. Bakhtin, *The Dialogic Imagination*, ed. Michael Holquist and trans. Carlyn Emerson and Michael Holquist (Austin: University of Texas Press, 1981).

45. Aimee, interview with author, December 30, 2002.

46. Everyday activism at GrrrlFest. 2003 GrrrlFest webpage (accessed September 9, 2003).

47. *RadioGirl*, WEFT, September 7, 2002.

48. Ibid.

49. For a similar description of this practice, see Kevin Leander's work on "identity artifacts"—that is, as "any instrument (material tool, embodied space, text, discourse, etc.) that mediates identity-shaping activity." Kevin M. Leander, "Locating Latanya: The Situated Production of Identity Artifacts in Classroom Interaction," *Research in the Teaching of English* 37, no. 2 (2002): 201.

50. Rebecca C. Hains, "Power(puff) Feminism: *The Powerpuff Girls*" (n.d.). Hains drew on the following sources: For information on *TV Guide*, "Briefs: Reed Business Information." *Multichannel News*, June 19, 2000, Business Source Premier. For information on viewers, see L. Moss, "'Powerpuff' quarter, *Multichannel News*, 21, no. 4, Business Source Premier.

51. Aimee, interview with author, December 30, 2002.

52. Despite the logo's excising of sexuality, the workshops provided an expanded format where organizers felt more comfortable addressing issues of sexuality both directly (e.g., workshops led by workers in the sex industry) and indirectly (e.g., discussions of fashion or characters in books). In this space, organizers could take up the doubleness of sexuality that RiotGrrrls explore, exposing, for example, girls' vulnerability at being sexualized and abused as well as girls' pleasure and power in their own sexuality. Like the dilemmas surrounding the GirlZone fashion workshops (see chapter 4), organizers chose to address sexuality within a timeframe that allowed more extended discussions.

53. For more on Sophia, see chapters 2 and 5.

54. Sophia, interview with author, July 10, 2000.

55. Sophia, interview with author, January 20, 2003.

56. Ibid.

57. Sophia, 2000.

58. This number reflects the GrrrlFest and GirlZone T-shirts sold over GirlZone's institutional life span. Aimee, e-mail to author, "Re: random question," February 20, 2006.

59. Joni, 2003.

60. Ibid.

61. Aimee, 2002.

CHAPTER 7. THE ECONOMICS OF ACTIVISM

Aimee, interview with author, December 30, 2002.

1. Two years after the GirlZone closed, Aimee became loosely involved with Portland's Rock Girl Camp in New York City, a highly successful activity that combined music business' desire for both good public relations and access to the next "big thing" with grassroots feminist activism's attention to girls. Girl-Zone, however, was not in an urban area, and Champaign-Urbana had few local businesses interested in investing in girls' organizations.

2. Eileen Green and Laurie Cohen, "Women's Business": Are Women Entrepreneurs Breaking New Ground or Simply Balancing the Demands of 'Women's Work' in a New Way?" *Journal of Gender Studies* 4, no. 3 (1995): 297–314.

3. Elaine Showalter, "Stop Whining, Just Do It. The Women's Movement Will Not Come Again, Warns One of Its Leading Lights, Elaine Showalter. But Women Could Improve Their Lot by Turning Entrepreneurial," *The Financial Times Limited*, October 18, 2003, 23.

4. Ibid.

5. Teresa Ebert, "(Untimely) Critiques for a Red Feminism." In *Post-ality: Marxism and Postmodernis*, eds. M. Zavardeh, Teresa Ebert and D. Morton. (Washington, DC: Maisonneuve Press, 1995), http://www.marxists.org/reference/subject/philosophy/works/us/ebert.htm, para 9 (accessed September 18, 2005).

6. J. Gregory Dees, "Social Entrepreneurs and Education," *Current Issues in Comparative Education* 8, no. 1 (2005): 53.

7. For how this impacts education, see the special issue of *Current Issues in Comparative Education* on social entrepreneurs, with particular attention to the review essay, by Maria Humpries and Suaznne Grant "Social Enterprise and Re-Civilization of Human Endeavors: Re-Socializing the Market Metaphor or Encroaching Colonization of the Lifeworld?" *Current Issues in Comparative Education* 8, no. 1 (2005): 41–50.

8. Dorothy Smith, *The Conceptual Practices of Power: A Feminist Sociology of Knowledge* (Boston, MA: Northeastern University Press, 1990).

9. Deborah Brandt, *Literacy in American Lives* (Cambridge, UK: Cambridge University Press, 2001).

10. Of course, the infusion of government monies and sponsorship of local activism was not new in the 1960s. While generally referred to as a relief program or perhaps as national service, the Civilian Conservation Corps (CCC) (1933–1942) could also be thought of as the government's largest foray into community activism. The CCC shaped how people thought about being a citizen and about the reciprocal relationship between individuals and the government.

11. For an extended example of how Republican administrations saw these programs as "Left" organizations that need to be defunded, see Kim Bobo, Jackie Kendall and Steve M, *Organizing for Social Change: Midwest Academy Manual for Activists*, 3d ed. (Santa Anna, CA: Seven Locks Press, 2001), 277.

12. Nancy A. Naples, "Women's Community Activism: Exploring the Dynamics of Politicization and Diversity," in *Community Activism and Feminist Politics: Organizing Across Race, Class, and Gender*, ed. Nancy A. Naples (New York: Routledge, 1998), 327–349.

13. Myra Marx Ferree and Beth Hess, *Controversy and Coalition: The New Women's Movement Across Three Decades of Change*, 3d ed. (New York: Routledge, 2000).

14. For a personal reflection on the pros and cons of this process, see Nancy A. Hewett, "The Glass Tower: Half Full or Half Empty?" in *Taking Back the Academy: History of Activism, History as Activism*, ed. J. Downs and J. Manion (New York: Routledge, 2004), 93–102.

15. Some argue that academic feminists more or less sold out their connections with community activism, creating an academic-activist split. Others argue that the institutionalization of women's studies was beneficial, ensuring feminism had a voice in a powerful social institution, reaching those who may be sympathetic to feminism but scared of the feminist label, and enabling activists' access to material resources that could help their causes in tangible and less tangible ways. For a range of arguments valuing women's studies, see Robyn Wiegman, *Women's Studies on its Own: A Next Wave Reader in Institutional Change* (Durham, NC: Duke University Press, 2002).

16. In addition to regional or community foundations, such as the Girl's Best Friend Foundation, there were national foundations focusing on girls and women, such as those affiliated with Sister Fund, *Ms.*, the National Organization for Women, the American Association of University Women, and The Third Wave Foundation.

17. Jung-Rim Kim. "The Answer to the Financial Needs of Women's Organizations?" *Common Concern* (March 2001), http://worldywca1.org/common_concern/mar2001/foundations.html (accessed January 15, 2005).

In her article, Kim draws on a *New York Times* article: K. S. Lombardi, "Mother and Daughters Raise Funds for Charity," *The New York Times* (May 2, 1999): 14WC, 6.

18. Stephen Lawrence, *The Foundation Center's 2002 Children and Youth Funding Update* (New York: Foundation Center, 2002).

19. Shirley Brice Heath and Milbrey W. McLaughlin, "Identity and Inner-City Youth," in *Identity and Inner-City Youth: Beyond Ethnicity and Gender*, ed. Shirley Brice Heath and Milbrey W. McLaughlin (New York: Teachers College Press, 1994), 1–12.

20. Mary S. Capek, *Women and Philanthropy: Old Stereotypes, New Challenges: Volume one: Women as Donors: Stereotypes, Common Sense, and Challenges* (Battle Creek, MI: The W. K. Kellogg Foundation, 1998a); ———, "*Women and Philanthropy: Old Stereotypes, New Challenges,*" vol. two: *Foundation Support for Women and Girls: "Special Interest" Funding or Effective Philanthropy?* (Battle Creek, MI: The W. K. Kellogg Foundation, 1998b); ———, *Women and Philanthropy: Old Stereotypes, New Challenges, vol. three. The Women's Funding Movement: Accomplishments and Challenges* (Battle Creek, MI: The W. K. Kellogg Foundation, 2001).

21. Capek cites various sources that address this issue, though none fully analyze if generic funding such as that focused on youth addresses or obscures female youth concerns proportionately. Capek cites: Women working in Philanthropy. *Doubled in a Decade, Yet Still far from Done: A Report on Awards Targeted to Women and Girls by Grantmakers in the Delaware Valley* (Philadelphia,

PA: Women Working in Philanthropy, 1990); M. Servantius. *Short Sighted: How Chicago-Area Grantmakers Can Apply a Gender Lens to See the Connections Between Social Problems and Women's Needs* (Chicago: Chicago Women in Philanthropy, 1992); C. V. Eberhart and J. Pratt, *Minnesota Philanthropy* (Arlington, VA: Feminist Majority Foundation, 1993); Michigan Women's Foundation, *Investing in Michigan Women* (Lansing, MI: The Michigan Women's Foundation, 1993); Molly Mead, *Worlds Apart: Missed Opportunities to Help Women and Girls* (Boston, MA: Women in Philanthropy/Boston: Women's Fund, 1994).

22. Molly Mead, *Why Such Low Funding for Programs for Women and Girls? Contrasting Views of Foundaiont Staff and Program Staff* (paper, 1997). Quoted in Capek, *Women and Phinadtropy* (2001), 6.

23. The Foundation Center keeps widely cited statistics. See, for example, E. H. Rich, ed., *Foundation Giving: Yearbook of Facts and Figures on Private, Corporate and Community Foundations* (New York: The Foundation Center, 1997). This statistic comes from the Foundation Center's Statistical Information Service, "Foundation Grants Designated for Special Population Groups, circa 2003" (FC Stats: The Foundation Center's Statistical Information Service, posted 2005) http://fdncenter.org/fd_stats/pdf/08_fund_pop/2003/16_03.pdr (accessed May 13, 2006).

24. According to reporter Erin Lukehart, GirlZone submitted 130 grants, receiving a few local and two national grants which provided GirlZone with seed money as well as the ability to encourage girls to explore technology and work with local businesses. Even acknowledging the odds against grassroots, girl-centered organizations in nonurban areas, Aimee commented in a radio interview that she found GirlZone's track record with grants and direct appeals to be "amazingly unsuccessful." Erin Lukehart, "GirlZone's Swan Song," *The Paper*, September 19, 2003. http://www.thepaperthewebsite.com/091903/girlzone%20 article6.aspk (accessed September 29, 2003); "'Good to Know' with Ondine Gross," WEFT Radio, October 13, 2003.

25. In chapter 4, I discussed how this grant proposal exposed the feminisms operating at GirlZone at its founding. In this chapter, I again use this foundational document but in this case I analyze how this grant proposal shaped organizers' practices in relation to their understandings of the economic viability of GirlZone.

26. Feminist sociologists Myra Marx Ferree and Beth B. Hess (2000) highlight the financial difficulties grassroots feminist organizations have when foundations provide seed money and then that initial sponsorship is withdrawn (e.g., services discontinue; organizations lose focus as they seek to match other funding possibilities). The history of GirlZone bears this out; yet this history also points out that at least sometimes the withdrawal of nonmaterial sponsorship is even more important.

27. Girl's Best Friend Foundation, "Guidelines" (Chicago: Girl's Best Friend Foundation, 1998), 2.

28. GirlZone follow-up Report to Girl's Best Friend Foundation, 1999.

29. For more on the proleptic power of this grant, see chapter 4.

30. United Way Of Champaign County, *Community Report 2004*, http://www.uwayhelps.org/resources/FINAL_annual_report.pdf (accessed May 9, 2006).

31. Aimee, 2002.

32. Jennifer Baumgarden and Amy Richards address this everyday aspect of activism as well as how activism can be integrated into everyday life economic realities. Despite this important move, which I applaud, I am troubled by their problematically individualistic focus of activism that diminishes the need for a more collective focus. Jennifer Baumgardner and Amy Richards. *Grassroots: A Field Guide for Feminist Activism* (New York: Farrar, Straus, and Giroux, 2005).

33. Aimee, personal communication, August 22, 2005.

34. "'Good to Know' with Ondine Gross"

35. Although organizers attempted other funding options (e.g., community solicitation letters and workshop fees), grant proposals were seen as the primary way to access the money needed for staff positions that could help make GirlZone institutionally viable. Years after GirlZone closed, Aimee commented that if she were to do GirlZone over again, she would focus instead on raising funds from the community (Personal communication, August 22, 2005).

36. Thomas James, "The Winnowing of Organizations," in *Identity and Inner-City Youth*, eds., Shirley Brice Heath and Milbrey W. McLaughlin, 187.

37. Of course, there are notable exceptions to this, such as the Ford Foundation's recent (2005) funding of "Difficult Dialogues Initiatives" on college campuses.

38. Capek, *Women and Philanthropy* (1998): vol. 2, 18.

39. Capek, *Old Stereotypes*, 2001.

40. What Capek calls "strategic rhetoric" nicely models what Michele deCerteau calls a "tactic," an art of the weak and not what he calls a "strategy," which deCerteau aligns with those in power. Michele deCerteau, *The Practice of Everyday Life*, (Berkeley, CA: University of California Press, 1984).

41. Deborah Mindry, "Nongovernmental Organizations, 'Grassroots,' and the Politics of Virtue," *Signs: Journal of Women in Culture and Society* 26, no. 4 (2001): 1187–1211.

42. Michelle Sidler, "Living in McJobdom: Third Wave Feminism and Class Inequity." in *Third Wave Agenda*, eds. Leslie Heywood and Jennifer Drake (Minneapolis: University of Minnesota Press, 1997), 33.

43. One prevalent strategy is to make explicit how feminist issues are imbued in other issues. This resonates with many younger women who forge as strong generational allegiances as they do gender ones. As Leslie Heyword and Jennifer Drake argue: "Because postboomer men and women have substantially narrowed the wage gap, because they are likely to occupy similar entry-level to mid-level positions in workplace power structures, and because these realities mean economic struggle, women now often have more in common with men of their own age group than they do with women of previous generations." While it is true that there is a feminization of poverty, in part because top wage earners are still overwhelmingly men, it is also true that most men and women are low wage earners. Similarly, while history has repeatedly taught the danger that gender might be occluded, it is necessary to, as Elaine Showalter argues, "give up the pleasure of ownership" of the movement and work with potential alliances and to demonstrate how feminist goals are weaved into the fabric of a host of issues, from the environment to a living wage to immigration (Gillis & Munford, 2004).

Leslie Heywood and Jennifer Drake. "It's all about the Benjamins: Economic determinants of Third wave feminism in the United States." In *Third wave* Feminism, eds. Stacy Gillis, Gillian Howie and Rebecca Munford. (New York: Palgrave, 2004), 13–23, quote from 16; Stacy Gillis and Rebecca Munford, "Interview with Elaine Showalter." In *Third World Feminism*, eds. Stacy Gillis, Gillian Howie and Rebecca Munford (New York: Palgrave, 2004), 60–64.

44. Elsa M. Davidson. "Report on Women's Philanthropy in the United States: Trends and developments" (Center on Philanthropy and Civil Society: The Graduate Center of the City University of New York, 1999).

45. For more on the girl crises, see chapter 3.

46. Capek, *Women and Philanthropy* (1998): vol 2, 15.

47. Ibid., 17.

48. Ibid., 18

49. Cited in e-mail: Aimee, "Fwd: Re: Girl Zone" e-mail, March 16, 2006.

50. While I agree with the trends Capek describes, the recent privileging of religion/morality in public policy and in that policy's economic manifestations (e.g., George W. Bush's "Faith Based Initiatives") complicate this trend.

51. Deborah Brandt persuasively addresses this issue in another context, namely, how those pursuing literacy bear the ideological freight of their sponsors, "Sponsors of Literacy," College *Composition and Communication 49* (1998): 165–185, 168.

52. Jung-Rin Kim, "Financial Needs of Women's Organizations," 2001, para 4. Kim makes her argument by drawing on the National committee for responsive philanthropy, "Payback times for women's group?" Are we ready? A Responsive Philanthropy Special Report (Washington DC National Committee for Responsive Philanthropy, 1999).

53. Women and Philanthropy in partnership with Jankowski Associates, Inc., *The Leading 100 New Foundations Funding Women and Girls, 2004–2005* (USA: Jankowski Associates, Inc, 2005), 5.

54. Jung-Rin Kim, "Financial Needs of Women's Organizations," 2001, para 2.

55. Amy Richards, personal e-mail, "help with resources," December 11, 2004.

56. Rebecca Walker, "Foreward: We are using this power to resist." In *The Fire This Time: Young Activists and the New Feminism*, eds. Vivien Labaton and Dawn Martin Lundy, pp. xi–xx (New York: Anchor Books, 2004), xvii.

57. Ibid., xx.

58. Aimee, 2002.

59. Aimee, "GirlZone closing up shop letter to read, share, and act on" (GrrrlFest organizers list serv. Sept. 9, 2003).

60. In addition to entrepreneurial feminism, there are of course other responses. For example, many recent activist movements, notably those against corporate globalization, tactically challenge global networks of capitalism by creating loose structures and affiliations for short-lived activist eruptions. Yet, these activist movements are seldom sustained beyond the event, or perhaps beyond a future eruption of another short-lived event. See, for example, Naomi Klein's *No Logo* (Picador: New York, 2002). For ongoing grassroots organizations, this decentralized activism is not a viable option.

CODA. SUCCESS AND SUSTAINABILITY

Quoted in e-mail, Aimee "Re: GirlZone," March 16, 2006.

1. Gina, personal interview with author, September 25, 1998.

2. Brian Mandabach, "Easy Listening: What's Missing on Colorado Springs' Public Radio Stations?" Colorado Springs Independent Media Center. August 30, 2001. http://www.csindy.com/csindy/2001-08-03/cover.html (accessed August 5, 2003).

3. Cynthia Kaufman, *Ideas for Action: Relevant Theory for Radical Change* (Cambridge, MA: South End Press, 2003), 296.

4. Some may see Aimee's obtaining a paid position devoted to bettering girls' lives a success, but while Aimee appreciated putting her graduate school research training to work in a context that supported girls, she was eager to return to more hands-on activism.

5. Aimee, personal interview with author, August 22, 2005.

6. Aimee, e-mail, "Fwd: Re: GirlZone," March 16, 2006.

7. Myra Marx Ferree and Beth B. Hess, *Controversy and Coalition: The New Feminist Movement Across Three Decades of Change*, rev. ed. (New York: Twayne Publishers, 1994), 147.

Bibliography

Abu-Lughod, Lila. *Writing Women's Worlds: Bedouin Stories*. Berkeley, CA: University of California Press, 1993.

Aimee. GirlZone *Girl Zine*. Winter 2000–2001. 1.2.

American Association of University Women (AAUW). *Hostile Hallways: The AAUW Survey on Sexual Harassment in America's Schools*. Washington, DC: AAUW Educational Foundation, 1993.

———. "Hostile Hallways: Bullying, Teasing, And Sexual Harassment In School." Report. Washington, DC: AAUW Educational Foundation, 2001, http://www.aauw.org/research/girls_education/hostile.cfm.

———. *How Schools Shortchange Girls: A Study of the Major Findings of Girls and Education*. Washington, DC: AAUW Educational Foundation, 1992.

———(Peggy Ornstein). *Schoolgirls: Young Women, Self-esteem, and the Confidence Gap*. New York: Doubleday, 1994.

———. *Shortchanging Girls, Shortchanging America*. Washington, DC: Greenberg Lake Analysis Group, 1991.

———. *Shortchanging Girls, Shortchanging America*. Washington, DC: Greenberg Lake Analysis Group, 1994.

———. "Tech Savvy: Educating girls in the new computer age." Washington, DC: AAUW Educational Foundation, 2000, http://www.aauw.org/research/girls_education/techsavvy.cfm.

———. *Under the Microscope: A Decade of Gender Equity Projects in the Sciences*. Washington, DC: AAUW Educational Foundation, 2004, http://www.aauw.org/research/microscope.cfm

———. *Voices of a Generation: Teenage Girls on Sex, School, and Self*. Washington, DC: AAUW Educational Foundation, 1999.

Anderson, Benedict. *Imagined Communities*. London: Verso, 1983.

Bail, Kathy, ed. *DIY Feminism*. Sydney, Australia: Allen & Unwin, 1996.

Bakhtin, Mikhail M. *The Dialogic Imagination*. Edited by Michael Holquist. Translated by Carlyn Emerson and Michael Holquist. Austin: University of Texas Press, 1981.

Barton, David, and Mary Hamilton. *Local Literacies: Reading and Writing in One Community*. New York: Routledge, 1998.

Baumgardner, Jennifer, and Amy Richards. *Grassroots: A Field Guide for Feminist Activism*. New York: Farrar, Straus, and Giroux, 2005.

————. *Manifesta: Young Women, Feminism, and the Future*. New York: Farrar, Straus and Giroux, 2000.

Baxandall, Rosalyn, and Linda Gordon, eds. *Dear Sisters: Dispatches From the Women's Liberation Movement*. New York: Basic Books, 2000.

————. "Introduction." In *Dear Sisters: Dispatches From the Women's Liberation Movement*. Edited by Rosalyn Baxandall and Linda Gordon, 1–18. New York: Basic Books, 2000.

Belenkey, Mary Field, Blythe McVicker Clinchy, Nancy Rule Goldnerger, and Jull Mattuck Tarule. *Women's Ways Of Knowing: The Development Of Voice, Self, And Mind*. New York: Basic, 1986.

Björkqvist, Kaj and Pirkko Niemelä, eds. *Of Mice and Women: Aspects of Female Aggression*. San Diego, CA: Academic Press, 1992.

Bikes Not Bombs. "Bikes Not Bombs Youth Services." http://www.bikesnot bombs.org/youth-prog.htm (accessed December 9, 2005).

Bingham, Mindy, Sandy Stryker, and Susan Allstetter Neufeldt. *Things Will Be Different For My Daughter: A Practical Guide to Building Her Self-Esteem and Self-Reliance*. New York: Penguin, 1995.

Blair, Kristine, and Pamela Takayoshi. "Introduction: Mapping the Terrain of Feminist Cyberscapes." In *Feminist Cyberscapes: Mapping Gendered Academic Spaces*. Edited by Kristine Blair and Pamela Takayoshi. Stamford, CT: Ablex, 1999.

Bleyer, Jennifer. "Cut-and-Paste Revolution: Notes from the Girl Zine Explosion." In *The Fire This Time: Young Activists and the New Feminism*. Edited by Vivien Labaton and Dawn Lundy Martin, 42–60. New York: Anchor Books, 2004.

Bobo, Kimberly, Jackie Kendall, and Steve Max. *Organizing for Social Change: Midwest Academy Manual for Activists*. 3d ed. Santa Anna, CA: Seven Locks Press, 2001.

Boston Women's Health Collective. *Our Bodies, Ourselves*. New York: Simon & Schuster, 1973.

"Brand Strategy Briefing: No More Growing Pains." *Brand Strategy*, February 7, 2005. Lexis-Nexis.

Brandt, Deborah. *Literacy in American Lives*. Cambridge, UK: Cambridge University Press, 2001.

————. "Sponsors of Literacy." *College Composition and Communication* 49 (1998): 165–185.

"Breast Implants: High School Graduation Gifts?" *Good Morning America*, American Broadcasting Company, June 15, 2004.

"Briefs: Reed Business Information." *Multichannel News*, June 19, 2000. Business Source Premier.

Brooke, Jill. "Girl Power." *Adweek* 39, no. 5 (1998): 18–19.

Brown, Lyn Mikel, and Carol Gilligan. *Meeting At The Crossroads: Women's Psychology And Girls' Development*. Cambridge, MA: Harvard University Press, 1992.

Brown, Adrienne Maree and William Upski Wimsatt, eds. *How To Get The Stupid White Men Out of Office: The Anti-politics, Un-boring Guide to Power*. Brooklyn: Soft Skull Press, 2004.

Bruce, Heather E. *Literacies, Lies, and Silences: Girls Writing Lives in the Classroom*. New York: Peter Lang, 2003.

Bunch, Charlotte and Sandra Pollack, eds. *Learning Our Way: Essays in Feminist Education*. Trumansburg, NY: Crossing Press, 1983.

Capek, Mary Ellen S. *Women and Philanthropy: Old Stereotypes, New Challenges*. Vol. 1–2. Battle Creek, MI: The W. K. Kellogg Foundation, 1998.

———. *Women and Philanthropy: Old Stereotypes, New Challenges*. Vol. 3. Battle Creek, MI: The W. K. Kellogg Foundation, 2001.

Carby, Hazel. "White Women Listen! Black Feminism and the Boundaries of Sisterhood." In *The Empire Strikes Back: Race and Racism in 70s Britain*. Edited by The Centre for Contemporary Cultural Studies, 212–35. London: Hutchison, 1982.

Carrington, Victoria. "I'm in a Bad Mood. Let's go Shopping: Interactive Dolls, Consumer Culture and a "Glocalized" Model of Literacy." *Journal of Early Childhood Literacy* 3, No. 1 (2003): 83–98.

Chesler, Phyllis. *Woman's Inhumanity to Woman*. New York: Thunder's Mouth Press/Nation Books, 2001.

Chow, Rey. "Gender and Representation." In *Feminist Consequences: Theory for the New Century*. Edited by Elisabeth Bronfen and Misha Kavka, 38–57. New York: Columbia University Press, 2001.

Cleaver, Joanne. "Girl Power." *Working Woman* 24, No. 9 (1999): 14.

Cole, Michael. *Cultural Psychology: A Once and Future Discipline*. Cambridge, MA: Belknap Press of Harvard University Press, 1996.

Cole, Michael, and Yrjo Engestrom. "A Cultural-Historical Approach to Distributed Cognition." In *Distributed Cognitions: Psychological and Educational Considerations*. Edited by Gavriel Salomon. New York: Cambridge University Press, 1993.

Congressional Commission on the Advancement of Women and Minorities in Science, Engineering and Technology Development (CAWMSET). *Land of Plenty: Diversity as America's Competitive Edge in Science, Engineering and Technology*. Arlington, VA: CAWMSET, 2000.

Conquergood, Dwight. "Performing as a Moral Act: Ethical Dimensions of the Ethnography of Performance." *Literature in Performance* 5 (1985): 1–13.

Cushman, Ellen. "The Public Intellectual, Service Learning, and Activist Research." *College English* 61, No. 3 (1999): 328–336.

———. "The Rhetorician as and Agent of Social Change." *College Composition and Communication* 47, No. 1 (1996): 7–28.

———. *The Struggle and the Tools: Oral and Literate Strategies in an Inner City Community*. Albany, NY: State University of New York Press, 1998.

Darke, Katherine, Beatriz Clewell, and Ruta Sevo. "Meeting the Challenge: The Impact of the National Science Foundation's Program for Women and Girls." *The Journal of Women and Minorities in Science and Engineering* 8, No. 3–4 (2002): 285–303.

Davidson, Elsa M. *Report on Women's Philanthropy in the United States: Trends and Developments*. Center on Philanthropy and Civil Society: The Graduate Center of the City University of New York, 1999. http://www.philanthropy.org/publications/online_publications/women_paper.

de Certeau, Michele. *The Practice of Everyday Life*. Berkeley, CA: University of California Press, 1984.

de Ras, Marion, and Mieke Lunenberg, eds. *Girls, Girlhood and Girls' Studies in Transition*. Amsterdam: Het Spinhuis, 1993.

Deak, JoAnn, and Teresa Barker. *Girls Will Be Girls: Raising Confident and Courageous Daughters*. New York: Hyperion, 2002.

Dees, J. Gregory. "Social Entrepreneurs and Education." *Current Issues in Comparative Education* 8, No. 1 (2005): 51–55.

Denizet-Lewis, Benoit. "Friends, Friends with Benefits and the Benefits of the Local Mall." *The New York Times Magazine*, May 30, 2005, 30.

Dill, Bonnie Thornton. "Race, Class, And Gender: Prospects For An All-Inclusive Sisterhood." *Feminist Studies* 9, No. 1 (1983): 131–50.

Doheny-Farina, Stephen. "Creating a Text/Creating a Company: The Role of a Text in the Rise and Decline of a New Organization." In *Textual Dynamics of the Professions: Historical and Professional Sudies of Writing in Professional Communities*. Edited by Charles Bazerman and James Paradis, 306–335. Madison, WI: University of Wisconsin Press, 1991.

———. "Writing in an Emerging Organization: An Ethnographic Study," *Written Communication* 3, No. 2 (1986): 158–185.

Douglass, Susan. *Where the Girls Are: Growing Up Female in the Mass Media*. New York: Random House, 1995.

Dowd, Maureen. "Mean, Nasty, and Missing." *New York Times*, February 27, 2002, sec. A, 21.

Driscoll, Catherine. "Girl Culture, Revenge and Global Capitalism: Cybergirls, Riot Grrrls, Spice Girls." *Australian Feminist Studies* 14, No. 2 (1999): 173–193.

———. *Girls: Feminine Adolescence in Popular Culture and Cultural Theory*. New York: Columbia University Press, 2002.

Dyson, Anne Haas. *Writing Superheroes: Contemporary Childhood, Popular Culture, and Classroom Literacy*. New York: Teachers College Press, 1997.

Eberhardt, Catherine Velasquez, and Jon Pratt. *Minnesota Philanthropy*. Arlington VA: Feminist Majority Foundation, 1993.

Ebert, Teresa. "(Untimely) Critiques for a Red Feminism." In *Post-ality: Marxism and Postmodernism*. Edited by Mas'ud Zavardeh, Teresa Ebert, and Donald Morton. Washington, DC: Maisonneuve Press, 1995.

Edut, Tali, with Dyann Logwood and Ophira Edut. "*HUES* Magazine: The Making of a Movement." In *Third Wave Agenda: Being Feminist, Doing Feminism*. Edited by Leslie Heywood and Jennifer Drake, 83–98. Minneapolis, MN: University of Minnesota Press, 1997.

Elbow, Peter. *Writing Without Teachers*. New York: Oxford University Press, 1973.

The Experience Music Project. "Riot Grrrl Retrospective." http://www.emplive. com/explore/riot_grrrl/index.asp.

Extreme Makeover. ABC. 2002.

Feaze. "Once So Sweet and Innocent." *Feaze: Morning Wood*. Urbana, IL: Mud Records, 1999.

Ferree, Myra Marx, and Beth B. Hess. *Controversy and Coalition: The New Feminist Movement Across Three Decades of Change*. Rev. ed. New York: Twayne Publishers, 1994.

————. *Controversy And Coalition: The New Feminist Movement Across Four Decades Of Change*. New York: Routledge, 2000.

Ferree, Myra Marx, and Patricia Yancey Martin. *Feminist Organizations: Harvest of the New Women's Movement*. Philadelphia, PA: Temple University Press, 1995.

Fields, Suzanne. "Mean Girls In The Mean Streets Of Middle School." *The Washington Times*, March 4, 2002.

Finders, Margaret J. *Just Girls: Hidden Literacies and Life in Junior High*. New York: Teachers College Press, 1997.

Findlen, Barbara. *Listen Up!: Voices from the Next Feminist Generation*. Seattle, WA: Seal Press, 1995.

Fine, Michelle, ed. *All About the Girl: Culture, Power, Identity*. New York: Routledge, 2004.

Firestone, Shulamith, ed. *Notes From the First Year*. New York: New York Radical Women, 1968.

Fong, Katheryn M. "Feminism Is Fine, But What's It Done for Asia America?" *Bridge: An Asian American Perspective* 6, No. 1 (1978): 21–22.

The Foundation Center, "Foundation Grants Designed for Special Population Groups, circa 2003." (FC Stats: The Foundation Center's Statistical Information Service, posted 2005) http://fdncenter.org/fd_stats/pdf/08_fund_pop/2003/16_03.pdr (accessed 13 May 2006).

Frazer, Elizabeth. "Teenage Girls Reading Jackie." *Media, Culture And Society* 9 (1987): 407–25.

The Freechild Project. "Home." http://www.freechild.org/index.htm (accessed December 9, 2005).

Friend, Tad. "Yes." *Esquire Magazine for Men* 121, No. 2 (1994): 48–57.

Frieze, Irene H., Jacqueline E. Parson, Paula B. Johnson, and D. Ruble. *Women and Sex Roles: A Social Psychological Perspective*. New York: W. W. Norton, 1978.

Frith, Simon. *Sound Effects: Youth, Leisure, And The Politics of Rock'n'roll*. New York: Pantheon, 1981.

Fritzsch, Bettina. "Spice Strategies: Pop Feminist and Other Empowerments in Girl Culture." In *All About the Girl: Culture, Power, and Identity*. Edited by Anita Harris, 155–162. New York: Routledge, 2004.

Garcia, Alma M. "The Development Of Chicana Feminist Discourse, 1970–1980." *Gender and Society* 3, No. 2 (1989): 217–238.

Gee, James Paul. *What Video Games Have to Teach Us About Learning and Literacy*. New York: Palgrave Macmillan, 2003.

Gere, Anne Ruggles. *Intimate Practices: Literacy and Cultural Work in U.S. Women's Clubs, 1880–1920*. Urbana, IL: University of Illinois Press, 1997.

————. "Kitchen Tables and Rented Rooms: The Extracurriculum of Composition." *College Composition and Communication* 45 (1994): 75–92.

Gilbert-Levin, Erica. "Class Feminist." In *Listen Up: Voices From the Next Feminist Generation*. 2d ed. Edited by Barbara Findlen, 165–172. Seattle, WA: Seal Press, 2001.

Gilligan, Carol. *In a Different Voice: Psychological Theory and Women's Development*. Cambridge, MA: Harvard University Press, 1982.

Gillis, Stacy, and Rebecca Munford. "Interview with Elaine Showalter." In *Third Wave Feminism*. Edited by Stacy Gillis, Gillian Howie, and Rebecca Munford, 60–64. New York: Palmgrave, 2004.

Girls, Inc. *Girls and Economic Literacy*. http:// www.girlsinc.org/ic/page.php? id=3.1.

———. "Girls Inc. Media Literacy." http://www.girlsinc.org/ic/ page.php?id= 1.2.3 (accessed 3 February 3, 2006).

Girl's Best Friend Foundation. "Girls Growing with Strength and Resilience in an Equitable World Brochure." Chicago: Girl's Best Friend Foundation, 1998.

———. "Guidelines." Chicago: Girl's Best Friend Foundation, 1998.

"GirlZone Participant Expectations." *GirlZine*: The newsletter for GirlZone news and events. January 2000, 4.

Giroux, Henry A. *Stealing Innocence: Youth, Corporate Power, and the Politics of Culture*. New York: St. Martin's Press, 2000.

———. "Teen Girls' Resistance and the Disappearing Social in *Ghost World*." *The Review of Education, Pedagogy, and Cultural Studies* 24 (2002): 283–304.

Glennon, Will. *200 Ways to Raise a Girl's Self-Esteem: An Indispensible Guide for Parents, Teachers, & Other Concerned Caregivers*. Boston, MA: Conari Press, 1999.

Goffman, Erving. *Forms of Talk*. Philadelphia: University of Pennsylvania Press, 1981.

Gold, Kerry. "Sex Sells Tween Fashion." *Vancouver Sun* (June 19, 2004): D4

"Good to Know" with Ondine Gross. WEFT Radio. October 13, 2003.

Green, Eileen, and Laurie Cohen. "'Women's Business'": Are Women Entrepreneurs Breaking New Ground or Simply Balancing the Demands of 'Women's Work' in a New Way?" *Journal of Gender Studies* 4, No. 3 (1995): 297–314.

Grossman, Lev, Nadia Mustafa, Deirdre van Dyk, Kristin Kloberdanz, and Marc Schultz. "Grow Up? Not so Fast." *Time 165* (January 24, 2005): 42–54.

Hains, Rebecca C. "The Problematics of Reclaiming the Girlish: The Powerpuff Girls and Girl Power." *Femspec 5*, No. 2 (2004): 1–39.

Hains, Rebecca C. "Power(puff) Feminism: *The Powerpuff Girls* as a Site of Strength and Collective Action in the Third Wave." n.d.

Harris, Anita. *Future Girl: Young Women in the Twenty-First Century*. New York: Routledge, 2004.

———. "Revisiting Bedroom Culture: New Spaces for Young Women's Politics." *Hecate* 27, No. 1 (2001): 128–139.

Hartley-Brewer, Elizabeth. *Raising Confident Girls: 100 Tips for Parents and Teachers*. Cambridge, MA: Fisher Books, 2001.

Hawkesworth, Mary. "The Semiotics of Premature Burial: Feminism in a Post-feminist Age." *Signs: Journal Of Women In Culture And Society* 29, No. 4.

Heath, Shirley Brice. *Ways with Words: Language, Life and Work in Communities and Classrooms*. Cambridge, England: Cambridge University Press, 1983.

———. "What No Bedtime Story Means." *Language and Society* 11 (1982): 49–76.

Heath, Shirley Brice, and Milbrey W. McLaughlin. "Identity and Inner-City Youth." In *Identity and Inner-City Youth: Beyond Ethnicity and Gender.* Edited by Shirley Brice Heath and Milbrey W. McLaughlin, 1–12. New York: Teachers College Press, 1994.

Hellmich, Nancy. "Girls Friendships Show Aggression At Younger Ages." *USA Today,* April 9, 2002.

Hernandez, Daisy, and Bushra Rehman, eds. *Colonize This!: Young Women of Color on Today's Feminism.* New York: Seal Press, 2004.

Hewett, Nancy A. "The Glass Tower: Half Full or Half Empty?" In *Taking Back the Academy: History of Activism, History as Activism.* Edited by Jim Downs and Jennifer Manion, 93–102. New York: Routledge, 2004.

Heywood, Leslie and Jennifer Drake. "Introduction." In *Third Wave Agenda: Being Feminist, Doing Feminism.* Edited by Leslie Heywood and Jennifer Drake, 1–24. Minneapolis, MN: University of Minnesota Press, 1997.

———. "It's All About the Benjamins: Economic Determinants of Third Wave Feminism in the United States." In *Third Wave Feminism.* Edited by Stacy Gillis, Gillian Howie, and Rebecca Munford, 13–23. New York: Palmgrave, 2004.

———, eds. *Third Wave Agenda: Being Feminist, Doing Feminism.* Minneapolis, MN: University of Minnesota Press, 1997.

hooks, bell. *Teaching to Transgress: Education as the Practice of Freedom.* New York: Routledge, 1994.

"How Does a Supermodel do Feminism? An Interview with Veronica Webb." In *To Be Real: Telling the Truth and Changing the Face of Feminism.* Edited by Rebecca Walker, 209–218. New York: Anchor Books, 1995.

Hull, Glynda and Katherine Schultz. *School's Out! Bridging Out-of-School Literacies with Classroom Practice.* New York: Teachers College Press, 2002.

Humpries, Maria and Suaznne Grant. "Social Enterprise and Re-Civilization of Human Endeavors: Re-Socializing the Market Metaphor or Encroaching Colonization of the Lifeworld?" *Current Issues in Comparative Education* 8, No. 1 (2005): 41–50.

Hutcheon, Linda. *The Politics of the Postmodern,* 2d ed. London: Routledge, 2002.

Hypatia: A Journal of Feminist Philosophy 12, No. 3 (1997).

Inness, Sherrie. *Tough Girls: Women Warriors and Wonder Women in Popular Culture.* Philadelphia, PA: University of Pennsylvania Press, 1998.

Jaggar, Alison M. *Feminist Politics and Human Nature.* Totowa, NJ: Rowman & Littlefield, 1983.

James, Thomas. "The Winnowing of Organizations." In *Identity and Inner-City Youth: Beyond Ethnicity and Gender.* Edited by Shirley Brice Heath and Milbrey W. McLaughlin, 176–195. New York: Teachers College Press, 1994.

Kaufman, Cynthia. *Ideas for Action: Relevant Theory for Radical Change.* Cambridge, MA: South End Press, 2003.

Kavka, Misha. "Introduction." In *Feminist Consequences: Theory For The New Century,* edited by Elisabeth Bronfen and Misha Kavka, ix–xxvi. New York: Columbia University Press, 2001.

Kearney, Mary Celeste. "Producing Girls: Rethinking the Study of Female Youth Culture." In *Delinquents and Debutantes: Twentieth-Century American Girls' Cultures*. Edited by Sherrie Inness, 285–310. New York: New York University Press, 1998.

Kim, Jung-Rin. "The Answer to the Financial Needs of Women's Organizations?" *Common Concern*. http://worldywca1.org/common_concern/mar2001/foundations.html.

Kirsch, Gesa E. "Ethics and the Future of Composition Research." In *Composition Studies in the New Millenium: Rereading the Past, Rewriting the Future*. Edited by Lynn Z. Bloom, Donald A. Daiker, and Edward M. White, 129–141. Carbondale, IL: Southern Illinois University Press, 2003.

Klein, Naomi. *No Logo: No Space, No Choice, No Jobs*. New York: Picador, 2000/2002.

———. "The Vision Thing: Were the DC and Seattle Protests Unfocused, or are Critics Missing the Point?" *The Nation* (July 7, 2000): 18–22, http://web23.epnet.com/DeliveryPrintSave.asp?tb=1&_ug=sid+019377EF52-4814-83E (accessed January 19, 2005)

Kress, Gunther. "English at the Crossroads: Rethinking the Curricula of Communication in the Context of the Turn to the Visual." In *Passions, Pedagogies, and 21st Century Technologies*. Edited by Gail E. Hawisher and Cynthia Selfe, 66–88. Logan, Utah: Utah State University Press and National Council of Teachers of English, 1999.

———. "Gains and Losses: New Forms of Texts, Knowledge, and Learning." *Computers & Composition* 22, No. 1 (2005): 5–22.

———. *Literacy in the New Media Age*. New York: Routledge, 2003.

Kress, Gunther and Theo van Leeuwen. *Reading Images: The Grammar of Visual Design*. London: Routledge, 1996.

Labaton, Vivien, and Dawn Lundy Martin, eds. *The Fire This Time: Young Activists and the New Feminism*. New York: Anchor Books, 2004.

Lamb, Sharon. *The Secret Lives of Girls: What Good Girls Really Do—Sex Play, Aggression, and Their Guilt*. New York: Free Press, 2001.

Lawrence, Stephen. *The Foundation Center's 2002 Children and Youth Funding Update*. New York: Foundation Center, 2002.

Lave, Jean and Etienne Wenger. *Situated Learning: Legitimate Peripheral Participation*. Cambridge, UK: Cambridge University Press, 1991.

"The League of Pissed Off Voters and You (Your Town, USA)." In *How to Get the Stupid White Men Out of Office: The Anti-politics, Un-boring Guide to Power*. Edited by Adrienne Maree Brown and William Upski Wimsatt, 184–197. Brooklyn: Soft Skull Press, 2004.

Leander, Kevin M. "Locating Latanya: The Situated Production of Identity Artifacts in Classroom Interaction." *Research in the Teaching of English* 37, No. 2 (2002): 198–250.

Lee, Shireen, "The New Girls Network: Women Technology, and Feminism." In *The Fire This Time: Young Activists and the New Feminism*. Edited by Vivien Labaton and Dawn Lundy Martin, 84–104. New York: Anchor Books: 2004.

Lemke, Jay. "Multimedia Genres in Science: Visual and Verbal Semiotics in Scientific Text." In *Reading Science: Critical and Functional Perspectives of Science*. Edited by J. R. Martin, 87–113. London: Routledge, 1998.

Lewis, L. E., ed. *Adoring Audience: Fan Culture and Popular Media*. London: Routledge, 1992.

Littman, Margaret. "Sugar, Spice And Not Very Nice: Girls' Cruelty to Girls May Be Very Old-school, but Experts Say It's Time to Start Taking These Mean Streaks Seriously." *The Chicago Tribune*, May 8, 2002.

Logan, Shirley Wilson. *We Are Coming: The Persuasive Discourse of Nineteenth-Century Black Women*. Carbondale, IL: Southern Illinois University Press, 1999.

Lombardi, Kate Stone. "Mothers and Daughters Raise Funds for Charity." *The New York Times*, May 2, 1999, sec. 14WC.

Lukehart, Erin. "GirlZone's Swan Song." *The Paper*, September 19, 2003. http://www.thepaperthewebsite.com/091903/girlzone%20article6.aspk (accessed September 29, 2003).

Mackoff, Barbara. *Growing a Girl: Seven Strategies for Raising a Strong, Spirited Daughter*. New York: Dell, 1996.

Mahiri, Jabari. *Shooting for Excellence: African American and Youth Culture in New Century Schools*. New York: Teachers College Press, 1998.

Mandabach, Brian. "Easy Listening: What's Missing on Colorado Springs' Public Radio Stations?" Colorado Springs Independent Media Center. August 30, 2001. http://www.csindy.com/csindy/2001-08-30/cover.html (accessed August 5, 2003).

Mankiller, Wilma. "Coda." In *The Fire This Time: Young Activists and the New Feminism*. Edited by Vivien Labaton and Dawn Lundy Martin, 291–293. New York: Anchor Books, 2004.

McDonagh, Deana, Nan Goggin, and Joseph Squier, "Signs, Symbols, and Subjectivity: An Alternative View on the Visual." *Computers & Composition* 22, No. 1 (2005): 79–86.

McRobbie, Angela. "Fashion as a Culture Industry." In *Fashion Culture: Theories, Explanations and Analysis*. Edited by Stella Bruzzi and Pamela Church Gibson, 253–263. New York: Routledge, 2000.

———. *Feminism And Youth Culture: From "Jackie" To "Just Seventeen."* Boston, MA: Unwin Hyman, 1991.

———. *Feminism and Youth Culture*, 2d ed. Basingstoke, Hampshire: Macmillan, 2000.

———. *"Jackie*: An Ideology of Adolescent Femininity." Birmingham CCCS Stenciled Paper, 1978.

———. *Postmodernism and Popular Culture*. London: Routledge, 1994.

———. "Shut Up and Dance: Youth Culture and Changing Modes of Femininity." In *Feminism and Cultural Studies*. Edited by Morgan Shiach, 65–88. Oxford: Oxford University Press, 1994.

———. "Young Women and the Consumer Citizenship: The Danger of Too Much Pleasure." Paper delivered as part of the AHRC Cultures of Consumption Programme, 2004. http://www.goldsmiths.ac.uk/departments/media-communications/staff/mcrobbie.php.

McRobbie, Angela and Jennifer Garber. "Girls and Subcultures." Reprinted in *Feminism and youth culture*. Rev. 2d ed. Edited by Angela McRobbie, 12–25. New York: Routledge, 2000.

Mead, Molly. *Worlds Apart: Missed Opportunities to Help Women and Girls*. Boston, MA: Women in Philanthropy/Boston Women's Fund, 1994.

Meadows, Susannah, Dirk Johnson, and Sarah Downey. "Girl Fight: Savagery in the Chicago Suburbs." *Newsweek,* May 19, 2003, 37.

Meadows, Susannah, and Mary Carmichael. "Meet the GAMMA Girls." *Newsweek*, June 3, 2002, 44–51.

"Mean." *Law and Order: SVU.* National Broadcasting Company, February 24, 2004.

Michigan Women's Foundation. *Investing in Michigan Women.* Lansing, MI: The Michigan Women's Foundation, 1993

Mindry, Deborah. "Nongovernmental Organizations, "Grassroots," and the Politics of Virtue." *Signs: Journal of Women in Culture and Society* 26, No. 4 (2001): 1187–1211.

Mintz, Steven. *Huck's Raft: A History of American Childhood.* Cambridge, MA: Bellknap Press of Harvard University Press, 2004.

Miriam "Want to be on the air? YOU GO, GIRLS: WEFT turns over radio station for kids' show every other Sunday." *The News-Gazette* (Champaign-Urbana, Illinois), February 11, 1999, B–8.

Mitchell, Melissa. "Radio Girl: Giving voices to youths." *The WEFT Revue,* Jan–Feb 1999, 3.

Mitchell, Sally. *The New Girl: Girls' Culture in England, 1880–1915.* New York: Columbia University Press, 1995.

Moraga, Cherrie, and Gloria Anzaldua. *This Bridge Called My Back: Writings By Radical Women Of Color.* Watertown, MA: Persephone, 1981.

Moss, L. "'Powerpuff' Quarter." *Multichannel News* 21, No. 4. Business Source Premier.

Munford, Rebecca "'Wake Up and Smell the Lip Gloss': Gender, Generation, and the (A)politics of Girl Power." In *Third Wave Feminism: A Critical Exploration.* Edited by Stacey Gillis, Gillian Howie, and Rebecca Munford, 142–153. New York: Palgrave Macmillan, 2004.

Naples, Nancy A. "Women's Community Activism and Feminist Activist Research." In *Community Activism and Feminist Politics: Organizing Across Race, Class, and Gender.* Edited by Nancy A. Naples, 1–27. New York: Routledge, 1998.

National Committee for Responsive Philanthropy. "*Payback Times for Women's Group?" Are we Ready? A Responsive Philanthropy Special Report.* Washington DC: National Committee for Responsive Philanthropy, 1999.

Nelson, Claudia, and Lynne Vallone, eds. *The Girl's Own: Cultural Histories of the Anglo-American Girl, 1830–1915.* Athens, GA: University of Georgia Press, 1994.

The New London Group. "A Pedagogy of Multiliteracies: Designing Social Futures." *Harvard Educational Review* 66, No. 1 (1996): 60–92.

"NGOs Score Victories at Bejing Women's Conference." *Interaction: American Council for Voluntary International Action,* http://www.interaction.org/library/mdbeiji1.html.

Ono, Kent A., and John M. Sloop. *Shifting Borders: Rhetoric, Immigration, and California's Proposition 187.* Philadelphia, PA: Temple University Press, 2002.

Oprah, April 24, 2002.

Pimp My Ride. MTV. 2004.

Pipher, Mary. "Mary Pipher, Ph.D," www.marypipher.net. Accessed December 18, 2005.

———. *Reviving Ophelia: Saving the Selves of Adolescent Girls*. New York: Putnam, 1994.

Pollit, Katha. "The Smurfette Principle." *New York Times Magazine*, April 7, 1991, 22.

Pomerantz, Shauna. "Grinding the Concrete (Third) Wave." *Sexing the Political: A Journal of Third Wave Feminists on Sexuality* 2, No. 2 (2002), http://www.iiav.nl/ezines/web/SexingThePolitical/2002/No2.PDF.

Porter, James E., Patricia Sullivan, Jeffrey T. Grabill, Stuart Blyth, and Libby Miles. "Institutional Critique: A Rhetorical Methodology for Change." *College Composition and Communication* 51 (2000): 610–42.

Prendergast, Catherine. *Literacy and Racial Justice: The Politics of Learning after Brown v. Board of Education*. Carbondale, IL: Southern Illinois, University Press, 2003.

Prior, Paul A. *Writing/Disciplinarity: A Sociohistoric Account of Literate Activity in the Academy*. Mahwah, NJ: Lawrence Erlbaum. 1998.

Probyn, Elspeth. *Sexing the Self: Gendered Positions in Cultural Studies*. London: Routledge, 1993.

Putnam, Robert. *Bowling Alone: The Collapse and Revival of American Community*. New York: Simon and Schuster, 2000.

Radway, Janice A. *Reading the Romance: Women, Patriarch, and Popular Literature*. Chapel Hill, NC: University of North Carolina Press, 1984.

RadioGirl. *Best of RadioGirl*. WEFT, August 29, 1999.

———. *WEFT*, October 1998.

———. *WEFT*, December 6, 1998.

———. *WEFT*, January 31, 1999.

Royster, Jacqueline Jones. *Traces of a Stream: Literacy and Social Change Among African American Women*. Pittsburgh, PA: University of Pittsburgh Press, 2000.

Russell, Rachel, and Melissa Tyler. "Thank Heaven for Little Girls: "Girl Heaven" and the Commercial Context of Feminine Childhood." *Sociology* 36, No. 3 (2002): 619–637.

Sadker, Mary, and David Sadker. *Failing at Fairness: How Our Schools Cheat Girls*. New York: Touchstone, 1995.

Schragge, Eric. *Activism and Social Change: Lessons for Community and Local Organizing*. Ontario, Canada: Broadview Press, 2003.

Scribner, Sylvia, and Michael Cole. *The Psychology of Literacy*. Cambridge, MA: Harvard University Press, 1981.

Segal, David. "The Che Cachet: An Exhibition Traces How the Marxist Revolutionary's Photo Inspired an Army of Capitalists." *The Washington Post*, February 7, 2006. C01 http://www.washingtonpost.com/wp-dyn/content/article/2006/02/06/AR2006020601950.html?sub=AR (accessed July 23, 2006).

Servatius, Mary. *Short Sighted: How Chicago-area Grantmakers Can Apply a Gender Lens to See the Connections Between Social Problems and Women's Needs*. Chicago: Chicago Women in Philanthropy, 1992.

Shandler, Sara. *Ophelia Speaks: Adolescent Girls Write About Their Search For Self.* New York: Harper Perrenial, 1999.

Sheridan, Dorothy, Brian V. Street, and David Bloome. *Writing Ourselves: Mass Observation and Literacy Practices.* Cresskill, NJ: Hampton Press, 2000.

Shiach, Morag, ed. *Feminism and Cultural Studies.* Oxford: Oxford University Press, 1999.

Shor, Ira and Paulo Freire. *A Pedagogy: Dialogues on Transforming Education.* South Hadley, MA: Bergin & Garvey Publishers, 1987.

Showalter, Elaine. "Stop Whining, Just Do It. The Women's Movement Will Not Come Again, Warns One of Its Leading Lights, Elaine Showalter. But Women Could Improve Their Lot by Turning Entrepreneurial." *The Financial Times Limited,* October 18, 2003, 23.

Sidler, Michelle. "Living in McJobdom: Third Wave Feminism and Class Inequity." In *Third Wave Agenda.* Edited by Leslie Heywood and Jennifer Drake, 25–39. Minneapolis, MN: University of Minnesota Press, 1997.

Signs: Journal of Women in Culture and Society. "Special issue: Feminism and Youth Culture" 23, No. 3 (1998).

Simmons, Rachel. "Aggressive Girls: Interview by Neil Connan." *Talk of the Nation,* National Public Radio, February 27, 2002.

———. *Odd Girl Out: The Hidden Culture of Aggression in Girls.* New York: Harcourt, 2002.

———. "Wild Things: Interview with Rachel Simmons, Author of *Odd Girl Out: The Hidden Culture of Aggression in Girls.*" *Dateline NBC,* National Broadcasting Company, April 9, 2002.

Smith, Dorothy E. *The Conceptual Practices of Power: A Feminist Sociology of Knowledge.* Boston, MA: Northeastern University Press, 1990.

———. *Institutional Ethnography: A Sociology for People.* Walnut Creek, CA: AltaMira Press, 2005.

Spellmeyer, Kurt. *Arts of Living: Reinventing the Humanities for the Twenty-First Century.* Albany: State University of New York Press, 2003.

———. "Education for Irrelevance? Or, Joining Our Colleagues in Lit Crit on the sidelines of the Information Age." In *Composition Studies in the New Millennium: Rereading the Past, Rewriting the Future.* Edited by Lynn Z. Bloom, Donald A. Daiker, and Edward M. White, 78–87. Carbondale, IL: Southern Illinois University, 2003.

Spivak, Gayatri. "Can the Subatlern Speak." In *Marxism and the Interpretation of Culture,* eds. Cary Nelson and Lawrence Grossberg, 271–313. Bassingoke: Macmillan Education, 1998.

Steedman, Carolyn. *Landscape for a Good Woman: A Story of Two Lives.* New Brunswick, NJ: Rutgers University Press, 1986.

———. *The Tidy House: Little Girls Writing.* London, UK: Virago Press, 1981.

Street, Brian V. *Cross-Cultural Approaches to Literacy.* Cambridge, UK: Cambridge University Press, 1993.

———. *Literacy in Theory and Practice.* Cambridge, UK: Cambridge University Press, 1984.

Swords, Faith. "These Girls Rock: Nothin' Fazes Feaze." *The News-Gazette* (Champaign-Urbana, Illinois), October 15, 1998, B8.

The Swan. Fox TV. 2004.

Taft, Jessica K. "Girl Power Politics: Barriers and Organization Resistance." In *All About the Girl: Culture, Power, and Identity*. Edited by Anita Harris, 69–78. New York: Routledge, 2004.

Talbot, Margaret. "Girls Just Want to Be Mean." *The New York Times Magazine*, February 24, 2002.

Taylor, Todd. "A Methodology of Our Own." In *Composition Studies in the New Millenium: Rereading the Past, Rewriting the Future*. Edited by Lynn Z. Bloom, Donald A. Daiker, and Edward M. White, 142–150. Carbondale, IL; Southern Illinois University Press, 2003.

Taylor, Verta. "Watching for Vibes: Bringing Emotions Into the Study of Feminist Organizations." In *Feminist Organizations: Harvest of the New Women's Movement*. Edited by Myra Marx Feree and Patricia Yancey Martin, 223–233. Philadelphia, PA: Temple University Press, 1995.

Thomas, Dorothy Q. "We Are Not The World: U.S. Activism And Human Rights In The Twenty-First Century." *Signs: Journal of Women in Culture and Society* 25, No. 4 (2000): 1121–1125.

Thorne, Barrie. "Re-visioning Women and Social Change: Where Are the Children?" *Gender and Society* 1, No. 1 (1987): 85–109.

Trading Spaces. TLC. 2000.

United Way Of Champaign County. *Community Report 2004*, http://www.uwayhelps.org/resources/FINAL_annual_report.pdf (accessed online May 9, 2006).

University YMCA Board of Governors. "University YMCA Vision Statement." University YMCA of Champagin, IL. (Adopted February 27, 2003) http://www.universityymca.org/vision.html (accessed 12 May 2006).

Vallone, Lynne. *Disciplines of Virtue: Girls' Culture in the Eighteenth and Nineteenth Centuries*. New Haven, CT: Yale University Press, 1995.

Wald, Gayle. "Just a Girl? Rock Music, Feminism, and the Cultural Construction of Female Youth." *Signs: Journal of Women in Culture and Society* 23, No. 3 (1998): 585–610.

Walker, Rebecca. "Being Real: An Introduction." In *To Be Real: Telling the Truth and Changing the Face of Feminism*. Edited by Rebecca Walker, xxviii–xl. New York: Anchor Books, 1995.

———, ed. *To Be Real: Telling the Truth and Changing the Face of Feminism*. New York: Anchor Books, 1995.

———. "Foreword: We Are Using This Power To Resist." In *The Fire This Time: Young Activists and the New Feminism*. Edited by Vivien Labaton and Dawn Lundy Martin, xi–xx. New York: Anchor Books, 2004.

Walkerdine, Valerie. "Some Day My Prince Will Come: Young Girls and the Preparation for Adolescent Sexuality." In *Gender and Generation*. Edited by Angela McRobbie and Mica Nava, 162–184. London: Macmillan, 1984.

Warner, Marina. *From the Beast to the Blonde: On Fairy Tales and Their Tellers*. London: Chatto & Windus, 1994.

White, Emily. *Fast Girls: Teenage Tribes and the Myth of the Slut*. New York: Scribner, 2002.

Whitely, Sheila. *Women and Popular Music: Sexuality, Identity, and Subjectivity*. London: Routledge, 2000.

Whittier, Nancy. *Feminist Generations: The Persistence of the Radical Women's Movement.* Philadelphia, PA: Temple University Press, 1995.

Wiegman, Robyn, ed. *Women's Studies on Its Own: A Next Wave Reader in Institutional Change.* Durham, NC: Duke University Press, 2002.

Williams, Raymond. *Problems in Materialism and Culture.* London: Verso, 1980.

Wiseman, Rosalind. *Queen Bees & Wannabes : Helping Your Daughter Survive Cliques, Gossip, Boyfriends, And Other Realities Of Adolescence.* New York: Crown Publishers, 2002.

Women and Philanthropy in Partnership with Jankowski Associates, Inc. *The Leading 100 New Foundations Funding Women and Girls, 2004–2005.* USA: Jankowski Associates, Inc., 2005.

Women Working in Philanthropy. *Doubled in a Decade, Yet Still Far From Done: A Report on Awards Targeted to Women and Girls by Grantmakers in the Delaware Valley.* Philadelphia, PA: Women Working in Philanthropy, 1990.

Yancey, Kathleen Blake. "Made Not Only in Words: Composition in a New Key." *College Composition and Communication* 56, No. 2 (2004): 297–328.

Index

Aaron (GrrrlFest logo designer),
117–118, 124, 173n9
Abu-Lughod, Lila, 34
activism, 2, 13–14, 21–25, 43; activist
organizations, 14, 82–83,
169n13; girl-centered, 34,
163n28; and girl power, 44–45;
grassroots, 16, 28, 36, 71, 136,
148, 152, 153, 157n25; lack of
information concerning, 14,
158n2; online, 13; professionalization of, 152. *See also* activism,
economics of; activism, feminist;
community organizations
activism, economics of, 127–129,
138–139, 140–144, 153, 179n26,
180n32, 180–181n43; conservative nature of funding institutions, 136, 137; and economic
discourses within granting organizations, 141–142; and entrepreneurship, 145–148; government
support of community activism,
130, 177n10; influence of New
Right policies on, 130, 177n11;
and institutional activism of
higher education, 130–131;
money raised by feminist foundations (1985 and 1994), 145
activism, feminist, 17, 24–25, 27,
29–30, 38, 58, 77–78, 82,
159n29; co-opting of, 107; designing new strategies for, 140–144;
Do-It-Yourself (DIY) feminist

activism, 28, 87, 110–111; in
South Africa, 141; strategies for,
139–140; success of, 166n11.
See also consumer culture,
feminist strategies for engaging
ad busting, 116, 118, 175n36
African American women, 15, 86,
175n30; and feminism, 58, 165n3
Aimee (GirlZone co-founder), 13,
14–15, 23, 26–28, 47, 63, 113,
134–135, 177n1, 182n4; and the
alignment of GirlZone with the
RiotGrrrl tradition, 111; career
accomplishments of, 27; on the
closing of GirlZone, 18, 147–148,
152; on the economics of Girl-
Zone, 127, 132–133, 143–144,
146–147; feminism of, 139;
and the GirlZone fashion show
debate, 74–75; on the logo and
slogan of GrrrlFest, 118–119;
on marketing strategies,
115; on music and GrrrlFest,
175–176n42; personality of, 27;
portrayal of GirlZone as providing choices to girls, 65–66; post-
GirlZone activism of, 152–153;
on the Powerpuff Girls, 120; as
the sole organizer of GirlZone,
16–17; split with Gina, 16; on the
success/sustainability of GirlZone,
151; on the United Way, 136–138
Ali (GirlZone/GrrrlFest facilitator),
149, 150, 153

197